Praise for *Healing with Nature*

"Rochelle Calvert is a warmhearted and direct guide to the healing that is possible through mindfulness and somatic practices combined with immersion in the natural world. *Healing with Nature* is full of practical and spiritual guidance for healing from trauma through what is already present — the wisdom of our own bodies and the embrace of nature and the outdoors. Her instructions are clear, thorough, and also radical: she turns us gently toward experiencing suffering while taking care to also nourish the capacity to turn toward safety. And she skillfully links our inner healing to the planet's suffering, showing a way to help cope with the heartbreak of our ongoing climate crisis."

— **Melissa Myozen Blacker**, Zen teacher, abbot of Boundless Way Zen, and former director of professional training at the Center for Mindfulness at the University of Massachusetts Medical School

"Combining mindfulness, somatic awareness, and the inspiration of nature, *Healing with Nature* offers a unique contribution that can aid in healing from traumatic events. Get yourself a copy, lean against your favorite tree, and let the healing begin."

— **Frank Ostaseski**, founder of the Metta Institute and author of *The Five Invitations*

"*Healing with Nature* is a wonderful book that invites us to reconnect with our hearts and minds through our senses and the natural world, affirming that we are part of the universe and not separate from it."

— **Bob Stahl, PhD**, coauthor of
A Mindfulness-Based Stress Reduction Workbook
(1st and 2nd editions), *Living with Your Heart Wide Open*,
Calming the Rush of Panic, *A Mindfulness-Based Stress Reduction Workbook for Anxiety*, and *MBSR Every Day*

"When faced with trauma, where do we look for support or healing? Rochelle Calvert has provided us with an accessible pathway to recovery in *Healing with Nature*. She draws on the inspiration of the natural world and shares exercises to help us connect more fully to our mind and body. The meditations and practices are a treasure of steps for living a fuller, happier life."

— **Sharon Salzberg**, author of *Real Happiness* and *Real Change*

"So many of us live in a de-natured condition, lost in the abstractions of a noisy mind. *Healing with Nature* shows us a path out of our hurt and into our heart, integrating the inner resources of mindful awareness with the outer resources of the natural world through Rochelle Calvert's wise, clear writing."

— **Martin Aylward**, author of *Awake Where You Are: The Art of Embodied Awareness*

"In *Healing with Nature*, Rochelle Calvert gently and patiently guides the reader to a deeply wise understanding of what trauma is and what health is, and to an appreciation of the power of nature to help us heal from one to the other. I especially appreciate the compassionate attention to the challenges inherent in moving toward and moving through the many layers of any trauma, and the inspiration to skillfully explore new possibilities in more spacious ways of living. The many mindful and somatic practices are easily accessible and reliably transformative. They provide a trustworthy path of healing into genuine aliveness, wholeness, and integrity in one's own being and in connection with all beings."

— **Linda Graham**, MFT, author of *Resilience: Powerful Practices for Bouncing Back from Disappointment, Difficulty, and Even Disaster*

HEALING

with

NATURE

HEALING

with

NATURE

Mindfulness and Somatic Practices to Heal from Trauma

ROCHELLE CALVERT, PhD

Foreword by Mark Coleman

New World Library
Novato, California

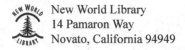

New World Library
14 Pamaron Way
Novato, California 94949

Text design by Tona Pearce Myers

Library of Congress Cataloging-in-Publication Data

Names: Calvert, Rochelle, author.
Title: Healing with nature : mindfulness and somatic practices to heal from trauma /
    Rochelle Calvert, PHD ; foreword by Mark Coleman, author of Awake in the Wild.
Description: Novato, California : New World Library, [2021] | Includes bibliographical
    references and index. | Summary: "A clinical psychologist, mindfulness teacher,
    and somatic experiencing practitioner offers nature-based mindfulness and somatic
    practices to help readers find peace and restore wholeness after trauma"-- Provided
    by publisher.
Identifiers: LCCN 2021008592 (print) | LCCN 2021008593 (ebook) | ISBN
    9781608687367 (paperback) | ISBN 9781608687374 (epub)
Subjects: LCSH: Psychic trauma--Alternative treatment. | Post-traumatic stress disor-
    der--Alternative treatment. | Nature, Healing power of. | Mind and body therapies.
Classification: LCC RC552.T7 C35 2021 (print) | LCC RC552.T7 (ebook) | DDC
    616.85/21--dc23
LC record available at https://lccn.loc.gov/2021008592
LC ebook record available at https://lccn.loc.gov/2021008593

First printing, June 2021
ISBN 978-1-60868-736-7
Ebook ISBN 978-1-60868-737-4
Printed in Canada on 100% postconsumer-waste recycled paper

New World Library is proud to be a Gold Certified Environmentally Responsible
Publisher. Publisher certification awarded by Green Press Initiative.

10   9   8   7   6   5   4   3   2   1

For the field of dirt across from my childhood home
For all traumas known and unknown

CONTENTS

Part 4: Healing Nature   211

FOREWORD

As a society we are beginning to wake up to the
depth and breadth of the trauma that pervades people, families, and communities. For far too long the trauma of war, violence, and abuse has left
scars that have not been kindly or effectively addressed. It is now time for
a different story, and this book offers a new possibility.

In this beautiful new work, Rochelle Calvert reveals, with the depth
of her psychotherapeutic expertise, how trauma can be held, worked with,
and healed. What distinguishes this book is how Rochelle draws on nature as a profound ally in the healing journey. As an Awake in the Wild
nature meditation teacher, Rochelle integrates many nature-based principles and somatic practices, applying them in innovative ways to address
trauma, showing you, in particular, how to ground yourself, be resourced,
and experience healing.

We know that for millennia people have gone into the forests, mead-
ows, and mountains for nourishment and rejuvenation. The Earth can
serve as a beautiful mirror, in that it can withstand tremendous destruction
and yet find the tenacity and creativity to regenerate and flourish. Now,
with the skilled guidance herein, you can learn how the natural world can
offer a safe space in which to both heal and find inspiration for understanding and recovering from the legacy of trauma.

Rochelle's background as a long-term meditator and mindfulness teacher very much informs her writing. Throughout these pages, she draws on the wisdom of mindfulness and its potential for improving our inner physical, emotional, and mental processes. Utilizing specific practices for cultivating awareness and an embodied presence, she shows how these innate tools can help you practically to understand yourself, your history, and how to work skillfully with the totality of your experience, no matter how difficult or painful.

Equally important, Rochelle has deeply trained in ways of the heart and draws on love and compassion as essential resources on the journey of healing. She is a loving, caring teacher who speaks from the depth of her own journey in how to hold and heal the tender traumatized parts of ourselves with loving presence.

You will also learn to explore how the embodiment of your healing with nature offers unique ways to heal the Earth. The Earth too has suffered and continues to suffer from trauma; opening to offer the gifts of your healing to the Earth will help to heal nature.

As someone who has spent years healing my own trauma, I wish I had had this kind of guide as I traversed my difficult path. Now, with Rochelle's clear and kindhearted guidance and the wonderful array of practices, tools, and techniques for working with trauma, you will find in this work an excellent resource for healing and genuine transformation, and an aid for healing the Earth.

Blessings on your healing journey.

— **Mark Coleman**, founder of Awake in the Wild
and author of *From Suffering to Peace*,
Make Peace with Your Mind, and *Awake in the Wild*

INTRODUCTION

One summer morning, the slopes of our canyon are cleared of dry grasses to reduce the fire hazard. Afterward, I am struck by how nature reacts. The birds chirp more erratically and fly in strange, rushed, excited patterns. The rabbits retreat to the bushes beyond the cleared area, an arbitrary thirty feet from the buildings, and peek out to see if it's safe to forage in the now-open landscape. The land looks exposed, raw, and vulnerable to the elements. My heart aches for a while. I know clearing the hillside provides protection, yet at the same time these acts cause disruption and chaos for my wild friends and the land.

In the days that follow, I see wildlife and the land begin to heal themselves. The birds find graceful new patterns of flight, singing with a tempo that simultaneously lulls and enlivens the hillsides. The rabbits have made new burrows deep in the sagebrush and succulents. And the soil begins to awaken as seeds are offered up and smells of tilled earth waft over the landscape, creating space for new life to emerge. I am reminded that nature has an inherent impulse to restore herself to wholeness. She will organize herself and respond with healing and new beginnings to whatever conditions arise. She does so with the support of her interconnected systems and with whatever resources are available.

Responding to Trauma with Care

Trauma is the response to a deeply distressing or disturbing event that overwhelms our ability to cope, causes feelings of helplessness, changes our sense of self, and diminishes our ability to feel the full range of emotions and experiences. Traumatic events are often unexpected. If we do not have the resources to cope and find a sense of balance, we may go on to have difficulty in our work, relationships, finances, health, and other aspects of life.

Traumatic experiences come in many different forms. The psychological community has classically defined traumatic events as including natural disasters, serious accidents, terrorist acts, war, combat, rape, and other violent personal assaults. But trauma can also arise from experiences of loss of control, like medical trauma (including life-threatening illness, surgeries, and childbirth) and the loss of a loved one. Betrayal, racism, bullying, abuse of power, helplessness, political unrest, pandemics, and the climate crisis may also be traumatic experiences for an individual or a society.

According to the World Health Organization, over 70 percent of people experience trauma, with an average of three events per person, and 78 percent of people who had a traumatic experience went on to develop posttraumatic stress disorder (PTSD).[1]

Trauma can leave us feeling disconnected from ourselves and from the rest of humanity. We may try to manage the difficulty by avoiding reminders of the experience, denying that it happened, or repressing the memories. This reaction can evolve into dysfunction in other areas of life and go on to cause greater suffering. We might begin to experience feelings of shame, which can lead us to avoid interacting with other people. The unseen psychological wounds of trauma are often regarded by others as something we should ignore. This can leave us feeling isolated and alone. We may try to sidestep the mental or emotional pain by avoiding upsetting situations. And we may try to soothe ourselves with habits like drinking alcohol, eating, or binge-watching TV.

Because trauma and its aftereffects can be so distressing and over-whelming, we may come to believe it's necessary to just "move past" what has happened. Our mainstream cultural approach to difficult experiences reinforces this idea of "fixing" and "moving on from" trauma. During a natural disaster like a flood, in which people lose their homes and can no longer meet their daily needs, society's typical response is to jump into action to restore the basics: food and shelter. The media covers amazing stories of overcoming hardship, and the larger community feels a sense of relief, believing we "got through it" and the problems have been resolved. While these short-term, practical responses are necessary and helpful and reflect human kindness, we often pay very little attention to the restoration of a person's psyche after trauma. As a society, we tend to want to hear about the distressing parts only if we can be reassured that the pain was alleviated.

In this context, it's easy to fall into the mainstream mindset of just getting on with life and hoping the passage of time will help us cope with trauma. But with traumatic experiences, it's not that easy. Even if the direct cause of the trauma has been addressed, a person's suffering can continue for months or even years, and others may not acknowledge it, because that would require them to feel discomfort too.

So we may deal with trauma by trying to get on with life, isolating ourselves, avoiding upsetting reminders, or looking for ways to numb the pain. All of these strategies are kinds of escape. While they may serve us in the immediate sense, they often cause other problems, and they don't restore us to wholeness or wellness. In order to heal from trauma, we must attend to it, and that means we must first turn *toward* the traumatic experience.

You may be thinking, "That sounds awful. Why on earth would I want to turn toward my trauma?" This is where the wisdom of the natural world can help. Nature has an intrinsic tendency to thrive, and it always works with and toward a traumatic or difficult experience to find a new way of being and restore health. We can see this in the way a tree grows back after a limb is torn off by the wind, or a tiny patch of grass grows up through a crack in concrete. In nature, healing is supported by interconnection. A young deer who has lost his mother may be helped by another member of the herd to ensure his survival. In the canyon where I live, when the land was unexpectedly cleared, all of life reacted together. Through the days that followed, the wildlife of the canyon found a new rhythm, new ways to forage and survive. The canyon began to restore itself to a new norm in response to the changes, with plant and animal life following the instinct to survive and thrive.

We humans tend to think of ourselves as separate from nature, but we are part of it. We too can learn how to attend skillfully to our traumatic wounds, find ways to heal, trust in our connections with others, and ultimately thrive and become whole again. We can move closer to our trauma, take care of it, and heal from its mental, emotional, and physical challenges. Trauma is not something to be ashamed of, to hide from, or to resist. When you choose to meet the experience with caring, responsiveness, and openness, you can heal from trauma, not just move on from it. From nature, we can learn to turn toward painful experiences and transform them into a more wholesome state of being.

My hope in this book is to share the support and inspiration of nature and to teach the skills and pathways needed for healing from traumatic experiences. By feeling the support of the natural world and deepening your connection to it, you can develop a greater sense of wholeness and well-being. You will reenter the stream of life with more health, ease, happiness, and openness to experience. As you do so, you will find a deeper sense of interconnection with all of life, giving you greater purpose, hope, and love for life.

The Aftereffects of Trauma

The human body has a natural system for responding to danger: the fight-or-flight response. When we detect a threat, the sympathetic nervous system increases blood supply to the muscles, increases muscle tension, dilates our pupils (for better vision), and accelerates our heart rate and breathing. All of these changes prepare us to take action to survive, by defending ourselves or fleeing. Once the threat is past, the parasympathetic nervous system slows the heart rate, increases intestinal activity, and relaxes the muscles. These shifts allow the body to resume functions like digestion, sleep, and sexual arousal, all of which are also important to our survival.

When this system works as it's designed to, we survive the threatening experience, and then life returns to normal. But in the days, months, and years after a traumatic experience, we may begin to experience a range of symptoms, affecting every aspect of our life.

Physical
- Hyperarousal of the nervous system: hypervigilance, tension, agitation
- Sleep disturbances
- Gastrointestinal difficulties
- Respiratory challenges, such as shortness of breath, panic attacks, or asthma

Mental
- Memory difficulties
- Ruminative thinking (continually thinking negative or challenging thoughts)
- Catastrophic thinking (exaggerating or ruminating on the worst possible outcome of a situation)
- Excessive or inappropriate feelings of guilt
- Intrusive thoughts, memories, or flashbacks
- Dissociation (feelings of detachment)
- Derealization (feelings of unreality)

Emotional
- Heightened anxiety, feeling on guard or fearful
- Irritability, agitation, or anger outbursts

- Feelings of shame or embarrassment
- Difficulty feeling positive emotions
- Feeling numb

Behavioral
- Excessive use of alcohol
- Compulsive or addictive use of illicit substances
- Overuse of screens: TV, computer games, devices
- Overexercising
- Self-harm, such as cutting
- Illicit activity, such stealing or unsafe sexual behaviors

Relational
- Withdrawal from or avoidance of close relationships
- Isolating or cutting oneself off from others
- Fear of trusting others or being taken advantage of
- Overreliance on relationships to feel safe

If we have a built-in system to protect ourselves from danger and then recover, why do some experiences cause us so much trouble in the long run? The answer begins with whether it was possible *during the experience* to take action to defend ourselves or flee. If we were able to respond, for instance by fighting back, taking shelter, running away, or calling for help, we may not experience further difficulties after the threatening situation has been resolved. When we can engage the resources of the body, mind, and heart to take action during a traumatic experience, we can re-establish equilibrium.

However, if, because of the nature of the traumatic event or the people involved in it, we cannot take protective action, we are more likely to experience distressing symptoms afterward. When the fight-or-flight system is engaged and yet we cannot do the things that are needed to ensure our survival, the trauma reaction gets "stuck" in the body. As a result, the sympathetic nervous system often continues to send out the fight-or-flight signals. Ultimately this may lead to symptoms like flashbacks, intrusive memories, hyperawareness of our surroundings, reliving the experience mentally, and feeling fearful.

When the sympathetic nervous system stays switched on, the parasympathetic system does not have a chance to perform its function of restoring regulation and maintaining homeostasis. This results in our feeling "on guard" and having difficulty sleeping, concentrating on work, and so on. Many of the symptoms of trauma arise because the sympathetic and parasympathetic systems have become imbalanced and are not able to turn on and off normally.

In addition to the fight and flight responses, we have a third evolutionarily developed way of attempting to protect ourselves from danger. When a threat arises that we cannot fight against or escape from, we may "freeze" instead. This adaptive reaction to a traumatic event can enable our survival when no other alternative exists. However, the aftermath of a freeze reaction can include continuing feelings and experiences of immobility and helplessness. And if freezing is our only way of coping with trauma — if we never find or engage a fight-or-flight reaction — we may end up stuck in this mode, experiencing symptoms like feeling numb, checking out, daydreaming, or dissociating.

Being unable to manage the danger can cause problems in a couple of other ways. The amygdala is a primordial part of the brain that detects and helps us respond to threats. In people who have experienced trauma repeatedly without being able to escape or cope, the amygdala is overworked. Over time it may become oversensitive, registering things as threatening because they are associated with past trauma, even when they do not actually pose a threat in the present. This continued overactivity of the amygdala sends signals to the sympathetic nervous system to keep it engaged, continuing the cycle of dysregulation in the body.

Some people who have experienced trauma have trouble recalling experiences or being able to perceive, feel, and think through them in a way that seems logical. These symptoms arise because of the effect of trauma on two regions in the brain, the hippocampus and the prefrontal cortex. Simply put, the hippocampus helps us with memory, and the prefrontal cortex helps us reason and make decisions. When we have experienced trauma that we cannot later manage or renegotiate, these areas of the brain are adversely affected. And, as with the amygdala, the effect on the hippocampus and the prefrontal cortex continues to stimulate the sympathetic nervous system, perpetuating the difficulty of returning to healthy functioning.

With traumatic events come emotions — fear, anxiety, worry, anger, frustration, irritability, sadness, grief, shame, and guilt — that may lead us to develop problematic ways of coping. We may try to avoid, ignore, or suppress these distressing emotions. For example, if we feel worry and anxiety, we may drink alcohol to manage those feelings. If we feel shame or guilt, we may throw ourselves into our work as a distraction. These strategies provide some temporary relief, but they are inadequate as a long-term solution, because they deprive us of the opportunity to cope with or resolve the difficult emotions. Over time, because the emotions are never properly processed, they likely will arise again and again, and increase in severity.

Traumatic events can also produce certain kinds of thoughts, such as believing that we're not good enough or not strong enough; negative thoughts about the event or the people associated with the trauma; rumination, difficult memories, and flashbacks; and confusion. Because these thoughts can be so upsetting and overwhelming, we may avoid, suppress, or ignore them. We may try to control our thoughts or distract ourselves. As with managing emotions, these strategies often fall short because they keep us from processing these thoughts and beliefs in a healthy and functional way. If we haven't developed healthy ways to cope with distressing thoughts and emotions, the impact of trauma on our psyche can lead to more dysregulation and dysfunction.

The experience of trauma affects our social connections, our relationships, and our view of ourselves. From infancy, we depend on cooperative relationships with others for safety and survival. We thrive and grow when we have a healthy sense of connection and support, as well as a sense that we have a valuable role in our tribe. When the nervous system is dysregulated because of trauma, it affects our social connections. We may view others as unsafe or untrustworthy. We may hesitate to share our feelings for fear of being excluded or not supported by the group. We may have difficulty making friends, maintaining friendships, or feeling safe and connected in our familial relationships. In turn, the disruption of these social relationships can leave us feeling isolated and different. We may come to see ourselves as victims, as not good enough, or as less than other people.

All these effects influence our view of ourselves and the story we tell about ourselves. They often limit our ability to engage meaningfully in the world and find pleasure, joy, and purpose in life. As with the physical, mental, and emotional aftereffects of trauma, the damage to our relationships and our view of ourselves can create further difficulties in life until we bring them back into balance.

Fortunately, there are approaches that can aid us in recovery. First, it is important that we acknowledge the traumatic event as challenging and seek help and support. It's helpful to have an action-oriented coping style — that is, to look for a positive way to address our inner difficulties. And finally, we may recover more completely if we look at the trauma as a learning experience, an opportunity to grow and change, and a reason to find greater purpose. You may recognize some of these characteristics in yourself already. But even if you have not yet done any of these things, you can do them now, and this book will help.

Ecosystems of Healing

Our nervous system and brain inherently seek to be in balance. We are made of nature. Our biology — our bones, our muscles, our organs — is of the Earth. And, just as many different systems regulate life on Earth — cycles of the moon, seasons, climates, and terrains — we too have biological cycles and systems. When we understand them, we can help our internal systems regulate themselves.

Our biological, psychological, and relational systems are the inner ecosystems in which we can cultivate harmony, health, and wholeness after trauma. The way to heal is to move toward the trauma, to be with it, to befriend it, to attend to the wounds and to things that are painful, difficult, and challenging. We can restore our inner biology, our psyche, and our relationship to ourselves and the world by cultivating mindfulness, body awareness, and connection to nature. Each of us has the potential to heal and fully experience life.

Mindfulness

As we learn to be present to what we are experiencing now with kindness, openness, and curiosity, we can develop skillful ways to experience life. Bring awareness to your breath now. Notice how you experience it — as shallow or deep, slow or fast, warm or cool? Paying attention to the breath as it is now is mindfulness. By being fully present and aware of our immediate experiences, we begin to see that we have choices — opportunities to step out of our habits and engage in new ways of living. Noticing the breath as slow and cool can give rise to more ease and calm. Learning to be mindful of the breath can invite new opportunities to experience your life.

Trauma can make us reactive in our biology, psyche, and relational experiences, leaving us feeling as though we are out of control, with no choices available. If we can learn to bring mindfulness to our sensations, thoughts, emotions, and interactions — if we can hold them in clear and kind awareness — we can engage in new and healthier ways of living. Mindfulness shows us that we can meet each moment without reactivity, judgment, or commentary, and this ability gives rise to more curiosity, openness, acceptance, ease, compassion, sense of mystery, joy, and love.

Mindfulness has been shown to help heal the body, the mind, and relationships affected by trauma.[2] Throughout this book I share practices that can increase your development of mindfulness and show you how it can help you resolve some of the patterns of reactivity in your biology, psyche, and relationships, enabling you to live more fully and meaningfully.

Body Awareness

Somatic experiencing (SE) is a body-awareness treatment approach developed by Peter Levine.[3] The theory behind SE is that trauma-related symptoms are expressions of sympathetic arousal — the stress response — that are residing in our bodies because we weren't able to defend or protect ourselves completely at the time of the trauma. The goal of SE is to learn to increase our tolerance of the body sensations, thoughts, and emotions related to the trauma, allowing the activation — the "trauma" — to leave the body. SE helps you meet the symptoms of trauma, renegotiate them, and find resolution to the trauma. Over time, your sympathetic and parasympathetic nervous systems regain the ability to engage when needed and then turn off again. Unlike the psychological form of exposure therapy, which requires that the details of the story of the traumatic event be retold and that the patient be "exposed" to difficult feelings from the event to reduce fear and decrease avoidance, SE does not require retelling the story. If the trauma is stuck in the body, then it is the body that needs to find the way to release it.

Somatic experiencing shows promise for healing PTSD, anxiety, depression, chronic pain, and secondary traumatic stress (which may be experienced by caregivers who work with trauma and trauma-related incidents, such as therapists, first responders, and frontline healthcare providers).[4] With SE's focus on body awareness, it is a great complement to the practice of mindfulness. In this book, I show how SE practices can open new pathways for healing trauma.

Nature

The average American spends 87 percent of their time indoors.[5] American adults spend more than eleven hours per day watching, reading, listening to, or interacting with tablets, smartphones, computers, and TV.[6] This engagement with the nonnatural world and disengagement from the natural world is associated with increases in rates of obesity, diabetes, and heart disease, among other problems. At the same time, interest is growing in the ways nature can restore our health and well-being. Research has shown that nature can improve vision, memory, and concentration; restore mental energy; relieve stress; reduce inflammation; sharpen thinking; and expand creativity.

Florence Williams, in her book *The Nature Fix*, reports the following findings from research into the benefits of nature for humans:

- After five minutes in a forest surrounded by trees, the heart rate slows, facial muscles relax, and the prefrontal cortex quiets.
- Water and birdsong improve mood and alertness.
- Spending fifteen minutes in nature can reduce levels of the stress hormone cortisol.
- Spending time in natural landscapes increases alpha waves in the brain, which are associated with calm and alertness.
- Spending an hour and a half in nature reduces preoccupation with problems and makes us feel more connected to others and the world around us.
- Spending five hours in nature per month can make us happier overall.[7]

Since nature benefits exactly those areas and systems of the mind and body that are affected by trauma, it makes sense to consider nature as a support in healing from trauma. We have forgotten that nature is essential to the survival and well-being of humanity. Disconnection from nature has left us feeling homeless, uprooted, and displaced. Since trauma often creates a feeling of displacement, returning to nature can help us experience ourselves and others more deeply and enjoy renewed feelings of health and wholeness.

A Path to Healing Trauma

Mindfulness in nature is the doorway to becoming aware, reducing our reactivity, and learning to feel compassion, kindness, and acceptance of our experiences. Somatic experiencing in nature can help us to reinhabit the body in a way that feels safe and restores balance in our brain, body, psyche, and relationships. And nature is the container and support for this healing. Learning mindfulness and somatic experiencing practices in the context of nature deepens the experience of healing and provides a source of support that is always with us.

In part 1 of this book, you will learn to practice mindfulness with nature to support calming and relaxing the nervous system, developing presence, and deepening awareness. Part 2 introduces you to the somatic wisdom of the body — looking at places in the body where trauma may be stuck, exploring how you can heal the body with the support of nature and learn ways of releasing trauma and restoring aliveness. In part 3, you will learn to integrate the teachings of mindfulness and somatic healing with awareness of nature to cultivate a deeper sense of wholeness and sustained well-being. You will learn to incorporate these practices into your life and communities and discover how to trust your own healing to live more fully. Part 4 offers ways to discover how your healing may restore health to others and to the Earth.

Each of the chapters offers teachings, practice support, reflection, activities, and stories. While the practices were created with an outdoor setting in mind, you are welcome to sit inside and practice near the support of nature (such as house plants) or near a window (open or closed). The practices offer opportunities to reflect and write, so you may wish to keep a journal. At the end of each chapter I include sections titled "Taking Care" (parts 1–3) and "Healing Continues" (part 4), which offers ways to integrate the practices into your life and suggestions that may help you on your path to healing trauma.

Everyone's path of healing is unique. Please feel free to adapt any of the practices in ways that serve your own needs. This might include letting go of a particular focus or instructions, modifying the practice to suit your body, or adapting suggested physical movements to practice in your mind's eye or with a different part of the body.

The stories of individuals presented here are intended to deepen understanding of the teaching and practices I write about. They feature individuals I have worked with who have given me permission to include their stories. I have protected their identities by using pseudonyms and altering some details.

If trauma is interfering with your life in significant ways, you may wish to seek professional help and use this book with the support of a therapist.

The Earth is and has always been here to support us. We are made of all the elements of nature. If we learn to connect to our inner natural way of being, we can connect more deeply to ourselves, and this in turn allows us to heal and to connect to others and the world. As we awaken and experience healing with nature, wholeness is restored. From this place of health and well-being, we can engage in life with greater openness, trust, creativity, love, care, and connection.

And now to explore your path to healing.

Audio Meditations

To download audio files of the meditations in this book, visit:

https://newmindfullife.com/meditations

Enter the password "healing."

Part 1

AWAKENING *in* NATURE

In every walk with nature one receives
far more than he seeks.

— JOHN MUIR

Nature is always revealing to us how it is to be alive — changing, evolving, letting go, surrendering, adapting, dying. These are beautiful lessons. If we are present in our own lives, we can awaken to our own true nature and experience being more fully alive.

Think of a time recently when you were touched by an experience of being with nature. Maybe you noticed the bud on a flower just about ready to burst into bloom, or the stillness and solidity of a tree you stood next to, or the gentle flow of water. As you connect to and learn to become fully present to these experiences, you can begin to feel that you too can experience a sense of innate well-being. The potential to bloom and open, the solidity and fluidity you perceive in nature are all present within, for you to connect with and experience.

By calling these qualities to our attention, nature supports our intention to be present. It allures our attention and invites us to be with this moment as it is. The heart of mindfulness practice is establishing a clear and kind relationship with what is here in this moment, skillfully responding to and engaging with life.

Traditional mindfulness practice is intended to support the development of awareness through specific meditations that emphasize cultivating awareness of the breath, the senses, the body, mind, and heart, and openness to all things. Students are often encouraged to explore these practices indoors, in a group setting. For some people (especially those who have experienced trauma), this learning format can be challenging, requiring more effort and giving rise to feelings of being stuck or unsafe. Practicing mindfulness in the support and community of nature can alleviate some of these difficulties.

Practicing mindfulness in nature also allows us to practice mindfulness *with* nature. Learning to experience awareness of the breath, the senses, the body, the mind, and the heart in a natural setting gives us greater access to our inner experiences. We are likely to feel more naturally present and curious about our inner landscape when we are supported by a natural landscape. Nature herself provides the container for a mindfulness practice that reduces the need to try or "do" and instead helps us to sense and receive what is arising and present within and around us. (I refer to nature as feminine because I experience her as a divine presence. You may choose to replace *nature* with another word or concept that resonates with you.)

We know that being in nature can slow the heart rate, reduce levels of stress hormones, and help our brains to orient to calm and natural alertness, all of which are conducive to the practice of mindfulness.

Mindfulness practice can be both formal and informal. In formal practice, you designate a specific period of time for meditation, during which you may sit, move, walk, stand still, or lie down to focus your attention in a particular way. To develop your informal practice of mindfulness, you bring mindful awareness to activities throughout the day, such as eating, drinking, showering, dressing, cooking, talking, driving, texting, and sending email.

Nature supports both formal and informal mindfulness. Beautiful outdoor settings can help us sustain and extend a formal mindfulness practice. Nature also draws us in with its colors, textures, and scents: we tend to be more present in an activity when we can feel the texture of leaves, smell the flowers, and appreciate the fine details as well as the vastness of nature. Awareness of nature supports our informal practice of mindfulness, teaching us to be present in our day-to-day lives.

By practicing mindfulness in nature, we begin to feel more fully alive and embodied — at home in the body. Many of us also often intrinsically feel at home in nature, and this sense of ease can help us learn to be present in all aspects of our life. As this sense of embodiment grows, we develop an increased ability to be kindly present to all that is arising in our inner landscape — in our sensations, body, mind, and heart — as well as in the external landscape, responding to what is happening as it unfolds. Mindfulness in nature gives us the opportunity to awaken to what is within us as well as around us, to heal and live skillfully.

If you have a history of unhealed trauma, it can affect your physical, mental, emotional, behavioral, and relational experiences. Feelings of being disembodied and disconnected may impede your ability to make wise decisions. By practicing mindfulness in nature, you awaken your inner sense of safety, well-being, and connection. You can learn to step out of the patterns of reactivity and being on automatic and into healing, wholeness, and healthy living.

The chapters in part 1 are designed to help you develop your mindfulness practice in and with nature. You will learn about, practice, and explore breath awareness, sensory awareness, body awareness, and element awareness. Mindfulness in nature can help you learn to relate kindly and respond to your true nature and potential. Take the time you need to integrate these practices into your life. Just as nature never rushes, you can follow your own natural rhythm to treat yourself patiently, kindly, and lovingly as you heal your inner landscape.

Chapter 1

BREATH AWARENESS

Every breath is a sacrament, an affirmation of our connection with all living things, a renewal of our link with our ancestors and a connection to generations to come.

— David Suzuki

Breath is a constant in every moment of our lives. It is the first thing we experienced as we entered life, and it is the last thing we will experience as life ends. This makes it a wonderful focal point or anchor to which we can tether awareness. When we learn to connect to the breath in awareness, we see how it can ground us, support our healing, and cultivate our capacity to feel fully alive.

Breath meditation is taught to support healing in various traditions. Breath symbolizes life, the power of the spirit, and transience and impermanence of life. The Bible identifies breath as spirit, which like the wind, is invisible, immaterial, and powerful. Yogic traditions are rooted in *pranayama*, techniques for regulating the breath to support health and spiritual growth. Neuroscience has shown us that breathing techniques can help our parasympathetic nervous system to provide regulation and healing to our brain and body.

Breath awareness is often the first meditation practice taught in mindfulness. It is a reliable way of connecting with *this moment*, a way to calm the mind and relax the body. By focusing on the breath, we can learn to observe all of the movements of the mind, the experiences of the body, and the terrains of our emotions. As we develop and sustain awareness of the breath, we can let go of reactivity and habits of following, clinging, or resisting, and relate to the experiences in a new, more open, kind, and loving way.

Nature can help us cultivate breath awareness. In nature, the body is often naturally inclined to breathe more deeply. Reflect on a time when you walked outside. Maybe the sun was out and a cool breeze was blowing. What impulse arose in your body? Probably a sense of opening in the chest and expansion of the lungs, taking in a deeper, fuller breath. The sights, sounds, scents, and sensory experiences of nature allow us to connect to our breath with more ease.

In supporting and healing trauma, learning to sense the breath as relaxing, calming, easeful, and uplifting is a good place to start. These qualities are inherent in nature. Attuning ourselves to nature supports our ability to experience these qualities within the breath and to help the nervous system to settle and feel grounded and supported.

Practice: Breath Awareness with Nature

Find a place outdoors relatively free of distractions where you can practice for ten to fifteen minutes. Ideally, choose a place that you feel reflects qualities of relaxation, calm, ease, and uplift — near a stream, in a spacious meadow, in a canyon, or in a park or backyard with local plants and wildlife.

During this and all the other practices in this book, you may choose to close your eyes if it feels safe and comfortable, to rest your gaze softly on something that feels supportive, or to open and close your eyes as you practice. You may wish to pause after each instruction below to practice what you have just read. You may also wish to access the recorded meditations by following the instructions on page 14.

Choose a supportive posture that allows you to sense the Earth beneath you, providing a feeling of stability and groundedness. Invite your spine to be alert, lengthened, and supported. Allow yourself to move or shift any parts of the body that are tight, tense, or contracted to enable the body to relax and open. You may choose to lie down, lean against a tree, or walk slowly. As you settle into your posture, become aware of what is around you — to the right, left, in front of, behind, above, and beneath you.

Attend to an expression of nature that you sense as helping to relax and release tension from your body: maybe the warmth of the sun, the coolness of the breeze, or the sounds of birdsong. Now bring attention to the breath. Become aware of the breath in connection with these expressions of relaxation in nature. Allow yourself to breathe slowly, noticing the inhale and the exhale. As you breathe, you may choose to make each exhale a bit longer than the inhale, and sense how this gives rise to relaxation within the body. Be present to the qualities of nature that offer relaxation and the qualities of the breath and body that allow you to feel relaxed.

Now shift your attention to the natural surroundings and the things that are giving rise to ease, bringing calm and peace to the mind: the coo of a dove, the movement of water falling softly over rocks, the winds hushing through the grasses. Become aware of the breath. Sense your breath in connection with one of these expressions of calm in nature. As you sense the breath, noticing calm and ease, observe what this is like in the mind. Attend to these qualities of nature and the way the breath is supporting ease of mind.

Now shift your attention to elements in your surroundings that you perceive as uplifting — things that open, inspire, and bring happiness or joy, such as a magnificently colored flower that is opening and reaching its head to the sky, a bird singing a melody of connection to his flock, or the clouds lightly moving and dancing through the sky. Invite your attention to notice the breath. Become aware of the breath in connection with these expressions of uplift in nature. Take time to observe each inhale and exhale, sensing any qualities of uplift, joy, expansion, or nourishment in the heart. Attune to the qualities of nature and the supportiveness of the breath to incline the heart to lightness, uplift, and joy.

In the last few minutes of the practice, decide which quality best supports your being present in this moment — a sense of relaxation in the body, calmness in the mind, or being uplifted in the heart — and allow your focus to rest in the movements of your breath and this quality of nature. Attend moment to moment to the breath in this way.

Gently open your eyes (if they were closed) and take in what you see around you. Move in whatever way feels orienting to nature and helpful in shifting into the rest of your day.

Afterward, consider writing in your journal about any experiences or insights you had during this meditation.

This practice cultivates awareness of a few qualities in the breath that can help establish your connection to nature and support your healing, but remember that nature is infinite, and our inner landscape has unique qualities and needs. Make this practice your own. When you are touched by an aspect of nature that exhibits another quality, such as exhilaration, quiet, or steadiness, take the time to be with it and breathe with it, sensing what arises around you and within you. Be open to what supports you best.

Natural Breath Awareness

Just like nature, the breath has its own rhythms and expressions. Steadying your attention and learning to focus on the breath supports being present to the moment. This allows you to better perceive and respond to your own needs and care for yourself. You also learn to observe patterns of reactivity or automaticity in your mind, body, and heart. You can develop a new relationship with these patterns, free yourself from them, and begin to create new ways of thinking, feeling, and taking action.

All these amazing possibilities arise from just bringing awareness to the breath naturally. In this moment, bring awareness to the breath as it enters the body. Notice its pace, the quality of its movement, its temperature, texture, and fluidity. Now, as you exhale, notice the way the breath shifts, releases, flows, and moves through the body. Continue, if you wish, for three more complete breaths. You may begin to notice that every breath, and every moment of the breath, is different. Attending to these differences provides rich opportunities for cultivating present-moment awareness. This is mindfulness.

As you bring awareness to the breath, you are likely to find that your mind wanders to thoughts of things that have already happened, anticipation of what is to come, or other distractions: sounds in the environment, difficult sensations in your body, or emotions such as boredom, anxiety, and sadness. These types of experiences can make it difficult for some people to cultivate mindfulness meditation practices like breath awareness. The important thing to remember when these experiences arise is that they are *part of the practice*. We have a mind that thinks, a body that feels sensations, a heart that expresses emotion. We often build habitual and reactive patterns of behavior to try to fix or manage difficult experiences. When we learn through attending to the breath to observe, let go of judgment, and experience presence, kindness, and appreciation for this moment just as it is, we can establish a new way of being that is not run by habits or automatic reactions.

For example, recall the last time you were worried about something: maybe your finances, strain in a relationship, or health concerns. When this thought arose, it likely led to many other types of thoughts about how to fix, manage, avoid, or control the problem ("I will make a budget," "I'll cut out things I don't need to buy," "I should have better spending habits," "I'm really no good at managing money"). Through mindfulness practices such as breath awareness (and other approaches discussed in later chapters), we learn that by steadying the focus on the breath, we can stay in the present moment. The same applies when we observe the mind wandering or running off. We can learn to observe these thoughts, gently and kindly acknowledge them, and then come back to a focus on the breath. As we begin to see that we have choices in our relationship to these reactive habits of mind, over time the habits fade away. Mindfulness practice becomes a trusted ally that supports us in changing habits and patterns of thought that have not served our well-being.

Nature supports our development of breath awareness by providing many experiences and sensations for us to attune to. We can feel support from sounds, temperatures, changing conditions, living things growing, plants photosynthesizing, wildlife gracing us with their presence. When we sit in nature, the environment supports us physically and spiritually, helping us steady our attention on the breath. Part of my daily practice is to feel the birdsong carried on the wind as I breathe in. I feel the vibrations, tones, and intensities of the songs of the birds in the wind, and I become curious about my own breath in the same way. I feel its vibrations, textures, and movements. As I inhale, I feel the support of nature, and as I exhale, I offer my support back to the natural world around me.

The breath-awareness practices offered here are designed to help you relax, calm the mind, quiet the heart, and establish feelings of being supported and nourished. You can practice them individually or in combination. Your practice may last only a few minutes or for twenty to thirty minutes, depending on what feels best to you. Practice in and with nature, choosing natural settings in which you feel connected, comfortable, and supported.

Practice: Natural Breath Awareness

The following practice can be done on its own, or you may start with the practice above for establishing relaxation, ease, and uplift and then begin this practice. Find a place outdoors that is relatively free of distractions and where you can sit for fifteen or twenty minutes.

Choose a place where you feel supported, grounded, and nourished by what is around you.

Choose a posture that feels relaxed and open and allows your breathing to be easeful, perhaps sitting or lying on the ground or resting against a rock or tree. As you settle into the posture and make adjustments for comfort, sense the ground supporting your body. Allow yourself to notice what is around you in nature, such as the quality and temperature of the air, its movement or stillness, or the scents and sounds carried by the air.

Now bring your attention to your breath. Notice the inhale and the exhale. Be curious about where in your body the breath feels easiest and most available to you — is this in the nostrils, the chest, the belly? Let awareness rest in this region. Notice the experience of each breath — the pace or rhythm, the temperature and texture, the movements and the sensations of the body associated with it.

It's likely that your mind will wander. Notice what is arising. Is your mind moving ahead to what hasn't happened yet, or rehearsing what has been? Are you solving problems, ruminating, judging, doubting, or questioning whether you are doing this right or should be having some particular experience? As you notice a thought arising, can you meet the experience with interest, without judgment, with kindness, gentleness, and acceptance, and then bring your attention back to experiencing this moment of the breath? What are the qualities of breathing that steady you in this moment?

You may experience difficult emotions, challenging body sensations, or distractions around you. Again, each of these is an opportunity to notice and meet what is here: the patterns of thought, habits, or tendencies you may experience of wanting it to be different, trying to change how it is, or resisting it. Can you invite a sense of curiosity, kindness, and compassion to this moment? Then gently return attention to the breath. Notice each breath as it moves in and out of the body. Feel how each inhale moves air into the body, pauses, and becomes the exhale, pausing again before the next inhale.

As you notice each breath, become aware of any expressions in nature that support your observing this moment. Maybe the breath follows the rhythms of the air flowing through the leaves of trees, or scents in the air awaken the nostrils and invite a deeper breath, or the moisture or aridity of the air allows the breath to move easily or choppily. Allow awareness to include a sense of not being separate but being supported in each moment by nature, breathing together with nature.

In the last few minutes of the practice, connect to the inner landscape of your mind, body, and heart. Notice what is present now. Is the mind a bit more still, less wandering? Is the body more relaxed or at ease? Is the heart more open and connected? What- ever is present, offer appreciation or gratitude for what you have cultivated in this practice. You may also choose to offer gratitude to nature and her support for you in this practice.

Gently open your eyes (if they were closed). Move your body — opening or closing the hands, moving the feet, allowing your eyes to take in what is around you. Carry the goodness of this practice into the rest of your day.

Afterward, consider writing in your journal about any experi- ences or insights you had during this meditation.

Challenges of Attending to the Breath

Although many people find breath awareness meditation helpful and easy to learn, some people who experience panic attacks or respiratory issues such as asthma find that a focus on the breath can exacerbate anxiety and lead to constricted or shallow breathing. Fortunately, there are techniques available that can help overcome these difficulties.

If it is difficult for you to find ease and connection to the breath as you are practicing breath awareness, here are some suggestions.

- Start small, perhaps by focusing only on one or two complete breaths, then move on to another practice or an everyday activity.

- Explore the places in your body where breathing feels easy, accessible, and available — maybe the nostrils, chest, or belly. Steady your attention on this region of the body for a few rounds of breathing.
- Use the support of nature. As you breathe, notice the temperatures of the air around you and the sounds carried on the air. Explore feeling the breath in your body in the same way that nature is expressing it around you.
- Take a walk. Notice the changes in your body and breath that occur as you walk more rapidly: notice scents in the air passing through the nostrils and the feeling of your body warming or cooling.
- Notice your breath while doing everyday activities. Focus on two or three rounds of breathing as you cook, exercise, dress, or work.

When you feel ready, learning how to breathe from the diaphragm can be helpful. This type of breathing stimulates the vagus nerve, which activates the parasympathetic nervous system and calms the body.

The diaphragm is a large, dome-shaped muscle at the base of the lungs. It wraps around both sides of the body and across the back. You can feel it by placing your fingers just below the lower rib cage and pushing inward.

Here is a simple exercise for exploring diaphragmatic breathing:

- Lie down on your back on a flat surface, such as your bed. Use a pillow under your head and another under your knees for support if that's more comfortable for you.
- Place one hand on your upper chest and the other on your belly, just below your rib cage.
- As you feel the diaphragm with the lower hand, see if you can become aware of the way it extends around the sides and back of your body as well.
- Breathe in slowly through your nose, letting the air in deeply and pulling it gently down into your belly. As your diaphragm

expands to draw in the air, the hand on your chest should remain still, while the one on your belly should rise.

- As you breathe out, let the diaphragm contract and relax. The hand on your belly should return to its original position.
- Continue to breathe this way for five to ten rounds of breathing. You will become aware of expansion and opening of the diaphragm in all directions as you inhale, and as you exhale, feeling the diaphragm deflate, contract a bit, and relax.

As you use this breathing technique, you will become aware of your parasympathetic nervous system engaging to calm your body. This sense of physical ease can help you develop an inner sense of relaxation that can aid in healing your trauma.

Mary's Story

Mary wanted to learn breathing practices to manage her increasing panic attacks and chronic anxiety. Although I explained to her that learning mindfulness through the experience of the breath might not be a good place to start given her history of panic attacks, she insisted she was ready.

We decided together to start with diaphragmatic breathing. I invited Mary to lie down and to focus on the movement of the diaphragm in the back of her body (this can be a helpful approach for people who suffer from panic attacks). As she practiced, she noticed that her diaphragm began to quiver and contract, making her feel unable to catch her breath. We were meeting near the ocean, and I suggested that she focus on the sounds of the waves and feelings of the breeze for a bit. As she moved her attention from the environment and then back to her breath, she became curious about why her diaphragm was constricting. As we discussed the question, we concluded that it might be a conditioned response to her recurring panic attacks and her limited awareness of what her body might need in order to feel safe.

In another session soon after this, Mary recalled a trauma that she had forgotten and suppressed: a tornado hitting her school when she was five years old. Her teacher had told the class to grab onto their desks as the tornado struck the building and tore it apart. She recalled the feeling of being pulled up and unable to feel safe. She also recalled that after the tornado, neither her teachers nor her parents talked to her about the experience or how to reestablish a sense of safety; they just encouraged her to move on and return to school once the building was repaired. Over the years, Mary had developed many strategies to manage this trauma stuck in her body, which manifested itself in panic attacks and anxiety symptoms. Over time, Mary has been able to establish calm and groundedness in her body through practices of grounding, orienting, body awareness, and pendulation (all described in later chapters), which have allowed her to experience more ease with her breath and to be comfortable practicing natural awareness of the breath.

Taking Care

Awareness of the breath may be experienced in numerous ways, ranging from exquisite beauty and interconnection to a sense of simplicity and quiet movements to feelings of extreme challenge, strain, or overwhelm. All experiences are okay. Through the practice of mindfulness in nature and the healing practices described in later chapters, you will learn to work skillfully with whatever feelings arise. If you find that these breath practices are not helpful now, feel free to move ahead to the chapters on sensory awareness and body awareness. Learn to trust the practices that are best for you. You can choose to return to this breathing practice when it feels right.

As you explore the meditation practices in this book and begin to feel the benefits of ease, calm, and relaxation, you may begin to feel a sense of lowering your guard. While this is beneficial and necessary in healing trauma, it may create internal conflict about how to proceed. The conflict arises when a part of you wants to decrease the overwhelm and stress associated with your trauma, but another part of you wants to stay on high alert because your brain has developed the patterns of fight, flight, and freeze as measures to keep you safe. You may find that you try to push experiences away, attempt to fix or analyze them, or look for ways to get rid of the discomfort you experience.

The practices described in this book will help you to work with these patterns and resolve the conflicts that are likely to arise. Be patient: remember that when these patterns arise, they are attempting to protect you as you have not known another way. As your body heals from the trauma, these patterns will fade. Be patient and kind to yourself as your healing journey unfolds.

Breath awareness can help you heal the wounds of trauma and feel your aliveness and your interconnection to all things. The breath is ever present to support you, to help you to let go of habits and patterns of your mind and heart that do not serve you, and to help you heal your inner landscape. Let breath awareness practice support you throughout your healing journey. Breath is the source of all life, and awareness of the breath can help you live your life to the fullest.

Chapter 2

SENSORY AWARENESS

Sensory perception is the silken web that binds our separate nervous systems into the encompassing ecosystem.

— David Abram

As I sit now, writing, I am in the canyon where I live in San Diego, California. It's spring, and it's amazing to be in the presence of the canyon: to see the bright yellow wildflowers, the canvas of green emerging in the leaves of the trees, and the hawk soaring on the waves of the wind; to *smell* the sweet scents of the moist, warm Earth and the fragrant perfume of the flowers; to *hear* the symphonies of birdsong — doves cooing, hummingbirds whizzing, sparrows chirping; to *feel* the cool wind gently touching my body and the steady, stable Earth beneath and around me, wrapping me in its embrace; and to *taste* the faint, sweet, pungent flavor of the pine trees around me. I pause, breathe deep, and feel how all of this as it enters each doorway of my sensory experience is allowing my body to feel alive, supported, and at ease. I rest in the beauty of all life in this moment.

Attuning to our senses — what we see, hear, smell, taste, and touch — can be a path leading us to awareness and experience of the present moment. Nature herself often allures and awakens the senses. Think of a time

33

recently when you were in nature and recall how your experience was shaped by what you saw, smelled, touched, and heard. Sensory awareness is a wonderful aid to establishing your mindfulness practice and healing trauma. Even if you have particular sensory doorways that may feel over- or underdeveloped, the practice of mindful sensory awareness can bring greater balance and ease into the experience of the senses.

Like the breath, each of our senses can be a tool for cultivating awareness. Focusing on a sense can allow us to feel supported. Consider the way a tree grows. As a seed, it nestles into the earth. As it sprouts, it is supported by soil, nutrients, water, and sunlight, slowly achieving its form as a mature tree and expressing its true potential and aliveness. Mindfulness grows in the same way. Starting small and vulnerable, you draw on resources that steady and support you — maybe the breath, external sensations, or sensations in the body. Gradually you become aware of your own growth: your mind may be less busy and your heart more open or joyful, and you may experience a sense of being more yourself. As you grow, you are able to recognize and shed habits and patterns that don't serve your well-being and to focus on new ways of being truly present.

Letting Go of Automaticity and Stepping into Sensory Awareness

Food (yes, food!) is a great way to awaken the senses. Eating stimulates all the senses. It is also one of the most conditioned activities in life, one that often becomes automatic and not particularly sensory. This makes food ideal as the focus of a mindfulness practice. And food is part of nature: everything we eat is the product of nature and a set of complex environmental conditions.

Consider strawberries. How many different ways have you eaten them? Do you like them, dislike them, or feel neutral about them? How did you form your opinions about strawberries? It's likely that in the past you had one or two particularly good or bad experiences of strawberries, and those sensory memories dominate your feelings about them now, to the point where you may not really be aware of the taste or texture of the next strawberry you pop into your mouth. This automatic response, or automaticity, limits how fully we can be present to experiences — not just of food, but of everything we encounter in life.

Conditioning is the way the mind processes past experiences and then expects and plans for similar experiences in the future. If you listen to the sounds around you now, you will probably identify them as natural or human-made. As you note the sound of a car or a bird, then your mind will immediately classify that sound as one that you like or dislike, based on past experiences. Sensory awareness practices give us a chance to change this automaticity, to let go of automatic judgment and be open to what we are experiencing.

I invite you to feel the way sensations are present in your ear now. Maybe you are feeling coolness, warmth, or the touch of air or hair on the external ear. Now shift the attention to the inner ear, sensing the vibrations or sound waves arriving to the ear from around you. See if you can be present moment to moment to the sounds arising and passing around you. When you bring awareness to a sense gateway, it opens the path to being fully present, not in automaticity, but to the actual sensations arising in *this* moment.

Let's go back to the example of our strawberry. Think what might happen if you are fully present next time you encounter a strawberry. By letting go of your automatic conditioning to the idea of strawberries and being fully present to all your senses, you may be able to discover new possibilities in that one strawberry. You may be able to choose a new and healthier relationship to your senses, body, and ways of connecting to food or life. Maybe you will notice the beauty and patterns of the seeds, the shades of pink and white, the sweet aromas, the brightness of the taste on the tongue.

Going beyond the sensory experience, you might consider other aspects of strawberries. Did you know that strawberries are a part of the rose family and that they were first cultivated in gardens during the Renaissance?[1] Consider how many hands have tended the one strawberry you eat. Who planted it, and where? How was the soil tended and the fruit picked, washed, and prepared for eating? How many generations of plants came before it to allow this fruit to come into existence? One strawberry plant lasts only five or six years. It takes eight to fourteen months for the plant to mature, and four to six weeks for a fruit to ripen after the blossom. How have the elements aided the growth of the fruit: water, the nutrients in the earth, the warmth and light of the sun, the environment that has given the plant space to grow? How many acts of pollinating bees and temperature swings from cool to warm brought this berry into existence? It took the infinite complexity and wisdom of nature to grow this one strawberry for you to experience.

From the deeper interconnection and sensory presence gained from this awareness of a small fruit, you can experience and savor your own well-being. This way of being present allows us to feel more alive, awake, and supported.

Practice: Sensory Awareness — Eating

This practice requires access to the outdoors (a window, patio, backyard, or park).

Choose a piece of naturally grown food, such as a piece of fresh or dried fruit or a vegetable. Notice what guides you in making your choice. There is no right or wrong choice here; the point is just to notice what habits or automatic judgments you may hold regarding various types of food.

Take some time to prepare the food. As you do so, bring attention to your hands. Sense the temperatures, textures, pressures, and densities as you wash the food, cut it, and pick it up or put it on a plate. Feel your hands and body being in connection with this piece of food.

Find a place outdoors, free of distractions, where you can explore this food with all five senses. You can choose to stay as long as you like with each sense. Going slowly will allow for a deepening of your inner experience and awareness. Place the food in the palm of your hand.

First, bring attention to your eyes, without looking at the food. Slowly close and open your eyes a few times, steadying your gaze on a natural object. Sense the muscles of the eyes moving, the light entering your eyes, and then your eyelids blocking the light.

Now sense shifting the eyes to look at the food. What colors, shadows, textures, shapes, and dimensions do you see? Turn the food in all directions, letting the light strike it at different angles. Let the eyes softly receive what is before them. As best you can, let go of needing to identify, label, or judge what you see.

Now move attention to the hand that is not holding the food, without picking it up from the palm of the other hand. (If you picked it up automatically before reading this, just smile — you noticed your habit.) Bring your first finger and thumb together and then apart, noting the sensations that arise. Notice the muscles that move, the pressure created, the warmth or coolness of your hand and the air.

Now pick up the food from your palm with the thumb and first finger of the other hand, noting the sensations and textures you feel. Is it soft, hard, sticky, smooth? Is it dense or light? Move it between the thumb and the first finger. Be curious and open to the touch sensations you experience.

Now shift your attention to your nose. Bring the food up to your nostrils. (If you've picked up the food to smell it already, move it away, and smile again.) Breathe in and out once through your nose. Notice how the nostrils expand, how air moves in and warmer air moves out. What aromas arise: sweetness, saltiness, pungency, earthiness, scents of spices? Notice whether your right and left nostrils experience different intensities of smell. Breathe deeply, staying present to what is arising. If you notice your mind moving to memories or distractions, bring awareness to the scent of the food in this moment.

Now focus attention on your hearing. If you observe the mind questioning or doubting whether this food has a sound, shift your attention to the ears. Notice the physical sensations of your external ears, such as air passing over, hair touching, warmth, or coolness. Now shift attention to the inner ear: become aware of the sensation of vibrations or movements of sound waves entering the ear.

Bring the food up to your ear. Holding it with the thumb and forefinger, move it back and forth while attending to sounds around you. Be curious about what arises. Do you hear a sound associated with this food? If the mind wanders off into stories or memories, gently bring awareness to this moment with this food.

Move the attention now to the sense of taste. Pause before you place the food in the mouth. Notice if there was an automatic sensation that arose in anticipation of tasting it. Bring your attention to the mouth and the tongue: notice tastes (which may be neutral, bland, or absent). See whether you notice moisture or textures on the tongue. Now place the food on your tongue, resisting the urge to chew for a few moments. Notice its flavors: sweet, salty, bitter, pungent. Notice its textures on the tongue or the roof of your mouth: is it smooth, rough, bumpy? Now move the food with your tongue and place it between your upper and lower teeth, noticing how your tongue automatically knows how to perform this action to enable you to chew. Bite into the food, with attention to the movement of your jaw muscles and tongue, the varying intensity of the tastes, the textures of the food, and the urge to swallow. Pause before you automatically swallow, and then bring attention to the actions of swallowing, feeling the engagement of the muscles of the mouth and throat. Notice the symphony of movements, tastes, and processes that bring food into the body. See if you can track the movement of the food down the esophagus into the stomach. Reflect on the fact that your body, which is made of nature, is now integrating this form of nature to become part of the body.

As you sit in nature, consider where this food may have begun its journey to you. If it is a plant-based food, consider the nature of the plant, where the seed might have sprouted, the conditions in which the plant grew, how many seasons passed while this one piece of food grew, how many hands tended and cared for this food, and how the elements of nature supported its growth. If you don't know the answers to all these questions, notice what feelings arise with not knowing, and just attend to what you know, feel, connect to about the food's journey. Offer gratitude for the food that is here for you now, nourishing you, supporting you, connecting you to life.

As you close this practice, observe the state of your mind, body, and heart. Connect to what has been cultivated by this practice. Offer gratitude to yourself for taking care of your being in this way.

Afterward, consider writing in your journal about any insights you had during this meditation.

Practice: Sensory Awareness — Walking

This practice encourages you to connect with your senses in nature, including sensing what arises within you, and to participate with nature as you encounter experiences that awaken your senses. It involves a twenty- to thirty-minute walk. If walking is not supportive of the needs of your body at this time, you may choose to move your body to connect with nature in ways that serve you best. This is a walk with no destination; let go of needing to get anywhere, and just be present to the experience of walking or moving while attending to your senses. You might choose a path in a local park or just stroll around your backyard or patio. If it's safe to do so, consider going barefoot. You can choose to focus on just one of your senses as you walk, or you can rotate through all of them: decide what serves you best.

Before starting to walk, stand with your feet about hip distance apart, or whatever feels comfortable to you. Bring your attention to the body, starting with the soles of the feet. Sense in awareness the points where your feet connect with the ground. Now shift up from the feet to the legs to become aware of feeling your muscles extended or contracted, the bones and joints aligned to hold your body upright.

Now become aware of the torso. Allow length in the spine, feeling the belly soft and the chest open. Let your arms rest gently by your sides. Now attend to the shoulders, neck, and head, finding an easy, relaxed posture. Let your head rest on the support of the body, legs, and feet. Settle into presence, feeling your body grounded, relaxed, and open.

As you begin to walk, attend to the sensations in the body. Go slowly; this walk has no destination. Feel the sensations throughout the body. Notice how each step is a symphony of sensations. As you shift, lift, swing, and place each foot, notice sensations arising, moving, and changing throughout the body.

Now bring your attention to the sense of touch. Feel the sensations of your feet touching the earth: smooth and rough textures, warm or cool temperatures, the solidity or unevenness of the ground. As you walk, attend to other touch sensations, like the moisture or aridity of the air brushing your skin. Explore the sensations in each region of the body, from the feet to the head. Be open to the particular expressions of connection with nature through touch: the coolness of a stone, the soft, light feel of a flower petal, the rough or smooth bark of a tree. Allow yourself to be present to what arises as you feel inwardly the sense of touch and the sense of connection to nature.

Now bring your attention to hearing. Notice the sounds around and above you. If you find yourself trying to identify, label, or name the sounds — for instance, distinguishing between natural or human-made — can you let go of the need to know what the sound is and simply be present to its arising and passing, coming and going? Be curious about the tones, the intensities, and the vibrations of the sounds. Let them pass through your inner landscape. If you become aware of efforts to analyze, judge, or compare one sound to others, notice this tendency as just a movement of the mind, then gently return to awareness of sound present in this moment. Rest in awareness of hearing nature arising and passing in your inner landscape.

Now shift your attention to the sense of sight. Invite your eyes to take in things near and far, above and beneath you. Notice how your mind likes to identify, label, or name what you see. Simply receive what you are seeing. Allowing your eyes to relax and soften, scan the landscape slowly and gently. Observe in what you see — the colors, shadows, plays of light, movement or stillness. If a particular sight draws your attention, slow down and allow yourself to explore in awareness what your eyes are taking in.

Notice what might arise in the heart in response to certain sights, such as a sense of being uplifted, warmed, or delighted. Be curious about what your eyes might be dismissing or avoiding (for instance, things that appear to be dying or decaying). Be present to emotions that may arise, like an ache, sorrow, or worry. Attend with kind awareness to the parts of the life cycle we may not want to see or take in. Allow yourself to receive nature through the eyes. Be present to the sacred beauty you are witnessing around you and within you.

Now shift to the sense of smell. Take three deep breaths in and out through the nostrils, attending to the flow of air and the scents it carries. Be open to what you notice. It may be a very subtle scent — the smell of soil, the sweetness of a flower, the bark of a pine. Let this scent be experienced in the body. Notice whether the body feels more awake, alive, or alert. Do you observe resistance, or a sense of seeking out a scent? Can you be curious, letting go of needing it to be a particular way, being present even to the absence or faintness of a smell?

As you continue to explore smell, bring your attention to the sense of taste also. If you can identify plants that are safe to taste, you may want to place a small piece in your mouth. Shift your attention between smell and taste. As you encounter smells, notice how the sense of taste may shift and how the body reacts. Does saliva increase or decrease? Do tastes such as sweetness or bitterness intensify or fade? As you continue to breathe deeply, consider breathing with the mouth slightly open, attending to the scents and tastes nature is offering to you. Feel how this connection between taste and smell is experienced within your body.

As you approach the end of your walk, stand still again. Feel the effects of the practice on your inner landscape. How do the mind, the heart, and the body feel now that your senses have been awakened? Offer gratitude to yourself and to the beings and expressions of nature that have supported you in this practice.

Afterward, consider writing in your journal about any insights you had during this meditation.

Daily Life with the Senses

Your senses are gateways that allow you to return to presence in any moment. You may find it easier to practice sensory awareness through everyday activities rather than through formal meditations. Here are a few suggestions to support practicing sensory awareness in everyday life.

When passing something in nature that allures you, stop and spend one minute looking at it. As you move through the day, attend to things you see often and regularly to observe them changing, noticing the minute differences. I like to observe trees in my neighborhood, taking time to see them in different lights as the time of day and seasons change.

Take a few moments to touch or connect to a plant inside or outside your home. Focus on the sense of touch, feel its leaves, petals, and stems.

When you are out and about, invite your attention to the sounds you hear around you or through the windows of your vehicle. See if you can notice the natural sounds behind the human-made sounds.

As you explore these practices, you may become more aware of the experience of being in your body. Various feelings may arise. Some experiences may feel restorative, calming, and easeful. Some experiences may feel difficult or challenging, perhaps evoking painful patterns, habits, memories, or feelings that you may have been unaware of, distracted yourself from, or suppressed. This is part of the journey: being present to the difficulty, learning to reexperience sights and sensations and relate to these difficulties in your mind, body, and heart, allows you to heal and create new ways of living. With each practice you are creating a new relationship with the traumas you have stored in your body and developing new, healing pathways.

Jennifer's Story

Jennifer had struggled with anxiety for most of her life. She sought help in reducing her anxiety in everyday activities like driving. As she began to explore the patterns of her anxiety, it became clear that it was linked to early childhood sexual assault. Because these experiences had occurred in a spiritual community, she had great difficulty closing her eyes and practicing any form of mindfulness meditation, as it would evoke fear, anxiety, and hypervigilance.

We decided together that a more effective way to heal her anxiety would be a practice that integrated awareness of the senses to everyday life and the support of nature. We began by taking walks and sitting outside, allowing Jennifer's senses to be naturally awakened by nature.

As she learned to explore sensory awareness in nature, she began to find ease and calm within her body. She found great comfort in practicing mindfulness while walking and attending to what she was seeing as she walked.

Over time Jennifer's anxiety lessened. She began to drive with greater ease and often enjoyed it, attending to nature and what she saw as she drove. As she developed her own mindfulness practice to heal from her trauma, she regained a sense of safety, agency, and well-being.

Taking Care

In exploring sensory awareness practices, you may encounter body sensations you hadn't noticed before or that you have been disconnected from. If this happens, do your best to be curious and present to the sensations you notice. What sensations are you experiencing? Where are they located in the body? It's best if you can stay with the descriptions of *sensations* of the body, rather than descriptions of the experiences as thoughts or emotions, as this will help you to explore a new way of understanding your body.

It can be difficult for those who have experienced trauma to realize that the conditions surrounding the trauma were out of their control. If this is the case for you, remember, you did your best to survive, using the resources available to you. You couldn't have known what you didn't know at that time. You are now giving yourself the gift of knowing yourself and the trauma differently. Be patient with this process. All of the practices in this book are meant to support you in learning how to safely reexperience your inner being, identify what needs to be healed, develop ways to heal, and step into a new way of living. Continue to offer to yourself in each practice the intention to meet what arises with compassion, gentleness, kindness, and ease. As best you can, let go of needing to fix or change what is challenging.

If your experiences during a practice feel too intense, shift your attention to something that feels soothing, such as an aspect of nature that brings you a sense of joy or calm. You may also choose to move to another activity, such as talking to a friend or loved one, listening to music, or reading a book. Healing is best approached by identifying and honoring what you need in any given moment.

Be open and be kind to yourself in this journey. Each practice, each stage of healing, and each moment can help bring you into your fullest sense of being. Let your senses be pathways of connection with nature and healing.

Chapter 3

BODY AWARENESS

The body always leads us home...if we can simply learn to trust sensation and stay with it long enough for it to reveal appropriate action, movement, insight, or feeling.

— Pat Ogden

Most of us live disconnected from our bodies, relying on our minds to navigate choices and actions. The body is where traumatic wounds are stored and often stuck. Yet it is also where healing occurs. The greater our awareness of living in the body, the better we can discover the places within us that hold stuck and unhealed trauma. By listening deeply to the body, understanding it, and attuning to it, we can begin to recover from trauma. A sense of connection to and appreciation of the body are fundamental to the experience of being alive. Body awareness can support your well-being, healing, and ability to live a life of meaning and purpose.

Appreciating the Complexity of the Body

The body is a beautiful, exquisitely complex system. From birth through death, this is where we live. The body helps to sustain our well-being by maintaining an inner homeostasis and helps us develop throughout life through its ability to grow and change. It also sends us signals when we need to heal. To appreciate some of its complexity, and to understand some of the mechanisms at work in the embodied experience and memory of trauma, let's look at some important components of the body: our lungs, diaphragm, muscles, and blood.[1]

- **Lungs:** The lungs bring air and blood into intimate contact so that the blood can carry oxygen to the body's cells and remove carbon dioxide. During a twenty-four-hour period, we breathe an average of 23,040 times. That adds up to more than eight million breaths per year and almost seven hundred million in a lifetime.
- **Diaphragm:** The diaphragm is the muscle between the chest cavity, containing the lungs and heart, and the abdominal cavity. Upon inhalation it contracts and flattens, expanding the chest cavity and pulling air into the lungs. On exhalation the diaphragm relaxes, contracting the chest cavity and pushing air from the lungs.
- **Muscles:** There are more than nine hundred muscles in the body, making up 40 percent of the average adult's total body weight. Muscles consist of elastic, electrically conductive fibers that support structures in the body and enable them to move. The smallest muscle of the body measures about one-twentieth of an inch. It's called the stapedius; it regulates the stirrup bone, which sends vibrations from the eardrum to the inner ear. The stapedius has the ability to dampen loud noise to prevent hearing damage. The strongest muscle of the body is the gluteus maximus in the buttock, which enables us to propel our body weight forward and uphill. The hardest-working muscle in the body is the heart.
- **Blood:** Our blood circulates throughout the heart, arteries, veins, and capillaries, carrying nourishment, electrolytes, hormones, vitamins, antibodies, heat, and oxygen to the cells of our body and taking away waste matter and carbon dioxide. Blood is

22 percent solids and 78 percent liquid. The human body contains eight to ten pints of blood. Every square inch of human skin contains twenty feet of blood vessels. Human blood cells travel sixty thousand miles per day.

Our bodies, like everything living in nature, are amazingly complex, consisting of multiple systems working together to grow, thrive, heal, and evolve. Being in nature offers a beautiful way to develop body awareness.

Body Awareness

Being present in the body supports your healing and well-being. Think back to a time when you were sick with a cold. The body may have sent you signals in the form of symptoms, such as coughing, sneezing, and fatigue. You may have chosen to respond by resting, taking medicine, and eating nourishing foods to help the body recover. This is a form of body awareness: observing the sensations and experiences in the body and responding skillfully. With practice, you can develop deeper and deeper forms of body awareness.

Most of us are never formally taught body awareness. When exercising, we may have received some training in specific aspects of body awareness — learning how to pay attention to our foot strike in running, or how to grip and lift weights, or how to move our arms and legs in a particular direction to stretch — but such instruction typically doesn't encompass awareness of sensations arising in and passing out of the body. The practices of breath awareness and sensory awareness presented in previous chapters help us notice the constant movement and changing of breath and external sensations. With body awareness, we become more attuned to the processes and sensations *within* the body. It can be helpful to view the body as new terrain to explore. Body awareness helps us become intimately connected to the locations, regions, and beautiful landscapes within.

Many of us have developed very automatic relationships to our bodies. When walking, we are often wrapped up in our thoughts (e.g., rehearsing what we said, or will say, in meetings or conversations) and miss the moment-to-moment experiences of our muscles and bones moving, our feet contacting the ground and propelling us forward, and our bodies moving through the environment. When you bring your awareness to the movements and processes of your body, such as walking, breathing, and blood circulation, you become more present in your body. You learn to observe its signals and respond in ways that enable you to calm yourself, heal, and find new ways of living. You learn over time to feel at home in, connected to, and trusting of this body. Body awareness is essential for undoing the traumatic conditioning and healing the wounds of your past.

Practice: Body Awareness in Stillness with Nature

Find a place outdoors that is relatively free of distractions and where you can sit or lie down for twenty to thirty minutes. Ideally, choose a place where your body feels held, secure, safe, and at ease (this might be in your backyard, in a secluded park, near a tree, in a canyon, or next to a body of water, large or small). As you move through this meditation, you may find particular places in the body difficult to attend to, or you may notice an absence of sensation. If this happens, you may choose to move on to another area of the body. At the same time, I invite you to be curious just for a few moments about these difficult or neutral sensations.

Choose a comforting and supportive posture, maybe lying down on a soft patch of earth or grass, or resting your body against a solid tree trunk. As you settle into the posture, bring your attention to the places where your body is in contact with the ground or the support — the feet, the legs, the torso, the arms, and the neck and head. Connect to the stability beneath you: can you allow your body to feel grounded and held up? Scan through the body to observe whether any tension is present, particularly in the jaw, neck, shoulders, back, or belly. Invite any tense areas of the body to soften, relax, and open.

Now bring your attention to the breath at the belly. As you inhale, notice how the breath opens, lifts, and expands the belly. As you exhale, the belly relaxes and falls back. Observe the sensations arising and passing as you breathe. Notice the temperatures, textures, pace, and movements as you breathe, coming and going, moment to moment.

Now shift attention from awareness of the breath at the belly to exploring sensations elsewhere in the body. Bring your attention to the feet, including the balls and soles, heels, arches, top and sides, and toes. Notice what sensations are present in the feet: you may feel pressure on the soles of the feet from the ground, or awareness of your toes touching, coolness or warmth from your shoes or the sun or breeze on bare feet. Continue to explore what arises. You may want to move the feet slowly, with awareness, to experience different sensations, then see if you can let the feet remain still. If you find your mind wandering, distracted by an experience in the environment or wanting to move ahead to explore another part of the body, kindly and gently let go of these thoughts and come back to awareness of the feet.

Now move up from the feet to the legs, Scan through the sensations you experience in your ankles, shins, calves, knees, thighs, and hips. Be curious about the sensations of the skin and of the muscles and bones beneath the skin, such as weightedness, contraction, length, and lightness, and sensations arising from contact with the earth, sunshine, or wind. If your mind begins to think in images about the experience of the muscles and bones, note that you are thinking, and bring awareness back to the sensations present in the legs in this moment. Be present to sensations arising and passing.

Shift your attention up from the legs to the torso, including the pelvic area, the belly, the chest, sides, and back. This is a vast region of the body to explore. Take time to be curious about each part.

Investigate the sensations that are present now. You may be more aware of sensations arising from the breath.

The torso is the site of many of our vital functions. Be open to noticing sensations of the digestive system, the expansion and contraction of the lungs, and the pumping of the heart as oxygen circulates through the body. If you encounter a sensation that is painful, contracted, or distressing, bring a sense of kindness and compassion to it. As best you can, let go of judgment or the need to push something away or fix it. Stay with these experiences as long as it feels right to you. You may also choose to attend to the sensations of vitality, aliveness, and breath in this region supported by the expressions of nature. Notice what is alive and present in this central part of your body.

Now bring awareness to the arms and hands, including the upper arms, elbows, forearms, wrists, hands, palms, fingers, and fingertips. Notice the sensations on the skin, supported by nature, such as temperature and sense of touch; notice the extension or contraction of the muscles; notice any pulsing, vibrations, or tingling at the wrist or fingertips. Shift your attention to the right arm and hand, and then to the left. If you notice any comparison or judgment arising, can you let go of it and simply meet the sensations as you experience them? We are typically most aware of our arms and hands when they are in motion: try keeping them still for a moment and becoming aware of the sensations that arise and pass in stillness.

Shift now to explore awareness of the upper body, including the shoulders, collarbones, neck (front, sides, back, voice box, and throat) and head (jaw, mouth, tongue, nose and nostrils, cheeks, eyes, eyelids and eyebrows, forehead and temples, ears, and the back, middle, and top of the head, including the brain). This is a very complex and intricate region of the body, housing four of the main sense organs and the brain that keeps us oriented to the world around us. Allow awareness to traverse and investigate each part of this region. Notice the textures, temperatures, and movements you experience. If you find your attention shifting to memories or stories, or if a challenging emotion arises (such as annoyance, anxiety, or sadness), these are part of the practice too. Be curious about and present to what arises — letting go of the need to figure it out, fix it, or change it — and then gently focus on the sensations in the upper body. Sense the sounds of nature arising and passing through the ears, light entering the eyes, scents wafting through the nose, the mouth receiving subtle expressions of nature riding on the waves of air.

Having scanned every region of the body, now expand awareness to the entire body. Allow awareness to be like the sun, illuminating every region of the body. Notice the waves of sensations present in your body now: feel, sense, and be present to the body as a whole. Now become aware of the breath permeating the entire body. Rest in this body, breathing, alive, supported by the presence of nature.

In the last few moments of the practice, feel the effects of experiencing your body in this way. How do your mind, heart, and body feel? Offer gratitude for what you have cultivated, tended to, and cared for in this practice. Also offer gratitude for all the expressions of nature that supported this awakening into body awareness. Gently open your eyes (if they were closed). Make gentle movements, such as opening or closing the hands and moving the feet, and allow your eyes to take in what is around you.

Afterward, consider writing in your journal about any experiences or insights you had during this meditation.

Challenges in the Body

Most people are disconnected from the sensory experiences of their bodies, as the body performs many functions automatically. We therefore expect the body to be there for us — until something is not working well or we feel pain. When this happens, we react with a desire not to experience pain, and we attempt to fix it by figuring out, planning, or analyzing how to change and relieve the sensation. While these strategies are helpful to our survival and getting through challenges, they don't give us a chance to experience a challenge or pain from moment to moment, or to use the body's own wisdom to discern the most skillful way to care for the body. Many of us have been conditioned to avoid difficult or painful sensations in the body. Even the body awareness practice can be very challenging for this reason. By understanding what habits are at work in our reactions to pain, and developing awareness of the tendency to avoid or distract and distance ourselves from the experience of pain, we can begin to identify patterns of disconnection.

Pain and Disconnection

Automatic patterns of disconnection to avoid bodily discomfort or pain are examples of maladaptive coping responses formed after trauma. If, during a traumatic event, you were unable to engage your body to find safety by running, fighting, or seeking shelter or protection, then the pain of this traumatic event becomes stuck in the body. You may feel disconnected from the parts of the body where trauma is stuck, or you may experience pain when you attend to them.

Over time, the patterns of disconnection associated with these traumatic events can affect your choices about how you view and take care of your body, the places or events you engage with, and the relationships you are willing to form. The practice of mindful body awareness gives you the opportunity to skillfully and kindly experience these bodily memories of trauma and learn new ways to work with them. You can begin to heal and discover a new way of living, free from the patterns of disconnection created by the trauma.

Skillful Ways to Support Pain and Disconnection in the Body

When learning to move toward pain, disconnection, discomfort, or any other challenge in the body, it's important to approach it with an attitude of kindness and compassion. These patterns developed as survival mechanisms to protect you from future trauma. Seeing body awareness as a means to fix, get rid of, or solve the difficulties you experience in the body is essentially the same approach that led you into the current patterns of disconnection from your trauma. As you awaken into your body, go slowly, and be patient and gentle with yourself as you learn to connect to the sensations of pain and disconnection related to your trauma. Bringing a kind awareness to your experience will open new opportunities to heal.

Nature offers great support for learning to work slowly and deliberately with difficulties. Life in nature expresses itself through myriad variations: intensity, dormancy, growth, decay, seasons, climates, and changing shapes, textures, and dimensions. Nature inherently *meets* and *moves toward* the prevailing conditions in each moment. Reflecting on this is a beautiful way to think about how you might meet the conditions of your inner landscape and thrive with them.

Reflect for a moment on a weed you have seen. I like to choose weeds that are growing up in the cracks of concrete in urban streets, but any weed will do. You probably have preconceived ideas about this weed: "That shouldn't grow there," "That's an ugly plant," "That weed is invading my beautiful garden," "How can I get rid of that weed?" These are also our habitual reactions to conditions in our lives that we don't like or are disconnected from.

If for a moment you could let go of these patterns of thought — judgments, comparisons, aversive reactions, the need for things to be different — you could consider that this weed is just a plant. If you paused to notice its colors, textures, shapes, size, leaves, and flowers, and were present to it just as it is, what might happen? It would likely reveal to you its beauty, strength, resilience, courage, and persistence, offering you a new way of seeing and relating to it. It is possible to see your inner weeds in this way too. You can use the teachings of nature as a way to consider inner difficulty or pain as opportunities to notice, let go of reactivity, feel, and connect to your body. Viewing your trauma differently can support your healing.

There are a few considerations to keep in mind when learning to attend differently to pain in the body. As you notice any painful sensations — aches, tension, soreness, sharpness, tightening, or other challenging states, bring your awareness to the way the mind reacts. Notice if there is a judgment, a fear, a dislike, a desire to change or fix the sensation, or a resistance, and notice how those reactions are experienced in the body. Often such reactions intensify pain. If you notice the mind reacting, let go and focus awareness on your breath or body sensations (easeful or challenging) as they are in the moment. This can open a way for moving toward the pain.

Another approach is to stay with the painful sensation for just a few moments and regard it with curiosity. It's likely that the mind will want to react. If it does, notice the mind moving: observe it with kindness and interest and then let go. Come back to being with the sensations just for a few moments to shift the reactive habit. By letting go of reactivity to the pain, you can choose to continue to be in stillness with it, or you may choose to move slowly and intentionally toward it.

As you turn your curiosity toward the painful sensations, it is helpful to bring an attitude of care and kindness. Let awareness gently hold the painful sensations, attending delicately and kindly to each expression (as you might to the leaves or flower petals of a weed) to feel and sense what it is like to hold these difficulties in a new relationship.

Another difficulty you may encounter when cultivating body awareness is a feeling of disconnection or numbness from sensations. This often occurs with people who have experienced traumatic events. Again, it is a survival mechanism at work. The last instinctive reaction if you cannot escape danger or trauma is to freeze. The mind overrides all other modes of response and disconnects itself from what is happening. This can be experienced as a sense of floating away, disassociation, or leaving one's body. Like the other reactions to trauma, this unresolved reaction can become stuck in the body. Over time it may be reinforced, and you learn ways to disconnect from your body.

As with painful sensations, you can learn to be present to disconnection, dissociation, or numbing experiences. This begins with learning to observe your patterns of numbing or checking out. For example, as you come to place your attention on a particular location in your body during a body awareness practice, you may become aware that your mind is wandering to random thoughts of what you did yesterday or what you have to do tomorrow, then drifting into fantasy, creating stories, images, or daydreams. This is the moment to focus your attention on your bodily experience of this disconnection. Do you notice a lightness, an absence of sensation, or neutral sensations in this part of the body? Noticing the reactivity of your mind to sensations of disconnection will open a new path for experiencing and exploring them.

You may find that memories arise and painful sensations are present. Again, this is a moment for noticing how the mind moves or reacts. From a nonreactive awareness, you can choose to do whatever feels most helpful. This might mean moving your body slowly in a particular way that feels helpful or focusing on something around you or in nature. As always, remember to bring an attitude of kindness and caring to what you feel in your body: this is where the transformation is taking place.

Jannie's Story

From early childhood through adulthood, Jannie suffered physical, emotional, and sexual abuse. Hoping to feel safe and at home in her body, she wanted to learn mindfulness and somatic practices to heal.

As she started to explore body awareness, she began to encounter many challenges, including feelings of hypervigilance, an inability to feel calm, tension, restlessness, achiness, and overwhelm. Jannie became concerned about how she could trust what she was feeling and learn to establish a sense of safety with body sensations.

I reminded her that these types of sensations had evolved to protect her and that learning to be aware of and present to them would take time. We explored practices that supported the needs of her body. She began by practicing with her eyes open rather than closed, walking, and focusing on the senses and sensations of just her feet. As she began to feel at ease with these practices, she was slowly able to expand her awareness to other areas of her body.

Jannie learned that she had to go slowly on her journey of healing, choosing practices that allowed her to feel safe, and not pushing herself to notice sensations that were too intense or that she wasn't feeling ready to explore.

As you learn these healing practices, it's important to establish how much exposure to sensations of distress or arousal you can tolerate while still feeling safe. If you feel too restless, anxious, or agitated — that is, if your nervous system is too hyperaroused — these practices may be challenging. The same is true if you are feeling too numb, dissociated, or checked out — too hypoaroused. Finding a window of arousal between these two states in which you feel safe requires learning as you go. We will explore this issue more in chapter 6. For now, stick with practices that allow you to feel safe, calm, and easeful.

The following practices of body awareness are designed to help you to move toward working with pain and disconnection. Remember, go slow, be patient, take your time. Just as nature has its own pace and process for healing, you can choose a pace and rhythm that are right for you.

Practice: Body Awareness — Walking in Nature

Find a place to walk outdoors for fifteen to thirty minutes that might not be your preferred setting. For example, if you prefer quiet mountain paths, you might choose an urban walking path. If you enjoy walking next to the ocean, you might choose to walk next to a small, slow-moving creek. The purpose of selecting this type of location is to allow your body to experience a setting that isn't full of the expressions of nature you might typically seek out. This will allow you to explore any tendencies you may have to avoid or distract yourself from inner experiences with outer experiences and to observe these patterns within the body.

Standing upright, bring awareness to the body. Attend to the breath, noticing it moving in and out in concert with your surroundings. Now shift attention to become aware of body sensations, scanning the entire body. Begin with the feet: notice the stability of the ground beneath you. Now slowly move your attention up into the legs, torso, arms and hands, and upper body. If you find tension or tightness anywhere, move in any way that helps your body soften and relax. Invite being present to your body, open to sensations arising and passing as you walk.

Now begin walking. Take your time — there is nowhere you have to go. Bring your attention to the way the body is moving and the sensations arising throughout the body as you move. You may find your attention drawn to external sights, sensations, and experiences that are beautiful — colorful, bright, alluring. Notice what sensations arise in the body as you perceive these examples of beauty. Do you feel a sense of expansion, uplifting, opening, relaxing? Invite yourself to receive these expressions of nature's beauty and observe how this feels in the body.

Now shift your attention to the ways you may have been distracting yourself from avoiding noticing things you do not perceive as beautiful — dead leaves, fallen branches, the bark of a tree, plain-colored rocks, or the earth beneath your feet. Bring your attention to these expressions of nature, noticing what sensations arise as you do so — maybe a feeling of contraction, a desire to look away, an urge to focus on other things that are more beautiful. As best you can, let go of this reactivity and steady your attention on these less beautiful expressions of nature. Notice their colors, textures, smells, and patterns. Stay with this part of nature that evokes habitual responses of distraction, discomfort, and avoidance. If you notice your mind wanting to move away, gently bring it back, remaining open to and curious about what you sense or feel within.

Continue to walk slowly. Each time you feel an impulse to turn away from what is arising in you and around you in nature, invite turning toward it, let go of the reactivity, and approach it with curiosity, wonderment, kindness, and caring. You can try this practice anytime you're walking when you feel too hot or too cold, see something that is decaying, or come into contact with a bug or crawly creature, weeds, rubble, waste, or trash. Everyone reacts aversively to different things: be open to what arises for you as you walk.

Toward the end of your walk, sit down somewhere. Slowly scan the entire body, noticing if there is any sense of discomfort, challenge, or pain. Draw on any insights given to you from nature that help you be present to the qualities, sensations, and expressions of this difficulty in your body. Be curious, kind, open, and caring to what you encounter.

Take the last few moments of this practice to feel how the mind, the body, and the heart may have shifted. Offer gratitude for what has grown within you. Close with appreciation for all the reflections offered to you by nature to support your healing.

Afterward, consider writing in your journal about any experiences or insights you had during this meditation.

Practice: Body Awareness — Moving Slowly with Nature

Find a place where you can spend five minutes inviting your body to move slowly and participate through the sense of touch with what you encounter. Choose something in nature that invites your attention, something you want to explore more intimately. It might be a hearty bush or beautiful flowering plant on the patio, a budding plant, a planter box full of creatures and life, or a well-established tree in a park.

Take a few moments to attend inward to sensations. Feel your body grounded and supported, alert, open, and relaxed. Begin now to connect to the object you are observing. Sense how the eyes are receiving this object — the colors, shapes, textures. Pause. Have you already lifted your arm and hand to touch it? This is reactivity of the mind. If you did, smile, and let's start again. Slowly extend your arm and hand to touch the object. Feel each movement, the pull of gravity, the way your muscles extend, contract, and reach, how your hand grasps, the way the fingers move together.

Pause before you touch the object. Do you have expectations about how it will feel, based on how objects like this are supposed to feel or have felt to you in the past? Can you let go of these expectations and be open to what you are sensing? See if you can let go and just be present to the sensations in your body as you make contact with this expression of nature. Let your hand and arm extend, one tiny movement at a time, to slowly reach out and touch it. Sense how the body receives this contact. Continue with slow, sensory-aware movements of touch as you connect to nature.

To end this practice, allow yourself to feel the effects of having slowly and intentionally connected with nature, and notice what is present in your body as you experience touch and connection. Close with gratitude for what has been cultivated in this practice, and offer gratitude to the object for its support and connection.

Afterward, consider writing in your journal about any experiences or insights you had during this meditation.

Body Awareness in Everyday Activities

Sometimes formal body awareness practices are too challenging for various reasons, and it can be helpful instead to bring attention to the sensations arising in the body in your daily life. The body's constant activity creates limitless opportunities for cultivating body awareness. Here are a few suggestions for practicing body awareness with nature in everyday life.

As you move through your daily routine, pause to bring moment-to-moment awareness to the sensations of the skin (temperatures, pressures) and the expansion and contraction of muscles. For example, when doing the dishes, notice the movements of the body — standing, moving your hands to access water and soap. As you handle the dishes, notice what sensations arise, such as warmth, wetness, slipperiness. Notice how your hands adjust their grip to hold wet dishes. As you scrub a plate, where in your body does the movement originate? What muscular sensations do you notice?

You can also practice body awareness when drinking water, feeling the movements of swallowing in your mouth and throat and the actions of your digestive and nervous systems. When you get dressed, notice your mind and body preparing for the coordinated movements of putting on clothes. In the shower, notice all the senses being awakened and the sensations in the body of feeling healthy, clean, relaxed, or invigorated. When you're emailing, notice the movements of your fingers, the coordination of your thoughts, and your mental and emotional attention to desired outcomes.

As you encounter nature throughout your day, notice how the body feels in different locations. Before you leave the house, scan your body, noting any sensations present. As you leave, scan again. Activities like getting into the car, driving, arriving at work, eating lunch, taking a break, leaving work, and returning home all offer opportunities for a quick body scan, enabling you to notice how sensations change in different places throughout your day.

Taking Care

Being embodied means that you cultivate a deep attention to, understanding of, and attunement to the body. This supports your well-being and healing, enabling you to live a life of meaning and purpose. Because much healing from trauma occurs in the body, practices of body awareness are foundational to that healing. By breaking habits of reactivity and attending skillfully to pain and places in your body from which you may have disconnected yourself, you will develop awareness of what is stuck and begin to heal.

The body holds both the pain of your trauma and the keys to healing. Honoring both is part of the process of healing. It takes time, patience, kindness, compassion, and gentleness to learn the terrain of your body.

As we continue to deepen the sense of body awareness in later chapters, you will learn how to transform the trauma that is stuck in the body. The only place we can begin is here, now. Be kind and patient with yourself on the journey.

Chapter 4

ELEMENT AWARENESS

It's said that when we die, the four elements — earth, air, fire and water — dissolve one by one, each into the other, and finally just dissolve into space. But while we're living, we share the energy that makes everything, from a blade of grass to an elephant, grow and live and then inevitably wear out and die. This energy, this life force, creates the whole world.

— Pema Chödrön

The elements — earth, water, air, fire, and space — are present all around us and within us: in our environment, in our bodies, and woven into the way we live in the world. Exploring the elements, we can discover how nature can heal trauma in deep, interconnected ways.

Element awareness is one of the key teachings in mindfulness. You can choose to focus awareness on these elements within your body. For example, when you breathe, you experience the element of air; when you sweat or salivate, you experience water; when you are warm, you experience the sensation of fire; and when you feel the weight of your body, you experience the force of earth.

In previous chapters we saw that by drawing on the support of nature and becoming present to our breath, our sensory experiences, and the body, whether in stillness or in motion, we can experience healing.

Mindfulness of the elements gives us another way to deepen body awareness and connect to the world and ourselves — one that provides new
possibilities for healing.

Exploring the Elements

When I first practiced element awareness, I knew the elements existed
outside me, but I was skeptical that I would be able to sense them within
me. A teacher I was studying with had introduced the element awareness
practice in an indoor setting. This helped me think about experiencing the
elements within my body, but it didn't give me the opportunity to *sense*
them. I decided to explore the practice on my own, in nature. I figured I
needed to be where the elements existed organically.

Sitting in my backyard, focusing on my breath, I began to notice that
the breath was accompanied by the wind around me. This drew me to
attend to air. I sensed the fluid motion of the breath as air moving within
me, just as it was moving around me. In my body, I felt, *Maybe there is
something to this practice.*

With curiosity — an important quality for this practice — I turned
my attention to the water in my breath, and I noticed that my breath was
soft and moist. Then I moved to fire, or heat. I noticed that the air I ex-
haled was warmer than the air I inhaled, and I also sensed that the push
of my breath had a warmth to it. Finally, I shifted my attention to earth.
Doubt came back into my mind. Where would I find earth in the breath?
Then I brought my attention to the places in my body that were holding
the breath: the nostrils, the windpipe, the lungs. I felt my body as a solid,
stable container, supporting, surrounding, and embracing the breath. As I
investigated space, I felt the opening, lifting, and expansion of my lungs,
and I felt a sense of spaciousness. As I ended the practice, I offered gratitude for the depth of my ability to breathe and for all of the elements that
supported my experience of breathing.

By deepening awareness of the breath, you allow yourself to be nourished by nature, moment to moment. Sensing how air carries oxygen to

all living systems and organisms brings an awareness of connection and support. When you feel the heat of your breath, you sense the vitality within you, and you also connect to the fire of the sun, which provides energy to sustain all life, including yours. As you notice the element of earth in the structures of your body, all supporting and holding your breath and being, you can also sense the forces of the earth around you — ground, trees, plants, animal and insect life — supporting and nourishing you. The presence of water in every breath we take reminds us that our world is made up largely of water and that in many different forms, water sustains all of the natural world.

As you breathe, you also experience a sense of space in the way the body opens, expands, lifts, and relaxes while breathing. That space allows you to feel life within you as well as the spaciousness in nature and everyday life. Awareness of space allows us to feel the movement of all the elements within and around us. We realize that we are not separate: we are made up of the elements. Each breath we take connects us to all the forces and elements in nature. The elements are here aiding you, caring for you, lovingly providing support and sources of healing.

Element Awareness in the Body

To practice mindfulness of the elements within the body, you bring your attention to the visceral sensations of each of the elements — earth, air, fire, water, and space — as they are known in your body. You can do this by noticing the connection between the world around you and experiences within the body.

Elements are often experienced in combination. For instance, saliva has an obvious association with water, but it is also the product of heat, air, and earth. We might also notice the element of water when we sense the pulsation, density, or fullness of our muscles or our organs.

We become aware of space when we perceive expansion, spaciousness, or a sense of openness. When we experience a moment of feeling that the body is not static or fixed but unbounded and fluid, we are open to noticing the vast space that is us. This also helps us to see that everything made of earth, air, fire, and water exists in the expanse of space itself.

Awareness of the elements in nature gives rise to a felt sense of the elements within the body. Over time, you can learn to sense your own elemental nature through the experiences of earth, air, fire, water, and space manifested in your body. As this awareness deepens, you begin to feel your connection with life itself and to make choices in your life that bring a greater sense of aliveness and well-being. You can learn to trust yourself.

You can practice element awareness both when sitting in nature and in motion. You may find it easier to focus your awareness on these elements within you during everyday activities like walking, eating, and doing chores. Typically we don't notice the elements as alive and present in our experience, but they truly are! For example, when you eat, each bite you take requires the water in your saliva to break down food, earth in your jawbones to chew, the fire of the digestive process to break down the food, and air to help you swallow it. All these actions take place within your body. And the elements are also present in the food itself: earth, sun, air, and water all help plants and animals to grow.

Here are three practices for developing element awareness. The first is done sitting or lying down in nature, the second while walking, and the third while engaging in a daily activity.

Practice: Element Awareness — Sitting

Find a place outdoors that is relatively free of distractions and where you can sit for twenty or thirty minutes. Ideally, choose a place that gives you access to all the elements directly, such as near a body of water, in an open landscape, or in a forest or canyon.

Choose a comfortable, supportive posture — sitting, standing, or lying down. Consider what your body needs: perhaps to feel closer to the earth, to have more connection to the movement of air or water, to sense the warmth of the sun, or to have space. As you settle into your posture, become aware of the sounds, light, smells, sights, and energy of the natural setting. Invite your body to begin to connect to these experiences.

Now direct your attention to the body. Notice all of the places where it is being supported: beneath you, behind you, in front of you, around you. Notice what sensations draw your attention as supportive — heaviness, lightness, warmth, coolness? Allow your body to relax, open, and settle into the support.

Shift now to bring awareness to any aspect of the body that you experience as heavy, solid, or stable. Notice these sensations as the presence of the element of earth. Investigate these aspects of the body that are earth — sensing the hardness of bones, teeth, and spine, the solidity of muscles and organs. Be curious and open to the felt sense of earth — solid, heavy, stable within this body.

Move your attention now to become aware of any quality of the body that you experience as light, moving, or uplifting. This is the element of air being sensed in awareness. Investigate the expansions and contractions of breath, the air circulating through the lungs, heart, and other organs in the body. Notice all the sensations arising from air coming and going in the body. Stay open to the feelings of lightness, movement, expansion, and letting go in the body.

Next bring attention to an aspect of the body you experience as warm (or cool) or pulsing. Notice these sensations as the presence of the element of fire. Be curious about the presence of energy and fire in the body — the pumping of the heart, the heat of digestion, the temperature of the body. Be open to awareness of fire as vitality and energy in the body.

Now focus on any aspect of the body you notice as water, moisture, or fluidity. Investigate the experiences of the body that are water — saliva in the mouth, sweat on your back, blood coursing through the body. Be curious about the felt sense of water and its role in the cohesion of all systems in the body.

Now attend to any quality of the body that you notice as spacious, open, or vast. Notice these sensations as the element of space. Investigate the sense of the space within and around the structures of the body, between the bones, muscles, and organs. Open your mouth slightly and notice the space between the teeth, tongue, and lips. Let go of needing to visualize or figure out the spaces inside your body, and just notice the feeling of that space.

For the last few minutes of the practice, choose the element that best supports your healing right now. Trust your intuition. Notice this element as it is present both in the body and around you in nature. Slowly shift your attention back and forth between the elemental sensations noticed within you and in your surrounding; allow a sense of interconnection and healing to arise.

As you bring the practice to a close, allow yourself to be present to anything that has shifted in your inner landscape. Be present to the qualities, attitudes, and experiences of the mind, body, and heart. Offer appreciation for what you have cultivated in this practice.

Afterward, consider writing in your journal about any experiences or insights you had during this meditation.

Practice: Element Awareness — Walking

To develop and deepen body awareness, it can be helpful to vary your posture during practices, shifting among walking, lying down, sitting, and standing. For this practice, find a place in nature where you can walk for twenty to thirty minutes. You may want to take a few moments at different points to just stand still and practice.

Begin by focusing on the body as you walk. Notice the experiences of the breath. Pay attention to what is received by the senses from your natural surroundings and to the sensations that are arising in the body.

Now shift your attention to each element in turn (earth, air, fire, water, space). Feel and notice each element arising within the body as you walk.

Become aware of each element as it is present in nature around you. At the same time, notice the presence of the same element in the body. With curiosity, move your attention between these outer and inner experiences of the element. Notice the connection with nature and within you when you sense the elements while walking. Allow yourself to investigate the elemental nature of all life around and within, not separate.

You may wish to make notes in your journal about anything you discovered during this practice.

Practice: Element Awareness — In Everyday Life

Practicing element awareness during everyday activities can help you feel more alive, present, and connected. Pick an activity such as cooking, eating, shopping, gardening, cleaning, drinking water, showering, brushing your teeth, or exercising as a focus for the practice.

Begin by slowing down to experience each step of the activity. If you are drinking water, notice the actions of getting a glass, walking to the faucet, turning on the water, filling the glass, turning off the water, and raising the glass to your mouth. Feel the water entering the mouth, the motions of swallowing, and the water moving into the body.

Now focus on the sensations associated with each element at each step. As you raise the glass of water to your mouth, notice the solidity and the structure of the hand holding the glass (earth); notice the movement in the arm and hand muscles that lift the glass to your mouth (fire); notice the hand and arm moving through space; and notice the sensations of breath, air, wet, coolness, and moisture as the water contacts the lips and mouth and you take a drink.

At each step, you might pause and reflect on a sense of connection and engagement with this activity and the elements. As you raise the glass of water to your mouth, for example, you might notice the element of air helping you breathe to bring water into the body and the energy (fire) in the movements of the mouth to transfer the water into the body. Consider the glass itself: made of earth, forged by fire in air and space. Consider the water in the glass, drawn from moving rivers, dropped from the air as rain, held in the soil, heated and cooled by the Earth's movement around the sun.

Continue slowly through the steps of this activity, feeling the sensations of element awareness and how the sense of each element allows you to experience this activity.

You may wish to make notes in your journal about anything you discovered during this practice.

Stephen's Story

Stephen struggled with trauma resulting from his experience of sexual assault and abuse. Growing up, he was removed from his birth family to be raised by distant relatives, and he never had a stable and secure home where he felt supported. As an adult, he wanted to heal from these childhood traumas.

We began by establishing body awareness, learning to tune in to sensations arising. We then explored element awareness practice near the ocean. Stephen noted that he was particularly drawn to air, feeling it as giant waves enveloping him in a gentle hug.

He reflected that he often felt he was floating or disconnecting from his body and that he enjoyed following these types of experiences. Through this insight, he discovered that he had evolved unconscious patterns of dissociation. These survival patterns enabled him to manage difficulties but were also affecting the ways he cared for himself and related to others.

Learning how to connect to the elements within us can give us a new way to connect to our body and expand our sense of awareness. It can also reveal hidden patterns and tendencies and provide insights into developing other ways of connecting to ourselves. Awareness of grounding, associated with earth, can support someone experiencing overwhelm or dissociation; air and movement can support someone who feels stuck; water and fluidity can release rigidity; and fire and sensations of warming or energizing can help reduce a sense of numbing and openness. Awareness of space can support someone dealing with feelings of contraction and narrowness.

Stephen decided that he wanted to start by practicing earth and fire awareness. He could see the benefits of learning to feel these elemental capacities within his body to support his healing.

Expanding the Sense of Loving-Kindness in Interconnection

As you begin to feel more supported through practicing element awareness, the wounded places of your body and psyche begin to heal. You may experience a greater sense of ease and connection within your body. You may notice that your heart and mind begin to soften and settle. You may notice yourself becoming more compassionate toward yourself and relaxing into the support of your interconnection with nature.

Element awareness in nature can be a safe way to develop a sense of relationship and interconnection. If you have experienced trauma, you may feel separate and isolated. Learning to cultivate a loving connection with nature can help overcome challenges of disconnection from yourself or others. The practice of loving-kindness is a way to support yourself in offering love to others in your life, to yourself, and to all beings. Loving-kindness practice involves reciting inwardly a set of wishes of well-being and love, each time with a different focus. It can help you to cultivate a sense of safety, health, joy, and ease and extend those feelings to others.

First, you direct the phrases toward someone or something you love and to whom you have a deep connection. We begin with a beloved person or entity as the focus because this is usually a direction in which feelings of loving-kindness flow naturally. It could be a family member, a friend, a pet, or a spiritual teacher. You can choose someone who is alive and present in your life now, or someone who has passed. You can also choose an expression of life in nature (a bird, an animal, an ocean, a mountain).

Next, you direct the phrases toward yourself. This may feel more challenging. Many of us struggle to offer loving-kindness generously and openly to ourselves. Whatever arises in the mind, heart, or body, allow yourself to be present with it in a loving way. There is no need to create any particular experience or to try to force yourself to feel safe, healthy, happy, or at ease. Through this practice, you learn to honor what is within you — all of it. This practice helps you let go of needing to fix or change things and instead learn to meet whatever is here without judgment and with openness, curiosity, and love.

Next, you offer the phrases to someone you don't know well — an acquaintance or someone you meet in passing, like a store clerk. Then you move toward offering loving-kindness to someone you find difficult. You may want to start with someone you've had a slight challenge or struggle with. Over time, you may even extend the practice to persons associated with your trauma.

Next, you offer loving-kindness to a community you know well and are close to — family, friends, people you work with, or your spiritual community — and then to all beings — as many beings and as many overlapping, interconnected communities as you like. You can include beings that walk and crawl on the earth, fly in the sky, swim in the sea, grow in the soil, the Earth herself, the planets of our solar system, the universe, and beyond.

It might be helpful in the beginning to pick only one or a few points of focus that you feel comfortable with. You can choose to expand the scope of the practice as you progress.

Loving-kindness is a traditional form of meditation. I've added to it by suggesting that you practice outdoors, with special attention to the natural world. Because nature herself invites your mind, body, and heart to open, it is a beautiful setting for learning to practice loving-kindness. As you have learned, focusing on the elements is a powerful way to feel your connection with nature and be supported by her. Including the elements as part of your loving-kindness practice may provide a safe and easeful way to experience healing and feeling fully alive.

I offer the meditation below with phrases that have been helpful in my own exploration of loving-kindness practice. If they don't speak to you, you can choose different ones that resonate with you. In the practice of element awareness, which elements have really helped you to connect more deeply to yourself and nature? What has felt healing, nourishing, and supportive? The answers can guide you toward the phrases in loving-kindness meditation that feel most supportive to you. Experiment and notice what best serves you in caring for your body, heart, and mind.

Practice: Loving-Kindness with the Elements

Find a location outside in nature that feels nurturing and supportive and where you have a space to yourself. Choose a place that is relatively free of distractions, where you can sit for twenty to thirty minutes. As you read the following instructions, pause after each sentence to practice what was read. Moving slowly through each instruction gives you time to fully sense the meditation.

Choose a comfortable posture in which you feel supported, grounded, alert, open, and relaxed.

Start by drawing the attention to the breath, noticing how it expresses itself in the chest. Sense the movements of the breath as it lifts up and releases the surface of the skin, the rib cage, and the lungs. Now sense the beating of the heart along with the breath, allowing yourself to radiate from the heart a felt sense of loving-kindness.

Call to mind someone in your life to whom you feel deeply

connected, someone you love, someone you adore. Hold this being in awareness, in your mind, body, and heart, and begin to offer them loving-kindness (reciting inwardly from your heart):

> *May you be safe, protected by the element of earth.*
> *May you be healthy and vital, nourished by the element of fire.*
> *May you be joyful, delighting in the element of air.*
> *May you be at ease and in balance through the element of water.*
> *May you know boundless love, held in the vastness of space.*

Allow yourself to be present to whatever arises as you recite these phrases inwardly.

Now call to mind the sense of your own being. Allow awareness to embrace all aspects of your body, mind, and heart, every cell, your whole being. And in the same way you offered ease and love to another, offer them to yourself:

> *May I be safe, protected by the element of earth.*
> *May I be healthy and vital, nourished by the element of fire.*
> *May I be joyful, delighting in the element of air.*
> *May I be at ease and in balance through the element of water.*
> *May I know boundless love, held in the vastness of space.*

Allow yourself to be present to whatever arises. Offer compassion and kindness to the essence of your being.

Now call to mind someone you don't know well. Holding the sense of this being in your mind, offer loving-kindness from your radiant heart to theirs:

> *May you be safe, protected by the element of earth.*
> *May you be healthy and vital, nourished by the element of fire.*
> *May you be joyful, delighting in the element of air.*

May you be at ease and in balance through the element of water.
May you know boundless love, held in the vastness of space.

Sense what arises as you connect and offer loving-kindness to someone you don't already know.

Now call to mind someone in your life you may have difficulty with (consider starting with someone who you have only a small difficulty with; later you can choose people you find more challenging). Hold this being in awareness, meeting any feeling of contraction, resistance, or turning away with deep compassion, and offer this being loving-kindness:

May you be safe, protected by the element of earth.
May you be healthy and vital, nourished by the element of fire.
May you be joyful, delighting in the element of air.
May you be at ease and in balance through the element of water.
May you know boundless love, held in the vastness of space.

Meet any feelings that arise with compassion, care, and forgiveness.

Now call to mind a community you are connected with, sensing each being individually and then collectively, remembering to include yourself. Now offer loving-kindness from the heart:

May we be safe, protected by the element of earth.
May we be healthy and vital, nourished by the element of fire.
May we be joyful, delighting in the element of air.
May we be at ease and in balance through the element of water.
May we know boundless love, held in the vastness of space.

Be present to the sense of connection.
Now allow yourself to reflect on all beings. Consider how every

being you are connected with is also connected with a community: people, pets, wildlife, trees, plants, ocean life. We can extend radiant, interconnected loving-kindness to all beings:

> *May all beings be safe and protected in interconnection.*
> *May all beings be healthy and vital, nourished in*
> *interconnection.*
> *May all beings be joyful, delighting in interconnection.*
> *May all beings be at ease and in balance in interconnection.*
> *May all beings know boundless love within our connection.*

As you bring the practice to a close, notice any shifts in your sense of connection to yourself and the world around you. Be present to the qualities, attitudes, and experiences in your mind, body, and heart. Offer appreciation for what you have cultivated in this practice.

You may wish to write in your journal about any experiences or insights you had during this meditation.

Practicing loving-kindness allows you to feel more kindly toward yourself, your past experiences, and future experiences life might bring. Over time, this practice leads to deeper connections with yourself and others and a greater sense of well-being. These can help the mind, heart, and body to heal.

Connecting Element Awareness to Thoughts and Emotions

Thus far, we have explored element awareness in the body through seated meditation, while walking, and during ordinary activities, and we have extended that awareness by practicing loving-kindness in nature. These formal practices offer a way to experience healing in our everyday thoughts and emotions, including those that follow from traumatic experiences.

When dealing with trauma, we often hold patterns of thoughts and emotions that can disrupt our lives and interfere with our ability to be present. We may get lost in thought; feel overwhelmed by anxiety, fear, or sadness; ruminate about things that happened in the past; or obsess about what may happen in the future. Any of these patterns can be alleviated by deepening our mindfulness practice and letting element awareness support our healing.

For example, if you are feeling lost or overwhelmed, or are struggling with chaos, then feeling the support of earth — touching the earth, holding a rock, lying on the ground — may help you. If you notice feelings of low energy, dormancy, tightness, or rigidity, then learning to feel heat or fire within and around you — standing in the sun or near a log fire — may boost your vitality and ability to relax. If you are feeling stuck, heavy, or burdened, then feeling the air on your skin or hearing the wind in the trees may uplift you and bring a sense of lightness. If you are experiencing agitation, anger, frustration, or irritation, then noticing and connecting to water — touching the dew on the grass, being near a river or ocean — may lead to a greater sense of ease and fluidity. And if you are feeling limited, uncertain, or doubtful, noticing the vast potential and experience of space around you and within you — raising your eyes to see the cloudscape or the night sky — may offer a way to be with these difficulties.

As you practice element awareness, you will come to know which of the elements best support your well-being. Learning to intimately connect to the elements can bring healing relief, support, containment, safety, ease, love, and compassion — whatever you need to release yourself from the trauma patterns.

By connecting to what we are made of and what we are connected to in nature, we see that we are much more than what our minds or emotion patterns might tell us we are. We are much more than our stories or our histories. Experiencing connection to nature helps us to release ourselves from our trauma and find a different way of relating to ourselves, to others, and to what is truly here. Through the practices in this chapter, you can begin to feel a sense of interconnection with the elements and open into the care and support of loving-kindness to heal the relational wounds of trauma.

Taking Care

Taking the time to feel, notice, and experience awareness of the elements within you and in nature can help you to feel more connected, nourished, and supported. Through these practices, you may be able to connect more deeply to parts of you that need healing. Your body, psyche, and relationships may be in disharmony after you have experienced trauma. Through element awareness practice, you come to know your own body, mind, and emotions more intimately, and this new depth of awareness can support healing by helping you regain a sense of regulation and connection.

Part 2

SOMATIC KNOWING
in NATURE

The natural healing force within each one of us
is the greatest force in getting well.

— HIPPOCRATES

Nature is composed of systems. Microbes, fungi, insects, grasses, plants, trees, wildlife, landscapes, terrains, and climates work in concert to sustain all life. You can see this if you spend a few minutes anywhere in nature — maybe a state or local park, in your backyard, or somewhere in your neighborhood. Consider how all of nature works together to support life: plants provide food and shelter for birds and insects, the birds nourish the flowers, the changing seasons support the life cycles of plants and animals, the climate and weather offer conditions that sustain life. Nothing is separate, and all the elements of nature support one another.

Living beings are part of a larger ecosystem but also have their own internal systems for growth and regulation. A tree has roots that draw water and nutrients from the soil and leaves in order to support photosynthesis. Its branches develop in different directions to grow toward the light, and its bark protects it from the elements and from damage by other living things. All life is constantly developing, changing, healing, and dying.

Your body is part of this web of living systems. Learning to see and feel your connection to it is part of the path of healing. And like all of nature, your body incorporates many systems that work in harmony to support your being alive. Developing awareness of and a healthy relationship with these systems can help bring wholeness into your life.

While nature's inherent impulse is to sustain life, sometimes natural systems are disrupted. We can see some of these effects at work in modern agriculture. Humans first developed organized ways of cultivating plants for food about twelve thousand years ago (very recently in the history of our planet), and these methods helped guarantee people access to food in harsh or barren seasons, as well as providing surpluses that could be traded among different groups for other foods or goods.[1] Over the millennia, as human populations expanded, agriculturists developed methods to increase efficiency and yield. These have come to include extensive use of artificial fertilizers and pesticides and intensive animal farming. While these methods benefit humans by meeting our needs for food, they have also come at a great cost: large-scale destruction of natural habitat; extinction of wildlife; pollution of the air, water, and soils; and depletion of naturally occurring soil nutrients, resulting in less nutritious crops. Our attempts to feed ourselves have ultimately gone against the flow of natural systems.

Similar things happen when we treat our bodies as a productivity system and don't consider the effects on our overall well-being. Depleting our internal resources in the pursuit of personal goals can lead to strained mental and emotional states, bodily dysregulation, and disharmony in relationships. This is particularly true if we try to push through, control, ignore, and suppress experiences of trauma.

The good news is that the body, like other natural systems, has self-repair mechanisms: it is inherently designed to organize itself toward healing. For example, the body has mechanisms for killing cancer cells, fighting infectious agents, and repairing damaged proteins, to name just a few. Our autonomic nervous system, the part that supports bodily functions that are usually outside our consciousness, is hard at work every moment to regulate our bodily functions and keep us in a state of equilibrium — keeping our blood flowing, digesting, sleeping, responding to threats (through the sympathetic nervous system), and calming us back down afterward (through the parasympathetic nervous system).

We have seen the value of establishing mindful awareness in healing from trauma. As you continue to develop awareness of your body, mind, and heart, you develop a sense of being "embodied"— present to and at home in your body from moment to moment, and feeling all mental, emotional, and physical sensations safely. This sense of embodiment helps us make healthy and skillful life choices. As you increase your sense of embodiment through awareness practices, you begin to heal your trauma.

Somatic knowing means awakening to embodiment, becoming intimate with the body's stored traumas, connecting to your inherent potential to heal, and choosing to transform old trauma patterns into new and healthy ways of living. Healing somatically means moving with awareness toward the trauma stored in your body, locating and knowing intimately the places in your body where trauma is stored, being willing to explore barriers related to the stored trauma, being open to new sensations and experiences in the body, and awakening new impulses for health and wholeness. In learning to move somatically, we draw on the support of nature to provide safety, care, inspiration, and guidance and to help us be patient, kind, and loving to what we meet within and around us.

The mind may have both fears and expectations about this process. When the body has betrayed you during traumatic events, or when it has been betrayed by others and by circumstances beyond your control, you can feel powerless, let down, and distrustful of the body. At the same time, the body inherently knows how to heal. You are part of nature, destined to be whole, capable of finding restoration, direction, meaning, and purpose. The practices described in the following chapters are designed to help you develop your somatic knowing. You will inhabit this body for your entire life. Learning to love, befriend, and care for it is a radical and courageous act. You have a right to fully inhabit your body, being present, connected, alive, and in tune with your highest sense of well-being. Your willingness to offer caring and kindness to your body supports you on your path, enabling you to reclaim your body and all the healing capacity that it holds.

Chapter 5

MOVING *toward the* TRAUMA

Forget your perfect offering
There is a crack, a crack in everything
That's how the light gets in.

— Leonard Cohen

Take a breath, and notice the sensations of air entering and leaving your body. Learning to inhabit the body from moment to moment is the path to releasing trauma that may be stuck in the body. Telling ourselves we should "just get over" our trauma or "move on" can leave us feeling stuck, reliving traumatic events that are long past. By identifying and moving toward the places in your body where trauma is stuck, you can let go of needing to relive the trauma or to ruminate on the what, how, when, and where of those events. Awareness can support exploring what is here and how to give it your care and attention in order to heal.

Practicing mindfulness in nature teaches us to be present to the breath, the senses, the body, and elements of the body to support our well-being and awaken within. These mindfulness practices have laid the foundation for a closer exploration of the traumas you have experienced and the places in your body where trauma may be stuck. Which of the practices you have engaged in have supported you best in being more curious and caring toward your body? Which natural settings and elements have supported you best in being more connected, intimate, and present with your body? We will build on these practices as we explore ways to heal trauma.

At first, your mind may interpret the idea of moving toward trauma as the need to confront or work through the trauma in order to be done with it. Yet moving toward trauma is an invitation, not a demand. It means bringing mindful awareness to the body to investigate and fully experience the sensations that are present, and letting what is here be felt and known. Ultimately somatic healing supports the rewiring, release, and transformation of the trauma that is stuck in the body.

This process can be challenging because unresolved trauma is often associated with patterns of reaction in our sympathetic and parasympathetic nervous systems that are not easily accessible to our conscious mind. The instinctive responses of fight, flight, and freeze have evolved to give us emergency exit routes to survive threatening situations. To move toward the trauma, you need to identify the patterns that are keeping your trauma stuck and learn to be present to these patterns — without engaging in the impulse to get away from, fix, or control them or check out entirely. In this chapter we focus on identifying and becoming present to the patterns that keep trauma stuck. In subsequent chapters we will look at ways to shift away from patterns of reactive impulses and toward releasing the stuck trauma, finding and restoring healing impulses in the body.

Everyone's experience of trauma is unique, and so are the patterns that we develop in reaction to trauma. A person may include any or all of the following reactive patterns:

- **Fight:** This is the need to fix or control a threatening situation. It may manifest as a feeling of being hot or charged up, with clenched jaw or fists; a desire to push, punch, or kick; fixed attention on something; thoughts of rage, revenge, blaming, or judging; or hostility and aggressive feelings or behaviors.
- **Flight:** This is the urge to avoid or escape a threat. It may be

expressed as nervous energy, restlessness, fidgeting, or agitation; a desire to move; a habit of scanning the environment and planning escape routes; an inability to sit still; a desire to be completely still; thoughts of anxiety, panic, and fear; and attempts to withdraw and get away.

- **Freeze:** This is the urge to simply shut down when a threat seems inescapable. It may include a sense of the body being unavailable or collapsed; a lack of sensation; feeling blank, constricted, frozen, numb, or paralyzed; feelings of fear or rage; and dissociation from one's feelings and actions even while engaging in correct social behaviors.

Do you recognize any of these patterns in yourself? If you do, remember that they are survival patterns, the attempts of your body, mind, and heart to protect you. It is healing to identify and move toward them. You may want to take a few minutes to reflect on which of these patterns tend to keep your trauma stuck. Inviting a caring, curious, gentle, nonjudgmental, welcoming attention toward these patterns will allow you to meet your trauma differently, creating space for something new to emerge.

You may already be aware of the places in your body where you have felt pain, discomfort, or numbing from the trauma you have experienced, and recalling the trauma may immediately evoke sensations in these places. You may tend to push these sensations away, think about them negatively, and avoid looking or feeling into these parts of your body. By bringing mindful awareness, kindness, and openness to these reactive habits and sensations, you can begin to see them as ways to move toward the places that hold the trauma.

Reflection: Moving toward a Traumatic Experience

Before you begin this practice, notice how the mind, body, and heart may be bracing or preparing for the idea of moving toward a traumatic experience. Choose an outdoor space that gives you a sense of support beneath, above, and around you. Take a breath, noticing the inhale and the exhale.

Now reflect on and call to mind one traumatic event you experienced. There is no need to recall all the details: just bring to mind a general recollection of what occurred, the thoughts or emotions you have about it, or behaviors that have arisen in your reactive attempts to manage, avoid, control, deny, or repress the trauma.

Now ask yourself, What would have helped me to find safety? Did I want to get away, to fight, to yell for help? Just come up with a few thoughts about what would have provided you with a sense of protection, safety, or support.

Notice whether this question gives rise to sensations in your body. Do you feel a bit tight, tense, stuck, unavailable? Where in your body are you noticing these sensations? Become curious about exploring the sensations, movements, and qualities of these experiences. Bringing your attention to the reactivity associated with this trauma and identifying what would have helped you feel safe can help identify places in the body where reactive habits may be stuck.

Consider writing in your journal about what you noticed or experienced during this reflection.

We explore this process in more depth at the end of this chapter. You may choose to return to this reflection when you are ready to explore other traumas to heal.

Resourcing

When learning to move toward trauma, we need not only to become aware of the patterns in our ways of managing trauma but also to find ways to ground ourselves and stay oriented in order to attend to what is arising. If you become too overwhelmed, your nervous system may shut down, either by becoming flooded with intense feelings, sensations, or thoughts or by collapsing, shutting down, and giving rise to feelings of confusion and disorientation.

Resourcing is the practice of inviting your mind and body to attune to sensations of safety, or simply things that feel good. These sensations can be small or large. They may be associated with connections to nature, the environment around you, people, objects, or sounds. Resourcing teaches our nervous system that it can come back to a sense of calm and safety after experiencing stress. When you feel resourced, your nervous system feels relaxed, at ease, calm, soothed, supported, held, and nurtured. These feelings provide a place to return to or reside in as you move toward trauma.

You may feel resourced by a particular natural setting or by some quality of nature, like the rustling of leaves in the wind, the security and stability of rock, the soothing current of water in a stream, or a graceful oak standing solidly with you. You may also feel resourced by specific activities, such as walking, swimming, gardening, singing, listening to music, or reading books.

I encourage you to make a list of the resources that help you stay balanced, steady, and present as you move toward your trauma. You may choose to engage in these forms of resourcing on a regular basis and to include them before or after the somatic nature healing practices you learn.

Staying Grounded

Grounding techniques can be helpful when you feel overwhelmed or flooded by emotional reactivity associated with activation from trauma. If you have ever experienced this type of distress, it's likely that someone tried to help you by suggesting that you bring your attention and awareness back into the present moment and your immediate surroundings. Helpful techniques can include holding something solid or focusing your attention on specific objects in your environment that are solid or steadily support your body. While these techniques are helpful, they are often used as remedies after feelings of distress and overwhelm have already arisen. For working with trauma, we want to cultivate a sense of steadiness and groundedness in a proactive way — to establish a sense of stability, safety, ease, and calm in your nervous system from the outset, so that the trauma that is stuck in the body can be skillfully experienced and healed.

As I sit writing this, I am again in my canyon and enjoying the aliveness of spring. For the past month, two ground squirrels have been busy on the hill, burrowing, excavating, foraging, and creating pathways beneath the earth. I have watched in wonderment and appreciation to see what their efforts would reveal. And yesterday about eight baby squirrels emerged from the earth. Tentative, curious, and playful, they were able to return again and again to the stability and safety of their burrow while beginning to explore the world. This is another example of the way nature models, reflects, and teaches us what we need to know. She shows us the truth of the importance of establishing a solid, secure, safe sense of ground. And, as you heal and transform trauma, you will need to create and draw on your own sense of groundedness within your body.

At this moment, where in your body do you feel a sense of groundedness, steadiness, stability, or security? Feel into the places of your body that have contact with the ground or a support — the feet, legs, and back. See if you can note two sensations that help you experience being grounded in your body (e.g., solidness, heaviness, stability, steadiness). This is the beginning of a simple awareness practice. At first this may be difficult, and you may struggle to identify places in the body where you feel grounded. This is okay; just keep your attention steady and curious to notice any sense of groundedness. You may notice it first in your feet or hands, or in the places where your body has direct contact with a source of support. Any sense of stability, steadiness, or groundedness will help you heal and transform your relationship to your body and trauma. Remember to be patient, kind, and gentle with yourself as you explore the practices.

Practice: Grounding Meditation

Choose a place outdoors where you can practice for fifteen to twenty minutes. Find terrain that feels solid, stable, safe, and steady, a place you can rest your body into. It might be against or under a tree, on or next to a rock outcrop, or in a canyon. It might be in your backyard, on your patio, or somewhere in your neighborhood. This practice is designed to help you sense these qualities around you and within your body; there is no need to try to force them to be here. Let them arise naturally.

Turn your attention inward. Choose a posture that allows your body to feel grounded, supported, alert, relaxed, and open. You might lie on your back, place your hands or bare feet on the earth, or lean against or curl your body into the terrain. When you find the posture that feels best to you, take time to slowly attend to the places in your body that are in contact with nature, such as the feet, legs, pelvis, back, arms, and head.

Notice where in your body you feel a sense of support, stability, safety, security, or solidity from this contact. Rest your attention here for a few moments. Be curious to explore this region of the body. What other sensations and qualities of groundedness might be present? If you find yourself trying to figure out analytically what is grounded or judging the sensations you are experiencing, let go and return to sensing the place in the body that feels supportive and steady in its contact with nature.

Now shift your attention to another area of the body that you sense as grounded. It may be another place in the body that is in direct contact with nature, or it may be within. Consider directing your attention toward parts of the body that you experience as dense, heavy, solid, or steady, like the bones, muscles, and organs. Become aware of the sensations of groundedness as they arise and pass. If your mind drifts to some other experience in the body, a distraction, or a movement away from the body, notice the shift and then gently return your attention to regions of the body that are grounded, steady, and solid. Continue to explore other parts of the body that feel grounded, noticing the various qualities of the sensations of groundedness.

Shift the attention now to noticing the environment you are in. What are the objects that feel most steady, grounded, and secure in the natural setting around you — the trees, the rocks, the land-scape itself? Take in the qualities of these grounded expressions of nature — their rootedness, their stability, their solidity, their density. Now explore where in your body you sense the same qualities. Shift the attention slowly between what is grounded in nature and what is grounded, steady, and secure within you. Take your time. There is no need to try to create or force these feelings to arise in your body.

In the last few moments of this practice, be present to the awareness of groundedness within you and around you. Sense the feelings arising in your whole body, mind, and heart. Offer gratitude for what has been cultivated in awareness, and offer appreciation to the natural setting that has supported your growing awareness of being grounded.

Afterward, consider writing in your journal about any experiences or insights you had during this meditation.

Orienting to Nature

We are wired to orient to our environments, to use all our senses to know what is around us, and to attend to what is most important to our safety and well-being. When we hear a loud noise, our ears and our eyes usually prompt us to attend to this stimulus. Being oriented to our environment is related to being grounded. Orienting techniques are often used to help a person experiencing distress associated with past trauma. Asking the person to list out loud a number of things they can hear, see, smell, touch, or taste can reorient them to the present setting and moment instead of reexperiencing the trauma. Again, these techniques are typically used as remedies, but orienting can also be a proactive way to establish a more constant sense of ease, calm, and safety in the nervous system. This state of calm supports the work of moving toward the trauma.

Like the rest of nature, we are primed to orient ourselves. Consider a flower following the movements of the sun, an animal stopping to scan the environment in response to a sound, or a bird chirping and taking flight in response to unexpected movements in its surroundings. This is how life survives.

Orienting is the process of engaging attention to the environment through the sense doors. The practice of orienting to nature builds on the practice of sense awareness presented in chapter 2. By attending with intention to what you hear, see, smell, and touch (and sometimes taste), you can allow your senses to guide you into a sense of steadiness and support.

Practice: Orienting to Nature Meditation

This meditation is designed to support orienting yourself to nature during the course of your day. It can be practiced formally for a period of five to ten minutes or informally by attuning to one or two senses for a few moments throughout the day. You may choose to practice outside or just shift from your daily activities while you are indoors.

Choose a posture that feels supportive: lying down, sitting, standing, or walking. Now turn your attention inward to notice how your mind, heart, and body feel in this moment. (Noticing the mind, body, and heart is a three-point check that orients you to your inner landscape. Remember to check again as new sensations and experiences unfold.) Is your mind busy, racing, planning, and anticipating, or is it still, quiet, and settled? Is your heart feeling stress, anxiety, worry, and agitation, or is there ease, light, and openness? Is your body tense, tight, and constricted, or steady, calm, and relaxed?

There is no need to judge, change, or try to fix the sensations you notice; simply welcome them.

Take a few moments to attune to your senses. Allow yourself to move your head and body to attend to what is in nature. You may want to turn your head from side to side to scan the environment all around you.

Now bring awareness to the whole body here in nature. Sense the earth beneath you and around you. Notice the textures of the ground beneath your feet, the solidity and presence of plants, rocks, and trees. Take in their shapes and sizes; notice the qualities of light, the fragrances of soil, leaves, and flowers. Orient and attend to the one sense (sight, smell, hearing, touch — or taste, to the extent that it is safe) that draws you to be present inwardly to the sense of groundedness here and the support of nature.

Now shift your attention to movement around you in nature: the wind stirring the trees, birds flying past, the movement of sunlight and shadow through leaves, clouds in the sky, the temperatures and texture of the air moving against your skin. Again, orient on the one sense (either the same one as before or a different one) that allows you to feel present to these movements of nature. Sense the ease, fluidity, and constant change in nature. Notice how orienting to the movements of nature increases your feelings of ease and acceptance of what is changing and unfolding within.

Now orient through your senses to expressions of calm and relaxation around you. Notice light that is subtle and muted, sounds that are soft and soothing, sweet and calming scents from the earth and plants, and the soft textures of grass, petals, and leaves. Orient to the sense that allows you to arrive into connection with nature's soft, restorative, peaceful expressions. Notice how orienting yourself to calm and peace in nature allows you to experience these sensations within.

As you close this practice, notice now the state of your mind, body, and heart. Observe how orienting to expressions of groundedness, movement, and calm in nature can help restore these qualities in your inner being. Offer appreciation for nature and for what has supported you in this practice.

Afterward, consider writing in your journal about any experiences or insights you had during this meditation.

Connecting to resources that support your well-being, cultivating a sense of groundedness, and orienting to nature gives you the support you need to safely explore the traumas stored in your body.

The Body as a Map of the Terrains of Trauma

If the body is the site of stuck trauma, then the body is also the map that points the way to resolving and healing the trauma. Awareness of your fight, flight, and freeze behavior patterns, examined earlier in this chapter, is a good place to start this exploration. The thoughts, emotions, sensations, and behavior patterns that arise in order to manage trauma are the signs to follow in the body, like markers on a map. They point to the places we can explore in order to heal.

Reaction to a traumatic event often causes parts of the body to brace, constrict, tighten, freeze, or become numb. As the body tries and fails to restore itself to homeostasis after the traumatic event, sensation patterns begin to arise. These patterns create stuck trauma in the body, which may manifest itself physically as a loss of range of motion or sensation in parts of the body, or areas of painful tension.

Learning to safely and mindfully note, describe, and be present with difficult sensations is the way to identify and explore the terrain of your trauma. This can be challenging at first, as the mind may remember experiences from the trauma or engage in attempts to figure out, change, or resist the sensations. Also, exploring this landscape may bring up emotions such as anger, anxiety, fear, rage, sadness, loss, and grief. All of these responses are okay: thoughts and feelings are part of the terrain. As best you can, simply notice these experiences arising — like a butterfly flying overhead or an ant crawling near your feet as you walk on a path — and, gently and without judgment, return your attention to the sensations of the body as you map your trauma.

Curiosity helps us to become more aware of long-held reactive patterns and also to rewire them. Every person's experience of trauma and reaction to it, like every terrain in nature, is different. Be open to discovering the unique terrain of trauma in your body.

When walking in a familiar place, we may realize after about fifteen or twenty minutes that the mind has been distracted, playing out past experiences or trying to plan for the future, so that we have barely noticed our feet moving or the path we are walking. In familiar settings, we often just go into automatic mode. In a similar way, our patterns of reaction may have become so familiar that we no longer experience them as challenging or a problem: we may hardly be aware of them. A sense of curiosity helps us really feel and become present to our internal landscape from moment to moment.

While exploring the terrain of trauma in your body, you also want to bring an attitude of kindness and compassion. This can prevent you from being trapped in the negative cycles of emotions, thoughts, and desires for things to be different. Remember that the contours of this terrain are the results of your efforts to survive. Treat them with reverence and respect. Creating a path through this landscape, drawing the map, placing signposts along the path, and smoothing the trail are all acts of care and kindness that will lead to the destination of healing.

Mapping your trauma entails returning again and again to exploring the sensations of your body. The organs, structures, and systems of the body present a vast terrain to explore, with many features and sensations to be noted. Body awareness will enable you to explore and map the places that hold your trauma.

Gwen's Story

Gwen experienced repeated physical abuse in a violent relationship during her late teens and early twenties. One incident in particular continued to cause her distress well into her thirties.

Gwen's abusive partner was driving a car with Gwen in the passenger seat, not wearing a seatbelt. The abusive partner slammed on the brakes intentionally, causing Gwen's head to smash through the windshield. Although she was able to leave the relationship safely, she later found it difficult to travel as a passenger in a car. If the car stopped or slowed suddenly, she would brace herself, attempt to stomp on an imaginary brake, and yell at the driver to stop, even though there was no obvious danger.

Through grounding practices and body awareness, she learned to map the terrain of her trauma. She identified sensations of contractions and jolts of energy in her head; tension, tightening, and numbness in the right side of her neck, right shoulder, and chest; and limited mobility in these regions. By becoming present to these places in her body, she became familiar with the flight and freeze patterns that had developed over years in response to this trauma.

By connecting to these patterns in her body with awareness, kindness, and steadiness, she began to reclaim a sense of agency and was ready to explore deeper healing practices to release this trauma from her body.

You may find it challenging to explore places that hold patterns of tension, disconnection, numbing, or immobility in your body, but these are precisely the places that hold the information you need to heal from trauma. Allow yourself to return again and again to the practices of this chapter to explore all of the terrains of your stuck trauma.

Reflection /Activity: Mapping the Body with Nature

For this reflection/activity, take your journal to write or draw what you discover. As you begin this reflection allow yourself a few moments to establish awareness of groundedness and orienting within your body. While walking or sitting in nature, focus your awareness on something that appears wounded, scarred, not growing, stuck, or trapped. This might be a tree with a missing limb, a fallen branch, a dead leaf, dried or brittle grasses, a plant rooted in concrete, or charred earth — whatever stirs your curiosity. Observe the details of this expression of nature, noticing what shapes, directions, and patterns it has taken. Let yourself reflect on the conditions that caused it to become like this. Now notice how some aspect of it is still surviving, like a fallen leaf or branch decaying and transforming to nourish the earth and become something new. Explore what aspects of the natural surroundings are supporting its survival and its connection with other life.

Now consider creating a map of your body and the places you know to be holding stuck or stored trauma. You might choose to draw your body, to make ephemeral art with natural objects, or find objects in nature that represent the experiences of your stuck trauma. Be creative and open to finding the form of expression that serves you best. Illustrate all the places in your body that feel stuck, along with the capacity of your body to survive and the ways that the intricate systems of your body sustain and support your being.

Now label your map: name and describe the sensations that reside in these regions of your body. Be creative and open with these expressions of sensation. Detail the temperatures, textures, pressures, movement or lack of movement, densities, and absences of sensation you experience.

This process can be challenging. If you become overwhelmed, you can always return to earlier practices to regain a sense of groundedness, calm, ease, and orienting to your environment. You can also always set aside this reflection and return to it when you are ready.

If you find yourself judging some aspect of the map you are creating, allow yourself to notice this thought, and then try to let go of needing to compare, figure out, analyze, or doubt the process. By noticing this challenge, you are already making space for something new to arise.

As you continue to map your trauma, return again and again to awareness of your body, a sense of groundedness. Take your time. What evolves and is created is as it should be — it's your map.

You may return to this reflection to explore other traumas that reside in different places in your body. You may also discover that different traumatic experiences are linked. This creates the possibility of exploring, mapping, and knowing a beautifully intricate and unique landscape. Return to your map to add to it as you deepen your practices and to create more ways to express the trauma in your body as you discover it.

By mapping the terrains of your trauma, you become more aware of what is held in your body, and this awareness helps you be present in everyday life and experience more possibility for choice. As you learn to notice where your body is reacting during difficult situations (e.g., noticing tension in the neck, shortness of breath, or constriction in your stomach), you can respond more skillfully, perhaps engaging in a practice of grounding or orienting that enables you to meet this pattern differently. Once you are aware of a particular location of stuck trauma, you might choose to track the sensations of this part of your body as you move through your daily activities.

The following chapters offer ways to use your map to deepen your healing, remain present to these patterns without engaging in reactive impulses, and find ways to release the stuck trauma from your body.

Taking Care

Turning toward trauma safely and mapping the terrain of your trauma, with the help of awareness, resources, and grounding and orienting practices, is a path toward healing. This may take time. Given that most trauma has become stored or stuck in the body over a long period, it also takes time to learn to reexperience and be present with it in a new and safe way.

The following chapters explore more specific ways to use the practices of this chapter — grounding, orienting, and mapping the body — to find healing and open yourself to new experiences. You can return to these practices again and again: they will help you travel safely and with curiosity in the landscape of trauma.

Chapter 6

FINDING *the* HEALING CURRENTS

Most people are afraid of suffering. But suffering is a kind of mud to help the lotus flower of happiness grow. There can be no lotus flower without the mud.

— Thích Nhất Hạnh

The lotus flower is one of the most ancient and deepest symbols. In Buddhist and Egyptian cultures, it represents beauty, magic, and the possibility of healing. It takes two years for a lotus plant to grow from seed to flower, and it grows only in murky and muddy waters. The lotus can endure scorching heat, blooming even in the hottest of summers, and it survives through the winter even when the water freezes over it. Individual plants can live for centuries, and seeds estimated to be approximately 1,300 years old have germinated into plants.[1]

When the mature plant blooms, the flower submerges every night into the murky waters and miraculously reappears the next morning without any residue on its petals. Each blossom lasts three to four days. Every day the blossom pushes its way through the muddy waters toward the sunlight, and the petals open one by one into the light of day, revealing beauty, strength, perseverance, and the capacity to meet life with ease and grace.

Growth, Grace, and Beauty in the Mud

Your trauma healing is like a lotus. The conditions that have brought you into this moment — the time, the darkness, the challenges of your lived experience — are also the conditions that can enable something magical and beautiful to emerge within you. Through these healing practices, you can be like the lotus flower, drawing strength, nutrients, and support from the mud of your traumatic history and awakening the beauty of your inner being.

It can be challenging to accept the idea that this mud of your past can give rise to beauty. You may have spent years creating reactive habits and patterns to suppress your trauma. In the previous chapter we explored ways you can become present to your trauma landscape. In this chapter we will deepen your capacity to stay mindfully present to your patterns of avoiding, resisting, denying, or clinging; you will learn to let go of needing to follow those patterns in any particular way and instead become open to new possibilities for healing.

This terrain may seem uncomfortable and unfamiliar, and you may feel uncertain about what will happen next. As these challenging feelings arise, you may feel pulled back toward familiar patterns and habits. Being willing to stay present to the mud and to meet the difficult or unfamiliar experiences with a kind, gentle, and compassionate awareness will enable healing to emerge like a lotus blossom. It takes courage, strength, and sometimes faith to explore the experiences of challenge or chaos in our body, mind, and heart.

Opening to New Currents of Healing

Consider a time when you went into a landscape or terrain with fixed expectations, but you discovered something else, growing amid conditions you didn't expect. Maybe you were surprised to see pine trees and lush forest, flowers in bloom, or a snowy landscape in a place you thought of as a desert. This type of discovery lends itself to seeing things anew, with delight, curiosity, and a heartfelt welcome. The same can happen with trauma. Opening your body, mind, and heart to new possibilities for healing requires presence and a willingness to let go of expectations of what is here or how it should be known.

Mindfulness gives us the opportunity to relate differently to life. As you've been practicing mindfulness of the breath, the senses, and the body — awakening new sensations, cultivating new ways to notice your body, establishing resources in the body, and learning where in your body trauma may be stuck — you have begun to experience new ways to inhabit your body and connect to the trauma it has stored.

Being open to experiences as they arise and letting go of the need to figure them out or understand them can help with the transformation of trauma. Analytical thinking helps us make decisions, pursue things we desire (such as careers and relationships), and learn about and understand our world, but these qualities of mind aren't helpful in working with trauma. If trauma is an experience stored in the *body*, then trying to have the *mind* understand it gets in the way, preventing us from making new discoveries or being open to new experiences.

We also have a habit of liking or not liking the experiences we encounter. This takes the form of seeking pleasant experiences and trying to hold on to them (which is unrealistic — they will inevitably end) and avoiding unpleasant experiences in life (which is also unrealistic — they will inevitably happen). These habits have contributed to the way your trauma patterns have formed in your body, mind, and heart. If you can learn to accept and be with both pleasant and unpleasant experiences without trying to amplify or resist them, you will be ready to meet the experiences that arise during your healing.

We also develop habitual reactions to neutral experiences. When we observe something that we categorize as known to us that we don't really have a strong feeling about one way or the other, we develop a habit of checking out from or ignoring it. This habit can become a coping mechanism for trauma, leading the body to feel disconnected, dissociated, or numb. As you learn to encounter these neutral moments as just experiences that are neither pleasant nor unpleasant, that are arising and passing, these reactive patterns can re-form into something new.

When you first explore these practices, you are likely to experience the initial sensations, emotions, and thoughts of hyperarousal — anxiety, restlessness, agitation — and /or hypoarousal — a sense of being on autopilot, checking out, or disconnection. As you become aware of and explore these reactive patterns, you can learn to stay present in your body at a level of arousal that is healthy for you. The intention in these practices is to stay aware of sensations, thoughts, and emotions arising and passing while also remaining calm and grounded. As you explore these patterns and expand your window of tolerance for these experiences, the reactive patterns can shift and release, bringing healing.

For the practices presented in this chapter, take time to consider which settings in nature will aid your healing. Choose places that give you a sense of support: perhaps a meadow full of tall grasses, birdsong, flowers, and plant life; a forest lush with mosses, trees, rocks, and wildlife; a place near the ocean or inland waters, steady with soft sands, rocks, aquatic life, and the sound of moving water; or a desert, vast, open, sandy, rugged, and full of underground and resilient life. Every landscape contains qualities and expressions of nature that can support your unique needs for healing. And each trauma you choose to heal may need a different environment. If you don't have access to a range of terrains, you can still consider them in your imagination and think about places where certain aspects of a particular terrain might be available to you.

Pendulation

The practice of pendulation, or oscillating your attention between different objects of awareness, is a core healing practice in somatic experiencing.[2] This practice builds on your practices of body awareness, grounding, and orienting. You first establish your awareness of an experience in your body that is grounded, steady, stable, and secure. If you can't find those qualities in your body, you may find them in nature: for instance, you may feel steadiness from leaning against a tree, feeling your back supported, the base of your body cradled, and your sense of security enhanced by the branches that rise above and around you. This helps your parasympathetic nervous system to engage, creating a sense of calm and ease to support you in working with the trauma.

Slowly and gently you then begin to move your awareness to the place in the body where you experience a sensation associated with your trauma, such as tightness, constriction, tension, or numbing. Invite your attention to stay present and become aware of the sensations in this part of your body. It's important to bring a willingness to just be with any of these sensations as it is, not judging, not needing it to be different. When you feel ready, bring your attention back to the place in the body that is grounded (or oriented to nature), and focus awareness on the sensations here. Again, there is no need to try to make your experience feel any different from what it is. Then you pendulate or oscillate attention slowly between the sensations in your body associated with trauma and the place you are sensing as grounded, with no intention of *changing* the experiences, simply allowing yourself to be present to any sensations that arise. You may choose to focus for only a few seconds on each place, or you may choose to stay for a while longer with the sense of groundedness and only briefly with the sensations associated with trauma. Gradually, as it feels supportive to you, increase the time you stay present with each.

This practice cultivates your capacity to be trusting, patient, and open. As you repeat it, space for healing will open. Often the feelings that arise are not familiar or predictable. You may experience a release or shift in the area associated with your trauma, a tiny movement elsewhere in your body, or a spontaneous, deep outward breath moving from your belly up into the chest — a signal of ease, calm, and relaxation in your nervous system. You can welcome these healing currents, letting your awareness become curious about the changes occurring in your body and the stored or stuck trauma.

With the practice of pendulation, it's important to *start small* and *work slowly*, gradually building up your capacity to attend to sites of trauma in your body. At first you may choose to practice only for a few moments and focus on bodily places of trauma that do not hold the most intense sensations. Developing this practice is like lifting weights at the gym. You wouldn't start out trying to lift the hundred-pound weights: you would start with what you can realistically handle and gradually increase your strength and capacity to lift heavier weights. Pushing too hard or trying to force, change, or expel the trauma that is stuck in your body is only another form of avoidance. Let yourself be open and present to each experience you notice, and gently, slowly, and kindly move your awareness toward it. Treat your trauma with care, respect, and regard as you transform it into healing.

Practice: Pendulation — Body Awareness

This practice supports learning to work with locations of stored or stuck trauma in your body. Start by practicing for two or three minutes, eventually building up to five to ten minutes. Begin by choosing areas of the body that hold only mildly difficult sensations, building up over time to focusing on more challenging areas and sensations. Choose a setting that contains an aspect of nature you find most supportive, such as water, birdsong, wildlife, trees, plants, or open space.

Choose a posture in which you feel grounded, relaxed, at ease, and open — lying down, reclining, sitting, standing, or walking. Feel what is supporting your body (above you, behind you, all around you) and what else is present in nature supporting you — the air, the earth, light, sounds.

Now begin to investigate your body, scanning slowly from your feet to your head. As you scan, notice any area that you sense as heavy, solid, steady, or secure. Rest awareness in the sense of groundedness in the body. If nothing in your body feels steady, stable, or secure, shift your attention, orienting to the sources of stability around you — anything that you sense as solid, steady, or grounded.

Now shift your attention to a part of the body where you are experiencing some challenge or a stored experience of trauma. Explore what sensations are here right now. Is there a sense of tightening, holding, gripping, contracting, stuckness, achiness, tension, pain, sharpness, dullness, numbing? Be curious about what is here. Notice whether sensations shift, change, or come and go in a particular way. If you find yourself wanting to change or alleviate the sensation, judge it, or check out, can you let go and try to simply experience the sensations as they are in this moment?

When you are ready, gently shift your attention back to the area of the body that feels grounded. Let yourself sense that groundedness. Notice whether the sensations in this part of the body shift, change, or expand in some way. After a few moments, gently and slowly move your attention back to the part of the body that holds trauma. Explore what sensations are here now, staying open, curious, and present. Slowly, and with the intention to remain present, invite your attention to pendulate between these places in the body. Stay with each place for a few seconds, observing how you are moving your attention back and forth between these places (slowly, easefully, and with curiosity, or trying to fix or change). As you attend to each of these places, allow yourself to rest in awareness to explore all the various sensations of this region.

During this practice, you may notice that your mind drifts. You may remember experiences, feel emotions arise, or notice new sensations in other parts of the body. This is okay. Simply take note of what arises, and then bring your awareness back to the selected areas of your body.

As you close this practice, expand awareness to the entire body. Do you sense a bit more space in parts of your body? Is your breath moving in a new pattern? Have shifts occurred in your mind, body, or heart? Some of the sensations you notice may be pleasant, relieving, and calming, and some may be unpleasant and agitating. These sensations are simply here for you to explore and to acknowledge as part of your path to healing.

Offer gratitude for this practice, for your courage, your intention to heal, and your ability to explore your body in this way.

Afterward, consider writing in your journal about any experiences or insights you had during this meditation.

Finding Movement and Touch

As you develop the practices of body awareness and pendulation to identify and attend to sites of stuck trauma in your body, you may begin to experience different healing currents in your nervous system. These provide you with an opportunity to use movement and touch to help you heal. The places that are holding trauma in the body are the places that could not be activated at the time of the trauma to help you find protection, safety, or security through running away, yelling, or fighting back. Through the practice of pendulation, of holding and caring for your trauma, you may experience an impulse to act to take care of your body in a new way, allowing it to resolve what it didn't get to do during the trauma. It's important to attune to impulses in the body that are arising during your healing practices, rather than what the mind "thinks" the body might have needed.

As you practice pendulation, you are likely to feel bodily impulses to move. Initially these may consist of small movements of your skin and muscles. As best you can, follow these impulses slowly and with awareness. Feel the sensations of the movements, going very slowly to ensure you are finding the healing current rather than moving into a familiar protective pattern.

The ability to identify and follow a healing impulse to move takes intuitive listening and a familiarity with the reactive habits of your body. Repetitive fidgeting, stretching, cracking, or movement — such as a habit of tapping on objects, twisting your hair, or shaking your foot or leg — may be a reactive habit that your body engages in for self-regulation or calming. It's important to acknowledge the parts of the body where these impulses arise, as they may be places of stored trauma, but engaging in these old patterns of regulation will keep the trauma stuck rather than release it. Through the practice of pendulation, awareness of what is arising within will guide the way to forms of movement that will help you heal.

Another impulse you may experience as you practice pendulation is a desire for support, connection, and touch. You may feel an urge to place a hand on the part of your body that is holding trauma, or to draw something close to you that feels supportive or containing. Touch lets our body register safety, connection, and soothing. Warm touch stimulates the release of oxytocin, the "cuddle hormone," which enhances a sense of trust and safe attachment.

Impulses for movement and touch are part of your body's own effort to release trauma. They can be explored through self-touch — embracing or placing your hands on specific regions of your body. Self-massage and self-touch have been shown to slow the heart rate and even lower levels of the stress hormone cortisol.[3]

Nature provides us with many opportunities for touch, connection, and movement. Think about touching the petals of a flower, dipping your hand into a cool stream, leaning your body against the rough, sturdy bark of a tree, or burrowing your feet into the sand. To experience the support of nature as you explore movement, you might gently lean your body into the steadiness of a tree trunk, push your feet or your legs into the solid earth beneath you, or let your chest, arms, and hands reach toward the sky.

Nature can provide cues to help you experience the healing currents that can release and transform your trauma. Take your time with these practices, allowing yourself to connect to what feels resourcing, supportive, and easeful to keep your nervous system regulated.

Alexandria's Story

Alexandria had struggled with forming safe and healthy intimate relationships for most of her life. As a child, she experienced physical abuse and abandonment by her father. In reaction to these traumatic experiences, Alexandria often engaged in patterns of freezing behavior and blamed her romantic partners when they did not live up to her expectations of a relationship.

In her initial attempts to heal from these early traumas, she often experienced feelings of being alone and scared. These led her to enter into a state of dissociation, numbing, or feeling like she was floating away.

As we worked together on her healing, Alexandria came to establish a connection with her body and developed the capacity to ground herself. As she learned the practices of pendulation, we were slowly able to begin exploring these "freeze" patterns.

During one session, Alexandria established a strong sense of grounding to the base of her body. She sat in my mobile therapy van with its doors and windows open, surrounded by blankets and pillows, in a setting of giant pine trees and an expanse of grass in the distance. As we slowly explored the freeze patterns, she identified a sense of floating in her upper body and head. Pendulating between this feeling and the sense of groundedness in her physical surroundings, she began to have sensations of feeling like a bird perched in a nest high in a tree. At first these sensations were linked to fear that the bird was falling from the nest. As we continued with the pendulation practices, she had the sense in her body and mind of being able to glide and fly away from her nest, of uplift and soaring, and of knowing how to return to the nest as she chose.

As she experienced the sense of being able to fly, Alexandria began to engage in slow rotations of her neck. She discovered that her body could relax and feel safe. She asked for support from the touch of my hand at the base of her neck (in somatic experiencing therapy, it is common for a therapist to offer touch support to aid the healing). As she continued to practice pendulation along with these neck movements, she spontaneously noted, "I just felt my amygdala drop. I didn't know that was possible." She had been aware of a tight, bound, and wound sensation at the base of her head and the top of her neck that shifted and released. She began to breathe deeply, with heat releasing from her neck and tension shifting out of her shoulders and chest.

At the close of this session, she reflected that her "freeze" patterns must have been her amygdala's attempt to protect her during the traumatic experiences of her childhood. With awareness of these patterns, she was able to work toward creating safety for herself and finding ways to remain present and engaged in her relationships.

Release Expressions

As you tap into the healing currents that arise with new movements and experiences of touch, you will feel the sensations of trauma being released from your body. These are often referred to as "discharge," or stuck energy releasing itself from the body. They may take the form of a sense of heat; spontaneous movements of the body; a deep, spontaneous belly breath; nausea, burping, or digestive gas; or tingling or pulsating sensations.

It's important to notice these release expressions and allow them to move through the body. They may give rise to additional impulses to yell, to stand up, to run, jump, and kick, or to feel your arms and hands push, grab, and squeeze. These bigger movements of release allow more stuck trauma to be released from your body.

You may choose to invite nature to be a part of these big impulses to move or touch. You might hug or squeeze a tree, paw or dig at the dirt, or yell to the beings in the landscape. Allow nature to support you in these release expressions. In chapter 8 we will explore ways to enjoy the new freedom and means of expression available to you as the trauma leaves your body.

Animals have an innate response after experiencing a threat to life: they literally shake it off, discharging the energy of the traumatic event. You might have noticed a dog shake his entire body after a distressing barking interaction, or watched deer flick and shake their tails and resume normal activity after a scare. These actions help to release trauma after a threatening experience so that the animal can resume normal activity.

We are animals too. Physically releasing trauma from your body leads to the transformation of your trauma and the activation of your innate capacity to self-regulate, organize, and restore your body to health and wholeness.

Practice: Pendulation — Body Awareness with Nature (Movement and Touch)

This practice incorporates the support of nature as you explore pendulation with body awareness, movement, and touch to locate and release stored trauma. It can last anywhere from a few minutes to thirty minutes.

Choose the aspect of nature that will best support you in working with this trauma (water, birdsong, wildlife, plants, open space). Take a comfortable posture, allowing yourself to meander, walk slowly, sit, or lie down and turn the attention inward. Note what is present in the landscape of your mind, body, and heart. There is no need to judge, fix, or change anything you notice. Now orient your body toward something in your surroundings that feels intuitively supportive — a tree, a particular flower or plant, a body of water, an area of earth, or a rock. Notice the sensations that arise in your body as you orient to this source of support: is there a sense of calming, ease, relaxing, groundedness, openness?

Now invite the body to connect to this form of nature (maybe through direct touch, or details of what is seen, heard, or smelled). Shift to notice how the body receives this as grounded within. Rest in awareness of this sense of groundedness.

Now move your attention to a place in the body that holds some experience of trauma. This might be a place where you currently feel tension or pain, or it might be a place that you know holds trauma. Notice the sensations in this region of the body, thoughts moving in the mind, emotions rising. Invite yourself to be present with the experiences that are here. Then gently shift your attention back to the part of the body that feels grounded. Stay with these sensations for a time, and then, when you are ready, return your attention to the place in the body that holds the trauma.

As you slowly and mindfully pendulate between these two regions of the body, be curious about the sensations and impulses that arise. If you feel an unfamiliar impulse to move or a desire for touch, follow it with awareness. Allow yourself to make small movements, or to touch the part of your body that holds the trauma; let the impulse guide you. You may feel a sense of ease or release; you may also sense tightening or constriction. Whatever arises, it's okay. Allow yourself to be present, pendulating and following with awareness what is arising.

Now shift your attention to the nature that surrounds you. In the same way you provided yourself with gentle touch support, let other qualities of nature support you too. Focus your attention on what in nature feels expansively grounding, secure, or steady — the roots of a tree, rock forms buried in the earth — and invite this sense of groundedness into your body.

Now observe aspects of nature that reflect to you the experience of the stored trauma in your body — the tightness of a closed flower bud, the dryness of grasses, the spines of cacti, a dead branch on a living tree. Notice what sensations arise in your body. Now sense and imagine this expression of nature in your body: tightness, constriction, aching, pain, heaviness. Let your body absorb and connect with this expression of trauma around you.

Now pendulate slowly, in your own time, between the expressions of groundedness and the expressions of stuck trauma in your body that are reflected in and revealed by nature. You may feel an impulse to move like nature, waving parts of your body like dry grasses in the wind, curling your head or body around as a flower opens to follow the sunlight, or moving as if your body is a branch growing from a tree. Let your body move in response to these expressions of nature. If you feel impulses for more touch and connection with nature, explore them in a playful and open spirit. You might delicately tap, poke, dig, rub, rest into, push, or pull the supportive forms of nature around you. Let your intuition guide you to touch, move, and feel new rhythms of healing in your body.

Continue to practice pendulation within your body and with nature, noting any shifts of your thoughts, feelings in your heart, healing currents in your body. Let go of needing to judge, change, figure out, or analyze what is arising. Connect to feelings of being newly embodied, at home, and alive in your body.

If you experience a sensation expressing a release of trauma, such as heat, nausea, tingling, or pulsing, let go of judging it or trying to figure it out, and just be present to what the body may want to do or is expressing. Follow the path of these sensations through your body. If you feel an impulse to stand, jump, run, yell, or kick, allow yourself to follow it. On the other hand, if you don't experience any release expression or any movement impulse, let go of needing it to happen. This is a *practice*. Be present to pendulating with awareness, holding your trauma kindly.

As you close this practice, invite your body into stillness and expand awareness to the entire body and to what in nature is present with you. Sense anything that has shifted, healed, or been released or restored. Offer gratitude for what has been cultivated and grown in this practice and for the way your body, mind, and heart feel now.

Afterward, consider writing in your journal about any experiences or insights you had during this meditation.

Taking Care

These practices support finding healing currents, releasing trauma from the body, and beginning to restore ease, health, and wholeness. This process takes time. You can return to these practices again and again. No two moments are the same. Learning to trust your intuition about what practices will serve you at different points is a part of the path of healing.

At times you may want to choose the practices of pendulation, grounding, and orienting yourself in nature, and at other times you may benefit more from practicing awareness of the breath, senses, body, or elements. Every time you engage in these practices, the experience will be different, leading you into new terrain on your healing journey.

You may also observe patterns in your approach to healing, such as wanting to move quickly through or avoiding certain practices. These are important: they are signposts that may point to different paths. Here are some considerations to support integrating practices into your daily living:

- Choose practices that feel nurturing, easy, and supportive to you today.
- Spend less time with practices that feel more challenging. Over time you can increase their duration.
- For your practices, return to the places in nature that provide you with a sense of ease, calm, and relaxation.
- On days when you feel more regulated and organized, consider practicing in new places in nature that may be unfamiliar and surprising.
- Practice for brief moments as you move in and out of nature or during transitions between work, school, and other activities.

This healing path is yours to create, travel, and care for. The journey takes patience, discipline, devotion to your healing, compassion, and kindness. Continue to follow your true path of health, wholeness, and aliveness as they emerge.

Chapter 7

NOTICING BARRIERS
in the INNER LANDSCAPE

In the middle of every difficulty lies an opportunity.

— Albert Einstein

We tend to approach the challenges in our lives as problems, things that are standing in the way of what we want. But if you reflect on various challenges you have faced and overcome, you may realize that you have come out on the other side feeling strong, accomplished, or relieved to be through it. Most of us don't consider that it is in the midst of the challenge itself that growth and transformation are taking place. In our automatic reaction of wanting the difficulty to end, we fail to perceive what the difficulty is offering or teaching us in the moment.

As you have increased your ability to move toward trauma, finding new currents of healing in your body, you have been meeting difficulties and challenges and learning that being present to these experiences creates new possibilities and opportunities for healing. As you continue on this path, you will also encounter new barriers that present you with new opportunities to learn. This is the normal course of healing.

The traditional sense of the word *barrier* is something that gets in the way, an object or obstacle that prevents movement or access. A language barrier is often seen as something that keeps people apart or prevents communication or progress. But barriers can also be seen as lines of division that highlight the contrast or difference between things. If we explore barriers — physical, cultural, or internal — from a different viewpoint, they may reveal deeper healing and wonderful, beautiful new truths.

In nature, barriers support survival. Beavers show us the benefits of creating barriers in the form of dams. The resulting ponds protect their lodges from predators like bears, wolves, wildcats, and otters and provide easy access to food, especially during the winter. The landscape also contains barriers between different climatic zones. This can be seen in the changes in plant and animal life as you move from a lush landscape to a more barren landscape. Here in southern California, the more moist, cool, temperate conditions near the ocean give way to the desert to the east of the coastal hills.

We can learn to look at barriers not as obstacles but as signposts inviting further exploration. The barriers created by the trauma you have experienced can become your teachers and your guides on the path of healing.

Several types of barriers are described below to help you understand how they may arise during your practice. I suggest reflections that you can integrate into your other meditation practices to work with these barriers as you encounter them.

Desire/Grasping

Grasping or desire is the feeling of wanting an experience to be different from or better than it is, or being attached to how something used to be. The mind is afflicted with habits of seeking things that are more comfortable or pleasant, but these habits only cause more stress and suffering. You might experience this inner barrier as a desire to have your trauma healed more quickly or to experience faster relief from difficult feelings or sensations, or as an attachment to a particular way of living or having particular experiences. The mind's need to grab, hold on to, and attach itself to a preferred experience can take limitless forms. As you explore this barrier, being curious about the movements of your mind, heart, and body as you cling, grasp, or attach will allow you to find a new way of relating to this experience and ways to experience more ease and be able to let go.

Consider the last time you went walking or hiking on a trail. Most likely you chose the trail based on a desire for a particular experience, such as seeing a beautiful vista, forest, notable landmark, or rare wildlife. Before starting out, you likely determined the length and difficulty of the hike and the availability of drinking water and bathrooms. These are all forms of grasping, of trying to ensure your comfort and the satisfaction of your desires. As you walked, you might have become so preoccupied with the accomplishment of reaching your chosen vista or destination or completing the hike that you missed the beauty of your surroundings: mosses on the ground, lichen on the rocks, tiny white flowers budding from the ground cover, or a sweet spider spinning her web above the waterline.

When we can quell the habit of the mind to chase and attach to what it thinks is better or more pleasant, we can experience the beauty and wonder in the experience of the moment. This requires a willingness to notice the reactive habit, to welcome the habit of desire with curiosity and kindness, and to simply be with it. This in turn is likely to require that you learn to be present to the grip of wanting things to be better, more comfortable, or exciting. As you do so, something new will open: maybe letting go, maybe ease or acceptance of the way things are.

Noting your reactive habits of grasping and desire allows you to experience your trauma in a new way and transform it into something healing. You will likely find less need to seek comfort, learn to be okay with how it is, and be able to let go of needing things to be different. With this shift you will experience a sense of being more at ease in your body and more open to and appreciative of the ways life is unfolding. As you develop your healing meditation practices, you can invite desire or grasping to be present, letting it arise and pass, accepting the pleasantness of the moment just as it is, feeling no need to hold on to or create anything.

Practice: Being Present to Desire/Grasping

Choose a place in nature to sit. Notice the need to feel more comfortable, to adjust your temperature in some way to help your body to feel more cool or warm. Notice whether you are seeking out something attractive to look at, like a flower instead of dry grass, or striving to hear birdsong or wind rather than mechanical sounds. As you notice these desires, observe how your mind, heart, and body react. Is the body grabbing and grasping to find comfort? Is the heart seeking more pleasant feelings to encounter? As you notice desire, can you let go of needing it to be different or better than how it is and let it just be a moment of pleasant arising and passing?

Dislike/Aversion

Dislike and aversion are rooted in the mind's tendency to reject, resist what is challenging, and avoid what is difficult. This barrier evolves when the mind, body, and heart become preoccupied with intense aversive feelings, such as discomfort, pain, and distress. Dislike/aversion and desire/grasping are two sides of the same coin. With desire and grasping, we seek ways to make things more pleasant: with dislike and aversion, we seek to avoid discomfort by resisting what is here. Over time these reactive tendencies of mind may evolve into more intense feelings such as hostility, resentment, and hatred toward ourselves or others. Exploring this inner barrier requires a willingness to move toward the dislike or aversiveness, meeting it with a sense of interest and kindness, and making space in the mind, heart, or body for other sensations to emerge.

We often experience dislike or aversion when we encounter things in nature that are dying or dead. Most human beings do not grow up with a curiosity about death. We are constantly seeking ways to live longer, better, and with more ease — and so we don't acknowledge that every breath we take and every moment we experience is one less in our lives. Living in avoidance of this reality builds patterns of aversion to the truth of death.

It's okay to experience resistance to this reflection on death arising: it is natural to not want to turn toward things that are painful, especially grief, loss, and death. Be kind and offer care to these patterns of body, mind, and heart. Noticing this reactivity and the urge to get away is the first step in exploring this barrier of dislike or aversion. As you learn to stay present to it, you can let go of the habit of turning away, and kindly explore what is here. This creates space in the heart for connecting more lovingly and seeing things anew and with curiosity.

Reflect on the last time you chose to explore and be present to the beauty, the mystery, the complexity of something in nature that revealed the presence of death. Maybe while out on a walk you saw a dead animal, the browning leaves of a weed, or a decayed and fallen tree. Recall whether you experienced any thought of how unpleasant it looked, a twinge in the stomach, tension in the shoulders, or an urge to look away.

If you have experienced trauma, it's likely that you have developed some patterns of dislike or aversion related to it. These might include attempts by the mind to reject or dismiss what happened; an aversion to challenging memories; avoidance of physical states, sensations, and scars; and hostility, rage, or hatred toward the trauma itself or people, events, and systems associated with it. These are all normal survival patterns that evolved in order to protect you from the pain and overwhelm that often accompany traumatic experiences, and they are likely to emerge during your practice. If you can learn to welcome these patterns and recognize what they have given you, you can come to see them differently. Let your heart, mind, and body be open to a new relationship to the dislikes or aversions associated with your trauma.

Practice: Being Present to Dislike/Aversion

As you sit in nature, direct your attention to something that is dying or dead — maybe a broken tree branch, dried or dead grasses, or the body of a dead insect or animal. Notice any movements of the mind to resist or avoid the sight, of the heart to feel disdain or sorrow, or the body to recoil or resist. See if you can be present to any impulses to resist, contract, recoil, or reject. As best you can, let go of the habit of judging things as bad or good. Allow the experience to be just a moment of transient unpleasantness, dislike, and aversion, and meet it anew, with kind awareness.

Restlessness/Worry

Restlessness and worry are associated with a mind, body, or heart that is agitated and unable to settle down. Often this barrier is experienced as discomfort, a desire to fix or change things, impatience, or a tendency to see things as deficient or lacking. The mind reacts with attempts to plan, prepare, analyze, anticipate, fix, and control the situation in order to prevent harmful things from happening to you in the future. This is a loving, protective gesture by your mind, but it is not rooted in truth or reality. There is no possible way to control or predict what will happen in the future.

To transform this barrier, you learn to welcome these expressions of restlessness and worry and see them as currents of energy moving through the mind, body, and heart, creating new possibilities for contentment, patience, satisfaction, and joy. This process requires patience and openness to experience. Trying to force these wholesome feelings to arise is another attempt to exert control.

Once, on a meditation retreat, I was sitting in meditation in a meadow in the Rocky Mountains in Colorado when the wind began to whip through the valley and over the mountain range. For an hour the wind seemed to blow right through the bones of my body. I felt restlessness, agitation, and worry. As I sat, I noticed old, familiar reactive patterns of my mind arising in response to my feelings of being out of control. I chose to remain sitting, welcoming the wind. Gradually I began to feel its vitality, rousing energy, and playfulness. I felt it lift me up, awaken me, delight me. I saw that this experience was the gift of my inner winds of restlessness, worry, and anxiety. Leaving the meadow, I walked, meandered, and danced into the mountain winds, relishing the contentment, joy, and vitality.

Practice: Being Present to Restlessness/Worry

As you sit in nature, bring your attention to an expression of restlessness around you — the whipping of the wind, the roar and turbulence of rapids, the buzz of a bee or hummingbird, or the appearance of straggling plants. Notice the intensity of the restlessness or worry you perceive. Notice how the mind may resist or want to change or fix it, how the body may feel agitated and restless, and how the heart may experience worry, anxiety, and distress. Kindly, without judgment, try to let go of any impulses to control, soothe, or change these feelings. Instead, welcome this energy. You may choose to move your body in concert with the restlessness and worry or to sit in stillness.

Tiredness/Dullness

The barrier of tiredness or dullness and boredom is associated with feelings of sleepiness, a lack of energy, or stagnation. Reactions to this barrier may include habits of remaining constantly active and moving on to the next thing, excessive sleep, or inertia and inactivity. Working with this barrier involves inviting awareness to be curious about the sense of tiredness, dullness, or boredom and letting go of needing to do anything in reaction to it — just being present to the experiences of it in your body, mind, and heart. It might seem paradoxical to notice, be present to, and experience tiredness and dullness, but this is the point — to notice the habits of doing and create space for something new, such as a new type of energy or a discernment of healthy states of body, heart, and mind.

The most obvious expression of tiredness or dullness in nature is the transition between day and night. The rotation of the planet supports dormancy and quiet as sources of rest, nourishment, and restoration. We can recognize and welcome this barrier as a state necessary for restoration and healing.

Feelings of fatigue and exhaustion following trauma are a reaction to the sympathetic nervous system being on high alert for extended periods. Often when people who have experienced trauma begin to practice mindfulness and somatic awareness, they experience feelings of sleepiness and wanting to rest. If this is your experience, take time to sleep when your body, mind, and heart ask for it.

If you notice continued feelings of tiredness and dullness as you practice, it may be because you have developed these patterns as a way to manage states of freeze or overwhelm. You might experience a tendency to check out, drift, or become dull, numb, or inert. Bring a sense of curiosity, interest, and exploration to these experiences. They may open new pathways emerging to release and heal you from stuck patterns of trauma and guide you into a healthier, more balanced energy state.

Practice: Being Present to Tiredness/Dullness

Sitting in nature, direct your attention to the quiet of night, the intensity of heat, the aridity of grasses, or the barrenness of a landscape that seems to be dormant or dead but is germinating beneath the surface. Sense how the mind may become sluggish or distracted, the body heavy, fatigued, or tired, the heart dull or numb. Shift your attention to exploring these energies. Notice how the urges of sleep, rest, or trying to summon up more energy arise. Welcome in awareness this tired or dull energy, letting go of resisting or following it and simply being present to it. Allow yourself to attend to this energy just as it is in this moment, inviting a skillful choice either to bring in more wholesome energy or to rest.

Doubt/Judgment

Your mind has developed to figure things out, to categorize, to evaluate, to judge. These amazing capacities sometimes lead to patterns that are not helpful in viewing yourself, others, and your experiences, including doubting, judging, and making assumptions. This barrier has evolved out of a need to know, to understand why or how things are happening, and to manage uncertainty. These patterns may lead you to question your own understandings of your experience. People often attempt to manage these patterns by habitually seeking external validation of their inner experiences, asking for confirmation, and comparing and contrasting their views and experiences with those of others.

Working with this barrier involves learning to observe these reactive states of mind. As you notice them, you can invite the questioning, doubting mind to be curious about itself. You can begin to see doubts and judgments as movements of the mind. As you become present to the mind, a choice arises to let go, to trust that this is how it is in this moment, and to accept that thoughts arise and pass in response to conditions that are themselves transient. As you develop awareness of your states of mind, and the stories and narratives that have formed around your experiences and the places where the mind is stuck, you are able to release yourself from the habits of judging and doubting, and a new sense of clarity and trust emerges.

Nature has no conscious mind trying to understand why it is the way it is. Plants and animals do not judge one as better than another, question their place on the planet, or behave as if they know more than others. Instead, all of nature works as a coherent, integrated, purposeful whole. All expressions of nature lean into the conditions of the environment, trusting their unique capacity to thrive, their resilience in changing conditions, and their reliance on and interconnection with all other life. When we enter nature, we might bring our questions, our doubts, and our judgments with us. But nature always reflects back to us the need to let go of these habits, which do not serve wholesome, healthy, interconnected ways of living.

Doubting and judgment are part of the reactionary patterns that evolve with trauma. In the events of trauma, you experience being out of control, highly distressed, and often uncertain, and the mind brings forward doubts and judgments in an attempt to protect you. To work with your patterns of doubting and judgment, you can practice letting them come and go like clouds in the sky. Clouds are constantly moving and changing in size, color, and density as a result of atmospheric conditions. Some are intense, heavy, and charged with electricity, and some are light, soft, and subtle. You can come to see that the patterns of your judging and doubting mind, like these clouds, arise and take their shape in response to constantly changing conditions. There is nothing to do: just let them arise, move, take shape, and pass into the next moment. As you develop this skill, you will come to observe the movements of your mind with curiosity, kindness, appreciation, and welcoming, and to develop states of mind that are calm and settled, opening space for a sense of equanimity.

Practice: Being Present to Doubt/Judgment

Sitting in nature, direct your attention to any experience of doubting, questioning, or judging. You may become aware of wanting to know the names of the birds, trees, or plants around you, wondering about exploring other natural settings, or judging what types of flowers, plant life, or wildlife you prefer. Can you meet the movements of the mind as they arise, seeing them as clouds passing through the sky, obscuring the spaciousness of your mind? As soon as you notice a thought of reactivity or needing to "know," to judge, to doubt, or to question, meet this thought with a kind, gentle, curious attention. Notice if the mind is making up stories, following, resisting, or drifting. As best you can, let go of needing to figure anything out, attach meaning to these thoughts, or associate or understand, and simply be present to your thoughts as fleeting clouds moving through the sky of your mind. Invite awareness to rest into this type of knowing, to be present to not needing to know, to be open and limitless, like the sky.

Each of these barriers, and the practices associated with them, presents an opportunity for exploration and healing. Returning to the meditation practices you have already learned can also help you in working with barriers and gaining new insights that will promote health and healing.

Juanita's Story

Juanita sought support when she was choosing to leave a challenging relationship she had been in for over twenty years. Married early in life, and with her three children now grown and with lives of their own, Juanita realized that the dysfunction of her relationship was something she could no longer endure.

As we began our work together, Juanita revealed something she said she had never told anyone before: she had experienced sexual assault by her father from her early childhood into her late teens. She was certain this abuse was related to the distress she was now experiencing.

Juanita learned from her Catholic upbringing not to speak up, to cope with difficult feelings by repenting her sins, and to be a dutiful daughter and wife. This early conditioning often led her to react to difficult experiences with flight or freeze patterns. She would often question or doubt the validity of her feelings and sought to avoid any sense of conflict or challenge.

Through body awareness and pendulation practices, Juanita learned ways to manage her feelings of anxiety and stress. When we began to explore her barrier of self-doubt, it manifested itself as a need to ask me for feedback. Rather than reassuring her of the validity of her experience, I invited her to become curious about these patterns of doubt and to try to locate physical manifestations of them in her body. As she explored in this way, she discovered that doubting emerged as movements of her mind, thoughts that swept away her awareness of her body and her knowledge of what was true for her. She likened the experience to a front of thunder and rain clouds in her mind. Through practices of awareness and somatic presence, she became clear that these doubting thought patterns originated from her trauma history. She began to see that these doubting patterns of mind were default patterns for coping with the challenges in her marriage and that these patterns developed as she had learned to cope with her childhood trauma.

Over time, through continued practices of body awareness, pendulation, and curiosity, Juanita learned to be aware of these doubting patterns of mind and to be fully present, no longer being swayed away from her sense of self and her ability to make decisions for herself even amid challenge and conflict. The more she was able to choose for herself what was best for her based on her experience, the more she was able to release herself from the stories of guilt and doubt that had formed around her experiences of abuse. She learned how to behave more assertively with others and to have acceptance and compassion for herself.

Ancestral/Family Patterns

We all have histories and connections to people, places, and cultures that influence our perceptions and ways of relating. In some cases these histories and connections feel welcome, supportive, and helpful, and in other cases they have left wounds, patterns of disconnection, or feelings of separateness. Our histories have instilled in us beliefs and expectations about roles, work, values, and family dynamics that inform how we see ourselves and how we relate to others. As we travel the healing path, it's important to identify which views, perspectives, and ways of being in the world are healthy and which we may want to transform.

Most of us have a sense of identity with the place where we grew up — its topography, vegetation, climate, and seasons. We also likely feel some connection to our ethnic heritage — our ancestors and the places our family has come from. We may also feel a sense of identity with the culture or religion we were raised in. All of these origins give us a sense of our place in the world.

Take a few moments to reflect on how your family history, the places you were raised in, your ethnic heritage, and the culture or religions you grew up with have affected you. Consider writing about how some influences have shaped your perspective in wholesome or helpful ways, and how others have created challenges for you. Remember, both kinds of influences are okay: together they have shaped who you are and how you experience the world.

Consider the place you are in now, as you read this book. This Earth has been here for billions of years, shaped by natural forces and by human activity. Reflect on the creatures that have come and gone from this land, both small and large, and the vast movements of the planet that have shaped and continue to shape the terrain.

Likewise, your life is the product of complex conditions, past and present, and many of these will continue to influence your existence and that of future generations. Trauma is often connected to histories. Whether you experienced trauma within your family, your community, your culture, or your environment, it has been part of your journey. When we perceive our history as a barrier, as a problem, we disconnect from a part of ourselves.

Learning to transform your relationship to these histories, and releasing any unwholesome aspect of a personal narrative or identity, is an act of love for yourself, your family, and future generations. If you notice you are holding tightly to, ignoring, or denying parts of your history, this is an opportunity to find a more wholesome way of relating to it and to see yourself, your family and ancestors, and your communities in a more complete and balanced way.

Practice: Being Present to Your History

Sitting in nature, take a few moments to feel and be present to the landscape. Take in the terrain, the landforms — mountains, hills, valleys, water, vegetation, birdlife, wildlife, insects, trees. Reflect on the beings present in and caring for this land — now and in the past few years, decades, and centuries. Reflect that you too are part of this history: your presence, your care, and your attention to this land help to sustain it. If you find yourself feeling separate from the landscape, notice what arises in the mind, body, or heart. Kindly and gently return awareness to sensing your connection with this land, your presence here, your history, and thoughts of all who have come before you and will come after you. Feel your connection to your family and your ancestors, known and unknown, who are part of your history and part of this beautiful, unique being that is you.

Taking Care

You are learning to care deeply for yourself. By identifying your patterns and barriers, seeing them clearly, and meeting them with kindness, you are learning to discharge unwholesome energies resulting from your trauma. This work creates space for new, healthier patterns to develop in your body, mind, and heart. It is a radical act of love and healing for yourself.

These new patterns take time to emerge and to be expressed. As you go about your daily life, be alert to and curious about new buds of healing that may be forming. You may notice more ease in being with what arises during meditation. You may feel more resilient in difficult situations or less reactive to situations that often provoked intense reactions. You may feel more creative or open to new ideas. You might find yourself wanting more connection, seeking to establish new relationships, or having more capacity to engage in daily life.

When you notice these or other signs of healing, appreciate them and offer gratitude to yourself. They are the fruits of your practice.

Chapter 8

AWAKENING *to* NEW IMPULSES

If you're brave enough to say goodbye, life will reward you with a new hello.

— Paulo Coelho

As you find the currents of healing in nature and your inner nature, you will experience new, beautiful impulses of awakening. Impulses are often thought of as strong, unreflective urges to act in a particular way. Acting on impulse, and without reflection, can lead to challenging and unhealthy habits (such as overuse of alcohol, drugs, foods, and work), or behaviors (such as yelling and suppressing or denying our feelings, sensations, and needs). These types of unconscious impulses may be part of behavior patterns associated with your trauma. But not all impulses are unhealthy or unconscious. As you develop your ability to be present and to perceive and follow what feels most helpful and wholesome, you create the space for new, healthy impulses to arise. The difference between unconscious and conscious impulses is that with the latter, we can choose whether to act on them, and we can discern what actions will be truly helpful in shifting us out of reactivity and habit. These impulses point the way toward new ways of living.

The release expressions or "discharge" sensations that you may have encountered during your healing practices are a type of impulse, one that helps you find new ways to experience your body, mind, and heart. These expressions often create urges within the body to move or act in a particular way. Maybe you've been exploring yelling, making loud noises, running, standing, kicking, pushing, and squeezing things as ways to release trauma from the body. Now is the time to integrate these new impulses into your healing.

These impulses may be felt in the way you experience your body, such as new sensations or a new sense of fluidity. They may express themselves as new patterns of mind — feeling less trapped, ruminative, or reactive — or as a flowering of the heart — feeling more open, vulnerable, and kind. When you learn to recognize these impulses, they can help you to create new patterns and ways of living and to explore new activities and ways of relating to others, expanding your ability to heal and be your fullest self.

Nurturing healthy impulses helps you learn to trust taking new, healing paths. It's like coming to a point on a familiar trail and seeing a faint alternative route. Because you know the terrain well, you trust that you are prepared to explore the new path. Developing this trust takes kind and patient listening to the new impulse, learning to embody and feel it, appreciating its arrival, and being willing to step into the unfamiliar.

Sometimes these new paths pose their own challenges, but the capacities you have developed for acceptance, letting go, curiosity, openness, discernment, patience, joy, ease, and trust will guide you.

Moving in Rhythm with the Body, Mind, and Heart

To learn what a new impulse feels like, we will examine the ways they are expressed in the body, mind, and heart. Each of the following sections is like a trail map, pointing you toward new terrain. While reading each section, take time to reflect on experiences and choices that were limited or inaccessible to you while your trauma was held in your body. Now, as you release that trauma and discharge its effects from your body, you can connect to a new sense of awareness and new choices.

Body

As you heal from trauma, you may begin to notice new sensations in parts of the body you formerly experienced as numb or dull. You may also be experiencing new desires to move the body — to stretch muscles or joints that had limited mobility. You may notice that your posture is more upright, solid, confident, and open, that your body feels more relaxed as you go about your daily activities, or that you can encounter challenging intensities in your body with more ease.

Consider a baby bird learning to fly. From the security of its nest, it can begin to explore the first movements of flight. Hopping from branch to branch near the nest, it feels its wings grow stronger and trusts in their ability to support it in flight. This is how your body may feel, experiencing new sensations, a sense of security, and the capacity for new movements. Give yourself permission to explore, delight in, and appreciate what is awakening within your body.

Chris's Story

Early in life Chris suffered a traumatic head injury after playing on a zip line. He hit his head directly on a tree, fell, and lost consciousness for a few moments.

As a young adult and into his thirties, Chris felt as though the left side of his body was unavailable to him. He struggled with various exercises to develop strength on his left side and often felt off balance when he sat because of a sense of disconnection or numbness there. He had sought support from many types of physiological therapies to heal, with moderate success, but he had read about somatic healing and trauma being stuck in the body and wanted support to fully heal from this event in his early life.

Developing his practices of body awareness and pendulation, and exploring new movements and release expressions in his body, Chris gained more awareness of the left side of his body. This began in an unexpected place: his left sit bone. Because he had assumed that it was his arms and hands that were implicated in the trauma (thinking that they had failed to absorb the impact of the collision), he had been focused on arm movements. It wasn't until he felt a sudden shift in his lower torso during a pendulation practice that he developed a curiosity about his lower body.

As Chris refocused his attention on his lower body, he found that the practices of feeling rooted to the earth, standing up, and extending his left leg to push against an object (my foot, which in his mind's eye became the tree that he struck in his fall), he began to discharge the stuck energy of his trauma from his body, and he experienced a new sense of stability and balance.

Practice: Unwinding and Awakening

This practice is designed to build on your previous practices and deepen the healing of the body and your connection to nature through movement. Integrating the somatic practices you have learned, you can begin to intentionally unwind stuck patterns into new movements and awaken your sense of innate natural wholeness. Consider practicing in an unfamiliar place in nature to awaken new impulses. Also consider what type of environment will feel most supportive for this purpose: an open expanse, an enclosed or secure space, or a place full of movement and change.

Begin in a standing position. Feel the contact of your feet with the ground. Gently sway the body forward and back, to the right and left, feeling the sense of groundedness in the earth. Now gently sweep your attention from the feet upward through the legs, the torso, the arms and hands, and the shoulders to the neck and head. Sense your body as alert and engaged, yet open, soft, and relaxed. Notice the natural rhythm of the breath moving through this alive, sensing body.

Shift your attention to the environment around you — the plant life, flowers, animals, insects, terrain. Notice how the elements of air, fire, earth, and water are supporting you in space. Sense your connection to nature — maybe the wind gliding over your body, the heat on your skin, the trees offering cooling shade and solidarity. Follow any impulse that arises in your body — maybe an impulse to move, to sway, to walk, to connect to your heartbeat. Feel how nature is touching and awakening your body.

Shift your attention freely between the sights, movements, and rhythms you observe in nature and what arises in your body. As nature awakens expressions in your body, move with them and follow them. Let yourself feel the body responding to nature. Listen deeply to your body, and trust its impulses to move.

Explore how things in nature are moving slowly, quietly, and softly, like a snail gliding along or a flower gently opening. Alternate between slow movement and stillness, and note the sensations you experience in these different states.

Now shift your attention to faster movements of nature, like the flow of swift waters, the wingbeats of birds, and flutters of wind stirring the leaves of trees. Allow your body to move freely and swiftly — fluttering, jumping, wiggling, and shaking — and feel these rhythms expressing aliveness through your body.

Now observe how the various fast and slow rhythms of nature coexist, and explore them in turn. Imagine you are like a river, winding through the terrain, flowing quickly along downward slopes, slowing as the terrain flattens. Note how the water changes its flow when it encounters rocks or other obstacles, and how the flow adjusts to changing conditions of the earth and the air. Let your body awaken, expressing the impulses coming and going within. Be open to moving your body in new ways.

At the end of your practice, sit down, shifting into stillness to observe what is here now. Your body may feel newly alive and awake, able to explore and stay with new and possibly challenging experiences. Let yourself feel the new buds of health starting to open in your being.

In closing the practice, offer gratitude and appreciation to all the expressions of life that you have observed and invited in.

You may want to write about any experiences or insights from this practice.

Mind and Heart

When the body holds stuck trauma, the mind and heart follow suit. The mind can form habits that seek to control, avoid, or disconnect from experiences that cause stress or overwhelm. The heart may constrict, limiting its capacity to feel open, vulnerable, or expressive; the emotional landscape can feel stunted or suppressed as a means of preventing potential future harm.

As you progress on your healing path, your mind and heart, as well as your body, will awaken to new impulses. Your mind may become quieter and less busy or charged. You may find you can be present to reactive states of mind without needing to do anything in response: your awareness of the movements of your mind is enough to shift them. You may also be better at pointing your thinking in a positive direction: you may be able to acknowledge that your reactive habits evolved in order to protect you, and you may be able to let go of judging them, instead practicing kindness or appreciation for their attempts to keep you safe in the past. And you may find your mind more curious and open to new experiences.

With new impulses awakening in the heart, you may be more receptive, more easily touched, more expressive, and more open and caring toward yourself, other people, and things in nature. You may experience a new awareness of joy, awe, wonder, appreciation, gratitude, care, and love. You may be better able to identify and connect to the emotional pain of your trauma and to stay present to these emotions, riding them like waves passing through your body and mind.

These qualities emerging in your mind and heart allow the old, constricted, or stuck patterns to dissolve and make way for new, healthier patterns. Be willing to explore, create, and invite these new patterns into being.

Practice: Healing Landscapes

This practice, which can take from ten to thirty minutes, is designed to help you cultivate wholesome, positive, healing states in your mind and heart. Choose a setting in nature that reflects the states you want to cultivate. It might be a garden full of budding flowers, a quiet, still place in the desert, or a place near the calming waters of a stream or river. You may choose to close your eyes, open and close them during the practice, or leave them open throughout.

Feel your body connected, grounded, and rooted in the place you have chosen. Find a posture that allows you to feel alert, engaged, and awake — lying down, sitting, standing, or walking. Now scan through the body to identify any place that may be holding tension, tightness, or contraction. If you find one, move your body in a way that allows you to open, relax, and soften your posture.

Bring your attention to the movements of your mind. Is it pulling forward into the future — preparing, analyzing, figuring out? Is it leaning back into what has already been — rehearsing, remembering, recalling? Can you let go of the habit of wanting to be in some other place or to have some other experience? Can you see your thoughts as just thoughts, and your mind as just a mind, feeling the contraction, push, and pull of your thoughts as sensory experiences? Let yourself experience the dynamic movements of the mind. If you notice feelings of acceptance, allowing, letting go, not judging, quieting, or spaciousness, stay with them as best you can. How do you experience these qualities throughout your entire being? Stay present to this experience.

Now shift your attention to nature for a few moments. Let your-self feel how she is reflecting these qualities and states of your mind. Feel how this reflection, offered from nature, is true in your mind now.

Bring your attention to what is present in your heart. What emotions are you aware of? They may range from challenging to calming to uplifting. Be curious about any challenging or negative emotion you perceive, which may be an example of the heart's clos-ing off, resisting, or contracting. Can you stay present to these emo-tions, seeing them simply as waves of energy and sensation passing through the body and mind? Notice that emotions vary in inten-sity and quality and in the way they are expressed as movement. As you stay with these emotions, note how feelings of kindness, care, compassion, ease, relief, love, and openness may arise in the heart. Notice how it feels to experience these wholesome qualities throughout your being. Rest in awareness of the heart.

Now gently shift your attention to the way these qualities and states of the heart are reflected in nature. Feel how this reflection, offered from nature, is true in your heart now.

In the final minutes of this practice, explore and feel the states of mind and heart that are present. Continue to shift your attention between the inner landscapes of your mind and heart and the land-scapes around you.

In closing the practice, offer gratitude and appreciation for the beautiful, unique, and growing health of your mind and heart and for the beauty and uniqueness of nature that support you on your healing path.

You may choose to write about your reflections or insights from this practice in your journal.

Emerging into New Ways of Living

Unresolved trauma can limit the ways we participate in daily life, leaving us stuck in habits and patterns of reactivity. As you heal, you may notice new desires and impulses to engage in different activities and relationships. Establishing intentions to follow these new impulses will support your healing.

Daily Life

When we have struggled with trauma, the patterns that form in order to protect us from more harm can restrict our activities, making our daily routines and habits more automatic and somewhat disconnected. We might develop habits of engaging only in very familiar activities — visiting the same store, going to familiar restaurants, gathering only with people we know well or feel safe with. We may also stick to routines in the way we dress, the hobbies we engage in (if we have hobbies at all), and even the things we eat. All of this habitual activity is a strategy to help us feel safe. However, this sense of safety is often false and can leave us feeling disconnected and disenchanted, unable to fully experience and participate in life.

As the mind, body, and heart begin to heal, we are likely to experience a desire to engage in new and different activities. We might feel an impulse to go into a new store or restaurant or feel a creative urge to learn to garden, explore photography, or create art. We might feel impulses to try new foods, explore new cultures, or dress differently. As these new desires arise, it is important to meet them with ease, balance, and openness.

Take a few moments to reflect on and write down any impulses you have felt to engage in new activities. Such impulses are often experienced as simple desires for things to be different, and little effort is required to engage in them. List both large and small shifts. Here are a few examples of different types of activities you may have found yourself wanting to try:

- **Self-care:** meditation, exercise, stretching, yoga, healthy eating, drinking water
- **Creativity:** drawing, photography, painting, sculpture, crafts, or making things with your hands

- **Self-expression:** dressing in new ways, changing your hairstyle, getting a tattoo, blogging
- **Exploration:** visiting new places, trying rock climbing, surfing, camping, or dancing
- **Reflection:** journaling/writing, reading, poetry, making time for quietness during the day
- **Nature:** gardening, learning about types of plants or wildlife, introducing sustainable living practices (recycling, eating organic or vegetarian food)

After you finish a mindfulness or somatic nature practice, you may notice that it points you toward healthier activities for the rest of the day. For example, you might notice during a practice that your body feels more awake, pulsing, and alive, and afterward you might experience a desire to take a walk or a hike. Notice the ways that formal practice supports the desire to live mindfully, somatically, and connected to nature.

As these impulses develop into concrete action in daily life, your new, healthy habits support the integration and transformation of your trauma.

Practice: Daily Life Activities

This practice helps you engage mindfully in the new activities that you may be inviting into your life. It entails a three-point check of body, mind, and heart.

First, notice the sensations and movements in your body as you engage in each step of the activity: for example, lifting your hands, grasping, bending, touching objects.

Second, bring awareness to your current state of mind. Notice whether you are meeting this state of mind with an attitude of curiosity and nonjudgment or whether you are reactive or automatic in your engagement, predicting or planning what will happen next.

Third, notice what is present in your heart during the activity.

Are you connected, open, and fully emotionally engaged, or closed, contracted, and disconnected?

This three-point check will ensure that you are approaching your new activities with awareness and presence. The more fully you engage with these activities, the greater the sense of expansiveness and wholeness you will experience in life.

Relationships/Community

Because trauma often occurs in relationship to another person, it typically creates unconscious patterns that lead us to distance and disconnect ourselves from others to avoid being harmed again. People who have experienced trauma may find it challenging to establish relationships and feel part of a community. You may have very few friends you trust and feel are available to support you. You may have had trouble establishing healthy romantic relationships. And you may have developed a preference for isolation or limited interaction with family or community. However, we humans have evolved to be part of a tribe. When we disconnect ourselves from our tribe, we end up less resilient and less able to flourish.

All forms of life are interdependent with other life. Trees provide shelter to birds; birds drop food that nourishes insects and the soil; the soil provides nutrients for the trees; and so the cycle continues. All things in nature thrive and survive through connection and mutual support. As you heal from your trauma, you will likely experience a new desire to experience this sense of connection by engaging with other people and reconnecting with your tribe.

The desire to connect may emerge in small ways at first. You may find yourself wanting to greet the store clerks you recognize and to connect to communities with which you share interests, such as spirituality, personal growth, or nature-based causes and activities. You may also be feeling impulses to reconnect with old friends who were supportive.

Depending on your personality and your experience of trauma, you may have a tendency toward being introverted or extroverted. You may have used this tendency as a coping strategy for managing or controlling unresolved trauma. As you heal, you may begin to notice a desire for more, or less, social engagement. This shift is connected to internal changes that are helping you feel more regulated, organized, and socially present.

This part of your healing may happen slowly. When people have harmed us, it is normal to feel trepidation and reluctance about connecting to others again. Not only do we need to heal within and learn to trust our inner resources, but we have to learn to trust others and be willing to feel vulnerable around them. Don't rush. Trust your nervous system to identify forms of connection, and people to connect with, that are safe and healthy. Consider reflecting on who your tribe is now. What qualities do these people embody? What lifestyle do they lead? How do they show support, care, and compassion? It may feel easier to reconnect first to parts of nature, wildlife, or pets before reconnecting to your human tribe.

Whatever pace, process, or path you follow, be guided by the healing impulses of feeling safe and wanting to connect with community. Feel how your body, mind, and heart flourish as you forge new relationships and connections. As these moments arise, be tender, caring, and loving toward yourself. Be patient, letting the healing impulses in daily life and relationships emerge naturally and without forcing. Chapter 10 discusses ways to nourish your health and well-being in relationships and community.

Taking Care

Your healing gives you the opportunity to forge your own path, to define and create the life you want to live. This process takes time and must be carefully tended to. As with seeds, the more you attend to and nurture the new growth within you, the more it will flourish. Celebrate the small and big changes that are emerging. Feel what it is like to be stepping into your new life.

Part 3

LIVING *into* YOUR ALIVENESS *with* NATURE

Nature is not a place to visit. It is home.
— GARY SNYDER

Nature calls us home to our true selves. She reminds us that we are part of nature, intimately connected to her, and beautifully unique. Your healing is leading you into the truth of your aliveness — the knowledge that you are whole, complete, and perfectly imperfect and that the essence of your being is love. As a result of your trauma, you may have identified with a particular narrative about yourself — being broken, not enough, not worthy, not lovable. These are stories the mind has created; they are not the truth of your being. In this part of the book, we harness what you have learned so far to shape a new narrative of health and wholeness, beauty, and love. You will learn ways to let go of the old narratives and open fully into a new self, one that isn't bound by your history.

In December 2019, the California Academy of Sciences published a list of seventy-one newly discovered plant and animal species. They included seventeen species of fish, fifteen geckos, eight flowering plants, six sea slugs, five arachnids, four eels, three ants, three skinks, two skates, two wasps, two mosses, two corals, and two lizards. These discoveries were made across five continents and three oceans. Scientists believe that 90 percent of the species on Earth remain unknown to humans.[1] This planet we live on is diverse, interconnected, and thriving. Just as forms of life on Earth evolve, we have the capacity to develop our own lives into new growth and discover our uniqueness.

You have been learning to cultivate mindful awareness, somatic knowing, and healing practices. As wholeness and health return to your body, mind, and heart, you regain energy, curiosity, and joy in living. This part of the book explores ways to use these new capacities to feel more alive and more connected with nature.

I invite you to let go of "knowing" how your new life will look. Thinking that the new narrative of your life is already written doesn't create much opportunity to encounter the new or unexpected. Beautiful new gifts may be surfacing as you heal, and if you hold too tightly to your expectations, you may not be open to seeing or receiving them.

As old patterns, narratives, and dysfunction leave your system, new patterns, rhythms, and ways of living emerge. As you gain a stronger sense of a healthy self, a new, healthy ecosystem will emerge around you. The Greek prefix *eco* refers not only to environment, habitat, or surroundings but also to home. As you begin to feel at home with your true self, you also feel more at home in your relationships and community. New relationships arise, unhealthy relationships dissipate, a new community of beings supports your flourishing, and you feel a new sense of ease and balance.

Species thrive and survive through their connections with other life. As we heal, we begin to embody connection, trust, and love. When we recognize these capacities in ourselves and all things, we find a new sense of peace in our oneness. If humans have identified only 10 percent of all species on the planet, think what additional beautiful mysteries of life lie beyond our current knowledge and understanding. The same is true of your healing and your transformation. This is just the beginning. As you recognize and feel your aliveness, you become aware of the endless possibilities and potential to heal and transform your life and all life.

In the coming chapters, we explore this sense of being alive and at home in a place that has always been here waiting for you.

Chapter 9

HEALING, HEALTH, *and* LIVING

He who has health has hope; he who has hope has everything.

—Arab proverb

Healing leads to health, and health leads to new ways to experience life. The journey you are on may reveal many new forms of healing for you to integrate into your life. This journey does not have an explicit end: you are hopefully only at the beginning of a beautiful, ongoing exploration to discover your truth, which is in essence wholeness, beauty, and love.

As you heal, it's important to reflect on and connect to what is here now, expressing itself to you. If you tend to focus on the next step in your healing, or want some bigger shift to arise, you may be missing what is already present. The exercise below offers a way to explore the qualities emerging from your healing.

Reflection: Healing

Allow yourself to breathe, pause, and feel your body, mind, and heart. Reflect and sense the qualities that have emerged through the healing practices you have explored. Have you noticed more patience, freedom from judgment and striving, kindness, care, openness, curiosity, acceptance, letting go, trust, safety, compassion, joy, love, or other qualities?

List each of these new qualities in your journal, leaving room to write or draw an image next to each. Reflect on and sense each quality within you. Does it take a particular form or image? Does it have an associated emotion, thought, or feeling? Does it have a color? Does it have a consciousness that speaks to and within you? As you continue to reflect, feel these qualities in your body.

Learning to appreciate, connect to, respect, and have gratitude for your healing is part of the experience and the journey. Awareness of your healing opens up possibilities for new patterns of living. Celebrate, celebrate, celebrate the healing you have brought about.

Each of us has a unique understanding of what health means to us, in its physical, mental, emotional, spiritual, and relational aspects. Our vision of health might take the form of a fit, vibrant body; a peaceful, serene mind; or a caring and vulnerable heart. Relational health might entail having many circles of friends and family who support one another or a healthy romantic partnership; and spiritual health might be defined as bliss, joy, oneness, or connection to God.

Reflection: Health

Allow yourself to breathe, pause, and feel your body, mind, and heart. Reflect on the various forms of health — physical, mental, emotional, relational, and spiritual — and write down a few words describing what each aspect of health means to you.

Now look over what you have written. Where are these ideas coming from? Are they associated with the way you grew up, the ways our society defines health, or expectations you may have set for yourself? Are they arising from your experience of your healing journey? There are many ways to define health, and none are right or wrong. This reflection is just an opportunity to see what is informing your understanding and experience of health.

Nurturing our health is a fluid, ongoing, lifelong process. All nature strives to be healthy and in harmony with the life around us. We all have an inherent desire to thrive and survive. As you heal and let go of the dysfunction and the reactive habits that once served as protective mechanisms for you, you make space for new ways of healthy living. Acknowledging what is past, and honoring it, is part of the journey toward healing and health.

As I sat writing this particular chapter, the peas from my garden had a story to offer. When I planted them in my backyard, I felt excited about connecting to the land in this way. After carefully placing each pea in the earth, I woke each morning to water them and tend to the soil.

After a week, the peas sprouted, and I felt delight, joy, and excitement. I sent them blessings and welcomed them into my garden. A few days later, I saw that three of the eight sprouts had disappeared. My first thought was that the squirrels had eaten them. My mind reacted with annoyance, upset, and frustration, and then my heart realized, well, the squirrels are hungry too — they need ways to survive and thrive.

I considered my options. I could let the squirrels eat my peas, since they often struggle to find food; I could plant peas elsewhere in the garden, though I could not be certain they would grow. Or I could build a shelter around the peas to protect them. I chose the third option. With some help I created a simple wood and wire structure to keep the squirrels away from the peas. Now the pea sprouts are growing, and the squirrels are foraging in other ways. The peas have reminded me that new growth must be supported and protected.

In the following practices and teachings, we will consider how you can support, nourish, tend to, and delight in your healing.

Inhabiting a New Body

As you heal, your body changes. You may have noticed new abilities to move — maybe a feeling of openness, a difference in your posture, or more energy. Your body is increasing its capacity to express itself. Sometimes the changes are very subtle, like a new awareness of a part of the body you hadn't known you could feel. And sometimes the changes are large. You may find yourself wanting to engage in physical activities you once felt some resistance to. You may also be newly aware of the energies of your body, knowing intuitively when it's time to rest, to be active, to go slow, or to speed up.

If you have not yet experienced these new capacities of your body, you can direct your healing into an exploration of body movement. Consider a physical activity you might be feeling a budding interest in, like surfing, rock climbing, hiking, biking, swimming, or yoga. Remember, no matter what the abilities of your body, with healing you can choose what feels alive and right for you. Allow yourself to be playful and open to exploring something new. You may want to return to an activity you loved as a child, or try something new that excites or intrigues you.

Your new body holds freedom, health, love, space, kindness, appreciation, and resilience. The following practices can help expand your awareness of the ways your body is transforming and awakening.

Being at Home in Your Body

The following reflection, activity, and practice are intended to be completed consecutively. Allow twenty to forty minutes to complete all three.

Reflection

Write down your definition of how you now inhabit or are at home in your body. Describe your body and qualities that are now present in it, and how you have felt recently while engaging in movement such as walking, yoga, stretching, or dancing. Describe your sensations, imagery, emotions, and consciousness of being present in your body.

Activity

When you've finished your reflection, it's time to dance! Spend ten to fifteen minutes in a place in nature, bringing a music source with you. Choose music that reflects what you are connecting to within your body: a solid, steady rhythm; a fast, vibrant beat; or a quiet, calm melody. As you turn the music on, begin to feel your body connecting to the music. Let your body move just as it wants to. Now invite your senses to connect to nature. See how she is dancing with you to the music, with the sway of branches, the crisp heat of sunlight, the solidity of the soil. Invite your body to express the felt sense of nature's rhythm and melody. As your body moves, inhabit your movements with awareness, resonance, and connection to nature.

Practice

Now invite your body to shift from your movement practice into stillness and quiet. Find a posture that is connected to the energy you feel now — maybe standing, feeling your rootedness in the earth; lying down to feel your connections to the Earth and nature; or sitting upright, alert and attuned to all the movements around you.

Allow awareness to move to the places in your body where you notice feelings of aliveness, such as the breath, heartbeat, or pulse. Feel how this aliveness is manifested in sensations, images, and emotions.

Now shift awareness more deeply into your body, like a pebble sinking to the bottom of a lake. You may notice your muscles, your bones, or the way your nervous, digestive, and respiratory systems operate and regulate themselves without your conscious effort. Feel the amazing expressions of your aliveness in your body. Notice any currents of energy, vibration, tingling, pulsation, or movement.

In the last few minutes of this practice, notice what it is like to feel at home in and present to the aliveness of your body. Appreciate and offer gratitude for the beautiful mystery of the living body, part of the mystery of living nature. If your eyes were closed, open them now. Observe how your body is now, and bring those qualities into the rest of your day.

Spacious, Not-Knowing Mind

As you heal, space opens in your inner landscape. You may notice that your mind is less reactive, less inclined to chase or resist certain states, and more settled, calm, or clear. When the body releases stuck trauma, the mind is more open, ready to move toward healthier and more positive thoughts. In challenging situations, you may experience less reactivity, agitation, fear, or withdrawal and more acceptance or patience. These shifts are signs that your mind is healing, releasing the habits and patterns of trauma.

As the mind becomes less reactive, you may begin to notice creative thoughts, insights about healing, truths about the health of your being, and openness to the ease and freedom of not-knowing. Not-knowing is a state of letting go of needing to know, of ease and curiosity toward uncertainty. We cannot truly know what the next moment will bring. Not-knowing invites us to experience each moment as fresh and unique.

If you take a glass of water, add a teaspoon of dirt, and stir it, the water is murky. If you let the glass sit, eventually the dirt settles to the bottom, and the water becomes clear. The mind operates in the same way. If we continue to ruminate on unhelpful things, our thought processes are clouded. The meditations and practices you have been learning are ways to help the dirt settle, leaving the mind in a clear and healthy state in which to relate to the world and see anew. Take time to notice what this new state of mind feels like.

As you begin to notice clarity, freshness, ease, and space in your thinking, you may want to seek new ways to engage the mind. You might consider learning something new — a language, a subject of study, a practical skill — or engaging in a creative activity such as painting, photography, or crafts.

As the Buddha said, "With our thoughts we make the world." With a mind that is more clear, open, still, and calm, anything is possible. Let yourself be open to new possibilities.

Presence in the Mind

The following reflection, activity, and practice are intended to be completed consecutively. Allow twenty to forty minutes to complete all three; take more time for the activity if you wish.

Reflection

Write about your experience of your new spacious, open, clear, not-knowing mind. Describe the sensations you notice: is the mind less tight, rigid, constricted, trapped, stuck? In the place of those sensations, do you notice more openness, lightness, spaciousness? Consider drawing an image of what the mind feels like now.

Activity

Now it's time to make nature mandala art! This activity can take as little as twenty minutes, or you may want to take a whole afternoon to walk and create. In Sanskrit, *mandala* means "magic circle." Mandalas are typically designs that are circular or have radial symmetry. They represent wisdom and deep connection to oneself and the universe.

Take a slow stroll around your backyard or neighborhood and collect items from nature that represent two patterns of mind: the old, constricted, stuck ways of thinking associated with your trauma, and the new, open, flexible patterns of thought you are experiencing now. Once you have gathered these items, find a place in nature (back at home or elsewhere) where you can use the objects to create two mandalas: one representing your old, reactive mind states and patterns, and the other representing your new, resilient, responsive mind states and patterns. Create your mandalas with abstract patterns, placing particularly symbolic objects in the center or around the edge. Use smaller or larger objects in creative ways to form the circles.

You may find it helpful to distribute similar items symmetrically around the design as you create it, or you may want to place items asymmetrically or in opposition. Follow your intuition in deciding what to bring into your magic circle.

Practice

When you finish your mandalas, choose a supportive posture in nature near the mandalas. Rest into the support of the ground. Allow your body to be alert and feel aliveness in connection with nature. Take care to relax and open any parts of the body that feel tense or constricted.

Now allow yourself to notice the breath as you inhale and exhale. Let go of needing to figure out, analyze, or make meaning out of what you created. Sense the vitality of the breath.

Shift your attention from the breath to rest in clear and kind awareness of whatever is present in this moment. If you notice a thought, sense what it's like in the mind as it arises and passes. You may notice sensations in your body, or external sounds, sights, smells, or touch sensations. Be aware of these as they arise and pass. If you notice emotions, feel what is present in the body as they arise and pass. If you find yourself reactive or judging, drawn by a particular thought, sensation, or experience, gently let go. There is no need to change, resist, adjust, or fix your experiences: rest in kind awareness of this moment, just as it is. Allow awareness to be present to whatever is here in this moment.

Resting in open awareness, feel what it's like to let go of needing to know, to do, to manage, to figure out. Just be present to life unfolding. Any time you notice that you are caught up in reactions of thinking, you can return to awareness of the breath, then let go of that focus and allow open and clear awareness of what is present and arising within and around you in this unique moment.

In the last few minutes of this practice, notice and appreciate your present states of mind — perhaps clarity, stillness, calm, openness, ease. How do these states of mind support your body and heart? Close with a moment of gratitude for your mandalas, nature, and the healing of your trauma. If your eyes were closed, open them, and move your body in any way that feels helpful. Take the goodness of your practice with you into the rest of your day.

When you are finished, consider leaving the mandalas behind. All things are impermanent and changing, and leaving these to the Earth is a gift to her and to yourself. Alternatively, you may want to keep with you one item from each to place on an altar at home to represent your healing journey.

Open, Caring, Receptive Heart

As the body and mind heal from trauma, the heart too will begin to heal, to open, to be more vulnerable, to care and offer healing to others. The experience of trauma often wounds the heart deeply. Challenging emotions such as distrust, disconnection, guardedness, and resistance arise to protect it from being hurt again. As you heal, releasing stuck trauma from the body and allowing the mind to feel calm, settled, and open, the heart will also seek to be more expressive and to explore and resolve emotions that may have been too difficult to process before.

You may already have noticed that the heart is beginning to find light, hope, and restoration from the healing practices you have engaged in. You might have become less harsh toward yourself or more accepting of what has occurred. You might also have noticed less anxiety, sadness, or grief. Perhaps you have found it easier to forgive or offer loving-kindness to people you find challenging. The heart has a boundless capacity for compassion, love, kindness, joy, and equanimity. As you begin to experience these feelings, take the time to appreciate them.

The heart's natural inclination is to expand, to connect, to feel. After a traumatic experience, however, it takes time to rebuild these capacities. Cultivating compassion toward yourself and welcoming joy into your life are good ways to start.

If you have felt a sudden release of trauma from your body or mind, you may also have noticed that your heart felt more open, relieved, and kind toward yourself. This is compassion, and it grows each time you practice. You are learning to offer empathy, acceptance, and caring to the wounds you have suffered and to recognize the challenges you have faced to heal those wounds.

Developing acceptance and compassion in the midst of experience creates new possibilities for joy, light, and uplifting emotions to emerge. These emotions are soothing and restorative to the nervous system as well as the heart. Cultivating them enhances healing. Nature can reveal these emotions: maybe you've found joy in the movement of trees, the play of light and shadows, or the sweetness of birdsong. Or perhaps you've listened to a friend talking about something good happening in their life, and your heart has lifted a little and felt joy for them. All these experiences can lighten and heal your heart.

Radiant and Loving Heart

The following reflection, activity, and practice are intended to be completed consecutively. Allow thirty to forty minutes to complete all three.

Reflection

Write about the open, caring, and receptive qualities you have noticed in your heart as you have healed from your trauma. List the positive emotions and sensations that you have experienced: maybe kindness, caring, compassion, joy, or ease. Does a particular flower, plant, leaf, or tree come to mind that represents the budding qualities of joy, kindness, compassion, and lightness in your heart? You may choose to write down descriptions of the sensory experience of these emotions or to draw or create images that express how you experience emotions within your body or as having a consciousness of their own (for example, as represented by a character or a form of wildlife).

Activity

This activity involves expressing the sensations of opening, budding, and blooming in your heart. You will need a few pieces of paper (or one large one) and a pencil. In addition, you will want to collect a few objects from nature. (Please consider asking their permission when you pick them or take them from their environment.)

In an outdoor setting near your home, look for three or four flowers, leaves, or branches that represent the emotions in your heart. You may find a flower that is in full bloom, its petals extended, representing complete openness; a fern frond that is beginning to unfurl; or a flower that has released all its pollen, representing generosity, compassion, and caring. Let go of needing your emotions to be a particular way — this is a representation of your emotions revealing themselves through nature.

Place each of your gathered objects onto the paper, and notice what qualities of your heart each one expresses. With your pencil, draw, trace, or create a rubbing of each item, feeling each quality as it takes form. Allow your creative heart to express what it wants. See the beauty and the boundless capacity of your heart.

Practice

Now choose a posture that feels kind and uplifting to you for a meditation. Feel your body grounded and supported by the earth and alert to the sights, sounds, sensations, and smells all around you. Let your body soften, relax, and open.

Now bring awareness to the body, orienting to the chest area. Notice the sensations that are present, such as temperature, textures of clothing, the rib cage rising and falling, the lungs expanding and contracting, the breath moving, circulation, the heart beating. Rest in awareness of the heart.

Now bring to mind the image of your being and a trauma you have carried. Allow yourself to become present to the challenges you have experienced and the wounds you have suffered in your body, mind, and heart. There is no need to call to mind the narrative of the trauma, just a representation and sense of the difficulties you have encountered. (It may help to call to mind the mandala you created of your old patterns and notice how these patterns are expressed in your body.)

Practicing compassion for yourself, say these phrases inwardly, noticing what arises as you do so:

I care.
I care about this trauma.
Through this caring, may this trauma be relieved and released.

Continue to repeat any or all of these phrases. Notice what emotions, sensations, mind states, and energies arise as you say these phrases. Be present to what emerges, both positive and challenging.

Notice this act of compassion as a radical act of care to liberate yourself from trauma. It is a gift to yourself that offers delight, joy, happiness, and contentment. Allow yourself to feel the effects of choosing to care for your heart in this way.

Now bring to mind an image of yourself lovingly tending to your trauma. Become aware of the compassion you have cultivated, and begin to recite these phrases inwardly:

May I be happy.
May my happiness continue.
May I be grateful for this moment of happiness or contentment within.

Continue to repeat these phrases. If you notice movements of the mind, or of the heart opening or contracting, kindly attend to whatever arises, and then return to the phrases. You may find it helpful to recite the phrases as you exhale. Stay with this practice for as long as you choose.

In the last few minutes of this practice, notice the effects of this practice on your heart. Is there more openness, warmth, caring, receptivity, sensitivity, contentment? Appreciate and offer gratitude for what has been cultivated and for your practice, for nature, and for your healing. If your eyes were closed, open them, and move your body in any way that feels helpful. Take the good from this practice with you into the rest of your day.

Berta's Story

As the daughter of undocumented immigrants who came to the United States to create a better life for her, Berta had developed a habit of always putting other people's needs before her own. Her parents often referred to the sacrifices they had made and the effort they had gone to in order to enable their children to experience the "American dream" and freedom. She often described putting herself first as "selfish" and "self-serving."

Throughout her life, Berta had experienced trauma as a result of the racism and systemic injustices her family had faced. She felt betrayed by and distrustful of systems that were supposedly in place to protect her. Her strategy for coping with these traumatic experiences was to work hard and work long hours, never question what she was asked to do, and forgo her own interests and needs for self-care.

As she learned to practice being present in her body with somatic healing practices in nature, she began to see her emotions differently and develop a new sense of self. She began to let go of the need to keep going, doing, and providing for others first. She experienced a new compassion toward herself and her parents for all they had endured, and she developed a desire to spend more time with things she finds soothing and healing, like creating art.

Over time she learned to balance the time she spent working with time for herself. Berta now regularly creates art that expresses her journey of healing, finding great joy and equanimity in her process. She no longer views this as a selfish act but rather as a deep, nourishing, and enlivening form of connection to others. She also teaches art, which gives her a sense of caring connection and another expression of her healing path.

Taking Care

Healing your body, mind, and heart will take you into new terrain, show you new vistas, and reveal the expansive waters of your inner being. This exploration requires your presence and willingness to attend in a loving, caring, open way to yourself and your experiences.

You can feel aliveness, openness, compassion, and joy in any moment. Here are a few suggestions for integrating the practices from this chapter into your daily life:

- Notice your body being touched by the wind, reminding you that you are alive.
- When you look up at the sky and see the cloud-scape or a great blue expanse, feel openness and spaciousness arising in your mind and body.
- When you hear a bird sing or see an insect land on a plant or flower, notice how the heart softens, appreciates the moment, and feels cared for.
- Feel how light shining on water, grass, or trees can lift, brighten, and bring joy to the heart.

Various expressions of nature may give rise to feelings of vitality, openness, compassion, or joy. Be curious to see what touches your body, mind, and heart. Any time your attention is caught by a special sight or sensation in nature, take twenty to thirty seconds to notice what you experience in your body, mind, and heart.

Your healing will reveal itself in your daily life, work, friendships, relationships, community, and contact with nature. Healing trauma allows you to create a new way of being. Delight in and welcome all the new expressions of your true nature.

Chapter 10

REEXPERIENCING RELATIONSHIPS *and* YOURSELF

Only someone who is ready for everything, who doesn't exclude any experience, even the most incomprehensible, will live the relationship with another person as something alive and will himself sound the depths of his own being.

— Rainer Maria Rilke

This journey of healing is taking you deeper into a loving connection to yourself and to all of life, including other people. Connection, in turn, brings transformative healing. Your growing sense of aliveness, spaciousness, compassion, and other beautiful states of being are becoming embodied within you and can be sustained by relationships with others.

Throughout our lives, we have connections with ourselves, the environment we live in, our family, friends, intimate partners, communities, cultures, and this planet. Up to this point in the book, we have focused on inner healing from trauma. In this chapter we will expand this healing to relationships with others. As you develop a new relationship with yourself, others will see you and understand you differently as well. Observing and sensing which relationships to nurture, and which are no longer serving you well and should be let go of, is part of the healing journey.

We will also explore how to redefine the story of your trauma. Learning to reexperience yourself and your connection in relationships with

163

balance, clarity, and intention can sustain your healing and take it in new directions.

Building Your Relationship Ecosystem

Living creatures thrive in a healthy ecosystem. For an ecosystem to be healthy and balanced, it needs an energy source (sunlight), living organisms (producers, consumers, symbiotes, decomposers, predators, and prey), inorganic material (water, soil, rocks), dead organisms, and natural boundaries (topographic, climatic, and biological).[1] When an ecosystem is operating at full health and capacity, it offers its inhabitants clean water, pure air, healthy soil, a stable climate, and nourishment for both body and spirit. It is resilient and able to adapt to changing conditions.

In your healing journey, you have been creating a healthy inner ecosystem by releasing trauma and associated patterns from your body, mind, and heart and exploring new ways of experiencing your inner landscape. Now it is time to explore how this healthy individual system can thrive in a larger ecosystem, among the inhabitants of the world around you.

Let's consider the components of your ecosystem, beginning with your energy sources. The fundamental energy source in a natural ecosystem is sunlight, which is converted by plants, fungi, and bacteria into energy that becomes available, through the food web, to other life.

What is your inner energy source? You might think of your vital energy as coming from your inner qualities: the light of awareness, your ability to practice kindness and compassion and to offer love, and your unique expression of self to others. By sharing grace, joy, sweetness, strength, and courage, you share these inner sources of energy with others. Maintaining your connection to this inner light, your sense of wholeness and goodness, enables your ecosystem to grow and thrive.

Which organisms in your ecosystem support health? In a natural ecosystem, producers, consumers, decomposers, predators, and prey all play roles in maintaining the health of the system. Viewing your relationships in a similar way can be helpful. Certain relationships in your life may use the energy you offer in ways that feel helpful and offer a sense of reci-procity: they provide you with energy in return. Others may need more energy or take energy from you, offering little in return. There is no need to judge these exchanges of energy — learning to discern how they sup-port the balance and health of your ecosystem is what is important. You may find that there are some relationships that you can lean into a bit more, while others will naturally shift or dissolve in order to allow your ecosystem to evolve and thrive.

There may also be dead organisms in your ecosystem. They might include past relationships that inflicted the trauma you experienced. Dead animals and plants are necessary to a natural ecosystem. Their decompo-sition releases nutrients like carbon and nitrogen back into the environ-ment to nourish other members of the ecosystem. You can consider past relationships associated with your trauma in a similar way: they contain stored or stuck energy, and as you let go of them and allow them to decay, they can become a source of energy and strength. After all, your unique existence would not be possible without those experiences of trauma and the relationships connected to them.

A healthy ecosystem draws from and reshapes its nonliving compo-nents: landforms, water sources, soil, and rocks. Your external environ-ment is your source of shelter, water, nourishment, and stability. Consider whether the place where you live is one that allows your ecosystem to thrive and find balance. Establishing an environment that is supportive, making adjustments as needed, helps your ecosystem thrive.

Boundaries in nature are the dividing lines created by different con-ditions of climate and terrain that determine what organisms live within a particular ecosystem. In your own life, you establish boundaries by creating physical, emotional, or mental space around you and choosing the degree of connection and separation between yourself and others. It's important to define and evaluate these boundaries. Certain people may no longer function well within your ecosystem. Learning to accept the passing of particular relationships and let them go is a part of the journey in healing trauma. Creating healthy boundaries will help you restore harmony and balance to your ecosystem, allowing your healing to continue.

Nourishing Your Ecosystem

The following reflection, activity, and practice are intended to be completed consecutively. You may want to set aside a few hours to complete all three, and you will need to gather a few items to create the living ecosystem suggested in the activity.

Reflection

Imagine your healthy ecosystem. Maybe this ecosystem is already in place, or maybe it is beginning to form but not yet complete. What are its energy sources? Who are the people who reside in it? What aspects of the environment around you provide you with shelter, security, and stability? What relationships have you allowed to dissolve and decay to provide you with sources of nourishment and energy? What does the landscape of your life look like? How are you living within it? How does it all work together to sustain life and health? Breathe and feel in your body, mind, and heart the experience of residing in a new, healthy ecosystem.

Activity

For this activity you will need a jar or bowl with a lid (consider an old pickle jar or mason jar or another wide-mouthed container that you can reach inside of), pebbles, soil, water, and plant cuttings. For these, you may choose mosses, succulents, ferns, and air plants. Include a portion of the roots if the plant has them, and consider asking for the plant's permission to cut it away from its origin.

Reflect on the nature of the container (how might it represent the boundaries you are creating?), where you want to gather soil (how might this soil represent your inner growth, with particular nutrients from a place you find meaningful?), and what types of pebbles and plant cuttings you will include (how might these represent the beings and landscape that support your own ecosystem?). Remember to include a cutting that represents you.

To create this ecosystem, place the pebbles at the bottom of the container, and cover them with a layer of soil. Dip your plant cuttings into water, and then place them into the layers of soil and rock. Cover your container with a lid. Place it in the sunlight to grow.

Let yourself be creative with this process. As you create, feel somatically the choices you make, as they represent your ecosystem of healing. You may choose to place this ecosystem somewhere special in or around your home where it can thrive and reflect the growth of your healing.

Practice

This practice explores all the elements of an ecosystem — energy, living things, decaying things, inorganic forms, and boundaries — in your inner ecosystem and the world around you, as well as your oneness with all things. Allow yourself thirty to forty minutes for this practice and a few more minutes to reflect, write about, and integrate the experience afterward. Choose a place in nature that reveals to you the aspects of a healthy ecosystem — where you feel the energy of the sun; the presence of insects, animals, plant life, and trees; and a connection to the landscape (landforms, water sources, soil type, rocks). Notice the decaying aspects of the land and the boundaries within which it all resides.

Choose a posture for your practice — sitting, lying down, standing, or walking — that enables you to feel a sense of groundedness, alertness, relaxation, and openness.

Become aware of the breath. Feel the breath entering your

body, carrying with it the warmth from the sun, the oxygen supplied by plants, the scent of the earth. As you breathe out, be aware of your body releasing carbon dioxide, participating in the exchanges of this natural ecosystem.

Bring to mind the energy within you: the breath circulating, the blood pumping, the nutrients being digested to provide energy, the nervous system regulating your bodily processes. Feel the energy that allows your body, mind, and heart to thrive.

Now shift your attention to notice the energy of the ecosystem around you: the heat and light from the sun, the vigor or motion of plants and animals. Slowly shift your attention between the energy around you and the energy within you. Sense how energy is flowing as one force, not separate.

Now become present to how your living being is expressing itself in this ecosystem. You might notice your breath mingling with the breath or transpiration of other living organisms. Reflect for a moment on how you are supported by other living organisms in your life — your family, friends, and community.

Now shift your attention to all the living organisms around you: insects, birds, wildlife, grass, shrubs, trees. Reflect on how each of these life forms is supported by all the other organisms of this ecosystem. Shift between awareness of your own living organism and all the living organisms you are connected to, holding them all as one living system, not separate.

Now reflect on your own being and all of the people who have come before you and are now gone who have made it possible for you to be here now. You may also reflect on past relationships that have dissolved and are no longer part of your ecosystem, which are also part of the history that has brought you to this moment.

Now bring attention to signs of decay or things that are dying or dead in the ecosystem around you, such as dry leaves, dead insects, bare trees, or the remains of wildlife. Slowly shift between awareness of the people who have gone before you and the decay in the ecosystem around you, feeling the interconnection to all stages of life.

Now attend to the inorganic forms that support your being — the solidity of the earth beneath you, your home, the structural systems that provide you with water and energy. Shift your awareness to the inorganic forms that support the ecosystem around you: the landforms that provide shelter and shade, the seen or unseen water sources, the qualities of the soil and rock formations. Slowly shift between attention to the inorganic structures that support your life and those that support this ecosystem. Sense all the conditions that interact to create this one physical world.

Now, attending to your own inner landscape, see if you can first notice the boundary of your skin — a boundary that supports and contains your inner being. Reflect on how your physical, mental, and emotional well-being is protected by the choices you make with your body, how you think and feel, and who you choose connection with. Now shift to noticing the natural boundaries of the ecosystem around you, noticing how life adapts to landscape and terrain, thriving or dying out where conditions change. Be curious about the way boundaries take shape and offer protection and support. Abide in awareness of your own physical, mental, and emotional boundaries and the boundaries of the terrain around you. Take time to sense the edges of all that is here, and remember that all of this is one. Be open to the sense of form and no form, distinction and oneness.

In the last few minutes of this practice, feel yourself existing in and with all of nature, with and as a part of all energy and life.

To end the practice, return to the breath. Feel and be present to the simplicity of an inhale and an exhale. Offer gratitude to yourself for practicing and for whatever has been cultivated through the practice, and for the beauty, vibrancy, health, and resilience of nature and our systems of interconnection.

Write about what you noticed and experienced during this practice. Did feeling your interconnectedness to this ecosystem provide you with insight, clarity, or support? Consider how what you discovered may help you define or redraw the boundaries and interconnections within yourself and in your relationships to others.

Allowing Change in Relationships

It can be difficult to decide and take action to shift our relationships. We expect relationships to satisfy our needs and desires for connection. Relationships formed in the presence of unhealed trauma are often strained, challenging, or dysfunctional because we unconsciously expect them to heal that trauma. By harnessing the power of your now-healed trauma, you can forge healthy relationships that allow you to flourish and connect to others in new ways.

Changing your relationships with family members can be challenging, especially if your experience of trauma occurred within the family. In order to survive, you may have developed specific ways to relate to your family that are based on fight, flight, or freeze patterns. Changing these protective patterns may feel challenging or uncertain. Using the practices that have helped you heal your trauma, you can find inner sources of support and safety that can help you establish skillful, nonreactive ways of relating to your family. You may find that you can assert yourself more intentionally, set healthy boundaries to safeguard your mental and emotional well-being, and come to feel compassion or forgiveness for family members who caused you harm.

Change can be difficult in intimate relationships as well. If you have experienced traumas related to issues of distrust, boundaries, or sexual abuse or assault from intimate partners, it can feel very unsettling to examine and change the ways in which you engage in relationships. With these types of traumas, you have likely developed various defensive strategies and ways of thinking in order to survive and feel safe. However, for an intimate relationship to flourish, we must have the capacity to be vulnerable, open to other perspectives, and supportive of our partner. As you feel more healthy, safe, and resourced, you can explore new ways of being present in intimate relationships.

Finally, as you heal from your trauma, you may notice a desire to change the ways in which you are connected to various communities. Again, because trauma impedes our ability to forge healthy relationships, you may have formed relationships with communities that engage in unhealthy ways of coping with stress, challenges, and unhealed trauma. Learning to shift away from the unhelpful dynamics of these communities can be challenging, especially if you feel affection and loyalty for people within them. Remember, your own healing can be a force for change within that community: you may be able to model a sense of self-worth and skillful ways to care for yourself that can help others. Your healing may also lead you to connect to new communities and to forge new relationships with people whose sense of purpose or direction in life aligns with your own.

Change is an opportunity to grow. Your healing can inform new ways to take action in your relationships that will allow you to grow and flourish. Be willing to stay with the discomfort as you consider how you might use your healing to make changes in your relationships. Embodying and offering your healing to others makes it a gift to all the people in your life, and to yourself.

Redefining Your Relationship to Trauma

As you begin to relate differently to the people in your life, you will also want to change and redefine your relationship with your trauma. Most people who have experienced trauma form a narrative about it. For example, you might have a narrative about being a victim or feeling taken advantage of, unworthy, not good enough, or any other number of unhealthy views of yourself. This narrative can become a part of your identity.

Your narrative about your trauma can define your actions and your relationships with others in small ways, like your choices about locations you visit or avoid or activities you choose not to participate in, or in large ways, like avoiding relationships and certain communities. If your narrative is based on the view that you are not good enough, you may choose relationships and act in ways that reinforce this view. The feeling that you don't deserve healthy romantic, family, or community relationships may have led you to behave in reactionary ways in your relationships out of fear of rejection. Apprehension associated with unhealed trauma may lead you to avoid particular people or groups.

Holding on to a trauma narrative may hold you to an old, protective sense of self and prevent you from being who you truly are — a vibrant, whole, beautiful self who can connect in healthy and intentional ways to others. Now is the time to reshape this narrative — to release a relationship with your trauma that no longer supports you and learn to see yourself differently in the new light of healing. As you heal, you can acknowledge that the trauma you experienced was a passing experience in your life, not a definition of who you are or who you can be. As you heal, you can awaken to a new, whole, healthy sense of yourself.

Over time, the narrative about our relationship with trauma decays or decomposes, not disappearing but transforming into something new, different, and perhaps less dominant in the landscape. A friend offered a story to me of a Monterey pine decaying on a trail she has walked for twenty years. After a difficult winter, it fell down parallel to the trail. At first, the branches blocked the trail. Then the branches were cleared to open the trail, but the fallen tree remained a landmark. Each year the tree decayed a little more (thanks to the fungi!), and eventually the surrounding vegetation grew up around and over it. Now a long ridge along the ground is all that remains of the old tree. Through the processes of nature, the tree has taken on a new identity and form in the community. In the same way, the healing process allows your trauma to decompose and dissolve, allowing you to step into a new form of self.

How does your new sense of self emerge, and what will it be? Your new narrative or identity has already been forming through your healing journey. You have been clearing the branches, allowing awareness practices to dissolve your old trauma narrative and identity. Now you can consciously turn to see the old view (the remains of the tree) and also the new view (the new growth emerging from the remains). You can allow yourself to find new ways of living and relating to others.

The path has been cleared, things that needed to dissolve and transform have faded away, and now it's time to move freely on your path. With your new view of yourself, you may feel empowered to pursue your passions, embark on a new career, or explore new relationships with the people in your life or with new people and communities. The possibilities will continue to expand with your healing.

Loving This Being

The following reflection, activity, and practice are intended to be completed consecutively. Allow twenty to forty minutes to complete all three.

Reflection

What are the narratives you have created about your trauma? Do they portray you as less than, not worthy, not good enough? Do they cast you as a victim or an oppressor? How do these views influence the way you live? How do they affect your relationships with others? Do you behave in reactive or entitled ways in certain situations or with certain people or communities?

Write down some of your thoughts about this trauma narrative (if possible on ecofriendly paper, as you may choose to dispose of it at the end of this exercise). Write whatever comes to mind, in whatever form you choose: fragmentary thoughts, complete sentences, images, single words, or a whole letter to yourself. Here are some questions and prompts for this inquiry:

- What is the story you carry about your traumatic experience? How has it defined who you are?

- The story of my traumatic experience causes me to feel and to think about myself as...
- When I think about my traumatic experience, I relate to myself as...
- From my traumatic experience, I carry with me the view that others see me as...
- What makes me feel stuck or limited in this narrative of trauma is...

It's time to let go of these patterns of how you think and feel about yourself. The whole, healthy self you have been restoring through your healing process deserves to be honored by not being seen through this lens. Your body, mind, and heart as they are now, in which you can fully be yourself, need to be welcomed and inhabited.

Activity

Take your writing and tear or cut up the paper into pieces of any shape and size you like. Make a picture by arranging these pieces to represent your body, showing the places that have held your trauma and what has been stuck within you, for example by balling up parts of the paper. Breathe in and breathe out onto these pieces. Watch them shift and change.

Now rearrange the pieces to create a picture that represents the challenging patterns of your mind that are associated with your trauma narrative. You might choose to throw the pieces into the air and watch them form chaotic patterns as they land. Breathe in and breathe out onto these pieces — watch them shift and change.

Finally, use the pieces to create a picture representing the painful feelings of your heart that are associated with these stories, for example by fraying the edges of pieces that contain painful words. Breathe in and breathe out onto these pieces — watch them shift and change.

Now it's time to let this story go. Find a quiet place in nature to say goodbye to it. Dispose of the pieces by a method that has some connection to the elements, so that the energy contained in this story can be given back to nature and the Earth. You may choose to burn them (being careful to protect yourself and the environment), to bury them in the earth, or to dissolve them in water and pour them away. They no longer need to be a part of the definition of you. The story is healed, released, and let go, allowing you to live fully the story that is unfolding now. Reflect on or write about what is present and possible now.

Practice

Choose a place that holds some aspect of nature that you associate with connection and love — maybe a special place or a particular tree, plant, or flower — or think of a connection with this aspect of nature. Settle into a comfortable, supportive posture.

Begin by bringing awareness to your breath. Feel the breath moving in and out of the body. Allow yourself to connect to the flow, the rhythms, the pace.

Now bring to mind the image of your being and an aspect of it for which you feel love, connection, adoration, or deep regard — perhaps the color of your hair, eyes, or skin, the shapes and forms of your body, or the different expressions and capacities of your mind and heart (such as your intellect, compassionate heart, or open mind). Acknowledge these as expressions of your inner light, things that are uniquely you, aspects of your wholesomeness, goodness, and beauty.

Now become present to this place in nature, where you feel love and connection. Become aware of all the details in this setting: the colors, shapes, expressions and capacities of nature, its unique beauty, wholeness, and goodness — its light.

Be present for a few minutes with the love that surrounds and inhabits both this aspect of yourself and this place in nature. Feel the love of being — alive, embodied, filled with unique light and goodness — within every cell of every being.

To end this practice, consider the new story of your being that is currently being written. Can you imagine how it will continue to unfold and reveal itself in your life, your relationships, your way of expressing yourself and being in the world? Create, imagine, and let go, trusting this new life unfolding.

Eli's Story

Eli experienced trauma from sexual assaults while attending boarding school as a teen. Over the years, Eli had come to view himself as a victim. He often felt a chronic distrust for systems, his family, and his relationships with others. He had been in multiple failed intimate relationships, felt disconnected from his immediate family, and now, as a parent, often struggled to feel like a good dad.

Over the course of two years, through the practices of mindfulness and somatic healing with nature, Eli's journey of healing unfolded. He was able to release himself from the fight and freeze reactions of his unhealed trauma and began to feel more alive and empowered. He was able to create healthy boundaries with his family of origin by asserting himself and stating his needs clearly; to form a functional, emotionally stable partnership; and to work to ensure the social, emotional, and physical well-being of his children. When the FBI approached him to take action against the person who had committed the assaults against him, he did so, and he also engaged with the school where the assaults took place in order to find justice and reconciliation.

Eli now views himself not as a victim but as healed, and as someone who has thrived and is stronger because of the experiences he went through. He has rewritten the trauma narrative that limited his way of living for so long and sees himself as an activist, an amazing father, and a person fully present in his own life.

Where will your healing journey take you in redefining your relationship with yourself? What ways of living will allow you to fully express your healing? How will your healing benefit the relationships you are in, the people you are connected to, and the communities you belong to and serve? Let yourself imagine what is possible.

Taking Care

Relationships have different forms, durations, intensities, and capacities to affect our lives. From a healthy sense of ourselves, not bound by the narratives of trauma, we can choose how to engage in fulfilling relationships with ourselves and others. This is a process. Take the time you need to rediscover yourself and to understand the relationships. Use the awareness practices in this book to support your investigation of what supports your healthy ecosystem.

As you heal, you will identify relationships that help you grow and that you want to maintain, and others that you may need to let go of. Allow yourself to adapt to new ways of being as you identify the relationships and communities that nourish, support, and enliven you. Be willing to reexperience the connections of relationships as you continue to heal.

Through your healing, you are learning to redefine how your trauma is expressed in your life, and this affects how you are showing up in the lives of others and how they are present in your own life. Letting go of unhelpful narratives creates space for balance, harmony, joy, and ease in your relationships with yourself and others.

Chapter 11

THE RHYTHMS
of NATURE

All life is a circle. The atom is a circle, orbits are circles, the earth, moon, and sun are circles. The seasons are circles. The cycle of life is a circle: baby, youth, adult, elder. The sun gives life to the earth who feeds life to the trees whose seeds fall to the earth to grow new trees. We need to practice seeing the cycles that the Great Spirit gave us because this will help us more in our understanding of how things operate. We need to respect these cycles and live in harmony with them.

— Rolling Thunder

Nature's rhythms reflect her wisdom. Rhythms are the currents of energy that create and sustain life. They include the birth and death of living things and the changing of the seasons. Rhythms are evident in the sounds, movements, and flows of energy within ecosystems. By learning to move in time with these rhythms, respecting and enjoying the cycles of ebb and flow, we can cultivate awareness, presence, clarity, and direction in life.

Your life has unique rhythms. Different stages of life bring different types of energies to help us navigate their challenges. As children and teens, we tend to have a lot of physical energy that helps us learn, explore, and process all our new experiences. In our late adolescence through early adulthood, our energy is directed toward self-discovery and the search for adventure, career, or stability. In middle and late adulthood, we may direct our energies toward helping our communities. In the final stages of life, our energy shifts toward reflection, wisdom, retirement, and letting go. Awareness of these shifting energy currents in us and around us can help us choose skillfully how to care for ourselves.

When we are disconnected from the rhythms in our lives, it can be more difficult to engage. If we are pushing ourselves at a time when we need to be slow and reflective, we can burn out. If we are quiet and resting during a time when life is asking us to engage and move, we might feel depressed. Unhealed trauma causes us to neglect or be unaware of these energies within us: instead of heeding them, we act out of reactivity and habit.

All of the rhythms in nature are here to help us develop, sustain, change, thrive, and let go. As your trauma is healed, you can discover and live according to the rhythms that serve you best. You have access to the deeper, more subtle energies within you. Becoming aware of these rhythms, respecting them, and trusting that they can guide you toward wholesome life choices is another step on the healing journey.

I grew up in a small agricultural town in central California (with a population of about six thousand). Across from our house were acres of open dirt and a ditch. I remember spending summer mornings playing in the dirt, building forts, creating things out of the mud and dried brush, and catching tadpoles. Summer days were long, slow, and hot. By midday the heat sent us kids back into the air-conditioned house to get Popsicles. In the evenings the air was cooler, sweet, and moist, and we would often return to the forts, creating an entirely new imaginary world.

I also remember spending most weekends out at our family farm, playing in the peach and nectarine orchards. In the fall we played in and among the stacks of wooden fruit bins in the barn that held the fruit during the summer harvest. At this time of year they became a three-story fort, reaching almost to the ceiling of the barn, which we would climb and sit inside. There we imagined traveling to mystical lands to meet creatures who would bestow magical powers on us. We would run and play hide-and-seek in the orchards. The smell of the soil wafted through the air, rich with the scent of decaying fruit left after the harvest to deposit nutrients back into the soil.

In the winters I remember the fog — the Tule fog of the Central Valley, too thick to drive through — and the joy of waking up to a "foggy day" school schedule, which sometimes meant school didn't start until after noon. I recall relishing the extra sleep, enjoying hot chocolate with my sister, and the way the entire town and community welcomed a pause in the busy routine.

In the spring, the sight of distant snow-capped peaks in the clear air awakened us to the new life emerging. For miles around, the orchard trees were blooming and opening their beautiful, delicate leaves to the sun. Like magic, the bulb of fruit formed, beginning its growth into a beautiful, juicy, ripe peach with its hues of orange, red, and yellow.

Growing up in a farming community against the beautiful backdrop of the Sierra Nevada, I learned to welcome each of the seasons and its lessons about life. To this day I value the slow pace of a hot summer day, the reflective beauty of the fall, the stillness of a foggy winter, and the delight of a spring blossom. These are the gifts of my childhood and the land I come from.

What connections with nature in your own experience have helped you attune to and flow with the rhythms of your life? Maybe you find these connections in the place where you grew up, maybe from other stages of your life. Everything on the globe responds to the light, the seasons, and the moon. Many cultures around the globe celebrate the summer and winter solstices, around June 21 and December 21, marking the longest and shortest days of the year (and the reverse in the Southern Hemisphere). The first known solstice celebration dates back to 10,200 BCE. These celebrations have anchored agricultural practices, spiritual connections, and rites of passage. Let yourself settle into and explore the rhythms of nature that support all life.

Inner Rhythms

The following reflection, practice, and activity are intended to be completed consecutively or done individually during a time of day that works best for you.. Allow forty to sixty minutes to complete all three.

Reflection

Choose a time period to reflect on — maybe the past few months of your life, your childhood, or some other period. Consider the types of rhythms you were aware of during this time. Did you notice connections to particular times of day, parts of the moon's cycle, or other natural rhythms? Perhaps there were times during this part of your life when your energy reflected a particular season: quiet, at rest, or still like the winter; full of energy, organization, and plans like the spring; active and achievement-oriented like the summer; or reflective, contemplative, and slowing like the fall.

Reflect on how these rhythms and seasons may have affected you. How have they been reflected in the feelings in your body, the movements of your mind, and the opening of your heart?

Do you notice new rhythms arising from the healing of your trauma? What do they feel like in your body, mind, and heart? If you wish, journal about what you are noticing.

Practice

We all have inner rhythms that vary from day to day, season to season, year to year, and decade to decade. This exercise is intended to help you to explore these rhythms. Choose a time of day that is appropriate for attuning to the particular rhythms you are exploring. If you are attuning to brightness in your inner rhythms, you might choose the early morning; for more energetic rhythms, you might choose midday. To focus on reflective, quiet, rhythms, you might choose sunset or the dark of night.

Find a location outside where you can sit comfortably or lie down and feel the supportive, stable presence of nature. Allow your body to feel grounded in the earth beneath and behind you. Feel the presence of nature around, above, and below you, and allow any tense, constricted regions of your body to relax and open. Move those parts of your body as necessary to release and soften them.

Now allow yourself to feel the rhythm of this particular time of day. Notice the qualities of the light and air (perhaps bright or dark, moist or dry), the movements in the landscape (stillness, awakening, rushing), and the expressions of nature's energy around you (birds chirping or soaring, animals burrowing or foraging, plants opening or closing their blooms and leaves).

Shift your attention to your inner landscape, attending to the sensations of your entire body. How is your body receiving and responding to the rhythms of this time of day? Do you notice a sense of opening, drawing in, lifting up, or relaxing?

Starting with the top of your body, invite awareness to be present to the head, face, and neck, including all of the sense doors that reside here — hearing, smell, sight, taste, and touch. How are you experiencing the energy and rhythms of nature and the day? Do you sense particular colors, sounds, vibrations, or movements? Welcome the connections between the rhythms around you and within you.

Now become aware of the middle of your body: the shoulders, arms, wrists and hands, chest, back, diaphragm, belly, and pelvic region. As you bring awareness to this area, notice the energy of sensations moving, ebbing, flowing, arising, and passing. Invite awareness to sweep through this region of the body like a paintbrush, sensing and awakening to the vibrations, rhythms, and movements. Sense how nature is expressing her rhythms and how rhythms are arising within you.

Be present to all the movements and rhythms you notice. If you find any rhythms uncomfortable — tight, constricted, dark, dense, heavy, pulsing, bellowing — let them be. As best you can, welcome with kindness and curiosity all the expressions of your inner rhythms. Let go of needing to figure out, change, resist, or fix anything.

Now shift your focus to the lower region of your body — the hips, thighs, lower legs, ankles, and feet. Feel and sense the surface of the skin, the muscles, and the bones Bring awareness deeper into the body, becoming aware of the qualities of the pulsing and vibrating energy of this part of your body. Notice the connections between these rhythms and those around you in nature.

Now expand your awareness to your entire body, from the soles of the feet to the top of the head. Be present to the moving, shifting, ebbing, and flowing energy of your body. Allow awareness to welcome all expressions of energy, in whatever form, shape, texture, image, or color you sense.

In the last few moments of the practice, rest awareness in the rhythms of nature around you. What rhythms do you feel and sense now? Do you notice any shifts in the qualities of the light, air, or landscape? Appreciate any shifts in energy within you too.

Close the practice by offering appreciation for what is here now and for the deeper knowledge of the rhythms within and around that this practice has cultivated.

Reflection/Activity

To complete this practice, you may want to reflect on and journal about your experience. Do the rhythms that you noticed in the practice reflect the particular cycle, season, or stage of life you are in now? Can you offer respect or regard to actions in your life that honor these rhythms? With new awareness of these rhythms, list three simple actions you can take to support your well-being: for example, you might consider going slower in a particular activity, or set an intention to move or be spontaneously playful.

When we attend to and attune ourselves to the rhythms of our inner landscape, we can choose to live more wisely and in greater harmony with our work, family, and communities.

Rhythms of Dying

In our focus on living, most of us spend a lot of energy and time thinking about our next experiences and accomplishments. We often evaluate our lives according to what we have achieved. While this kind of thinking is helpful for orienting us and engaging with life, we forget that every moment we are alive, we are also dying.

The moment some achievement is completed, it is also finished, gone, dead. Each breath is one less in our lives, one step closer to the last breath we will take. Most human beings don't take time to reflect on this truth, as it can elicit difficult feelings of fear, uncertainty, sadness, grief, and loss. If we can learn to trust in the beauty, mystery, and love that are inherent in the uncertainty and impermanence of life, we can live each moment more fully.

Death is an integral part of the rhythms of nature. Expressions of impermanence, birth, and death are everywhere in nature. For example, if you walk through a healthy forest, you will find baby trees only a few feet tall. You will also find the midlifers, reaching intently toward the sky, spreading their branches wide. And you will see trees that are dead or dying — withered, fallen, decaying into the earth. These dying trees are the ones that support new life by returning their nutrients to the soil. And amid the dying or dead forms of nature, you will often find new, small sprouts of life. In the same way, it is necessary for parts of your life to die away to make rich soil that enables new things to emerge.

As you heal from trauma, you can see it as a part of your life that is being allowed to die and support new growth. You can appreciate the new space, clarity, ease, and lightness that are emerging in its place.

Death is happening at every moment. Learning to appreciate, welcome, allow, reflect on, and contemplate death along with all the other rhythms in your life can help deepen your healing and allow you to connect to vitality and joy.

Moments of Birth and Death

The following practice and reflection/activity are intended to be completed consecutively. Allow twenty to thirty minutes to complete them. Before you begin, allow yourself a few minutes to reflect on birth and death. As best you can, let go of the associations, meanings, and thoughts traditionally associated with birth and death and turn your awareness to the uncertainty, impermanence, and ephemeral nature of each moment.

Practice

Find a location outside where you can sit, lie down, stand, or walk. Feel the supportive presence of nature beneath you, around you, and above you.

Begin by establishing a sense of groundedness, alertness, relaxation, and openness in your body. Now orient your attention to the breath. Notice the simple movements as you inhale and exhale. Allow awareness to feel the changing, flowing, coming, and going of each breath.

Now shift your attention to notice the movements of the fresh, new, alive, vital qualities of each breath. Sense the shifting upward, the arising, the uplifting, the beginning. Rest awareness in feeling the birth of each moment of breath. Be curious if this beginning is present in the inhale, the exhale, or both. If you find the mind wandering or feel yourself trying deliberately to sense or create these qualities, try to let go and meet each breath as it arises.

Now shift your attention to the movements of the releasing, passing, and dying qualities of the breath. Sense the letting go, the falling away, the ending. Rest awareness in feeling the death of each moment of breath. Be curious about whether the dying and passing away is present in the exhale, the inhale, or both. If you have trouble being present to these qualities or encounter fear, contraction, or resistance, meet those experiences with kindness.

Welcome the feelings of the birth and death of a breath with awareness and openness. Feel what is new, what is awakening, what is released, and what will never be again.

Now shift your attention to what is exchanged with nature in each breath. As you breathe in, you receive oxygen that has been released by other forms of life. As you breathe out, you give back carbon dioxide to all life. Each breath is a moment of exchange of what is dying and complete for what is alive and beginning. Rest awareness in this reciprocity of the rhythms of life.

In the last few minutes of the practice, notice what is present in your mind, body, and heart after feeling the qualities of change, life, and death that are present in each breath. Offer gratitude for whatever has been cultivated in this practice.

Reflection/Activity

To complete this practice, reflect on and write about what qualities this practice has cultivated in your mind, body, and heart. How might trusting the rhythms of birth, change, and death support you in living more fully?

List three simple actions you can take today that will increase your awareness of birth and death around you. You might choose to stop to observe a dying plant, touch or connect to something in nature that is just beginning its life, or appreciate the exhale as you engage in an activity.

Harmony in the Rhythms of Life

When we experience harmony, we sense balance and ease. If you have experienced trauma, you have likely felt aspects of your inner life to be off balance, chaotic, or distressing, preventing you from experiencing harmony. As you are healing and developing new, healthy inner rhythms, you have more capacity to develop balance and peace in your life.

The First Nations and Inuit peoples of North America have deep respect for the land that sustains them and feel sacred ties to it. They see themselves as living *with* the land, rather than *off* the land.[1] To live in harmony is to know and trust the Earth and her ability to provide, to teach and offer wisdom, and to sustain the cycles of life. Feeling this reverence and connection to the Earth can also help us develop reverence and care for our own being.

The events and conditions around us are out of our control. Equanimity is a sense of inner calm, well-being, vitality, integrity, and confidence in the face of whatever we encounter. It is equanimity that brings inner harmony and enables you to act with a deep regard for your own being and everything around you. When you can sense clearly your patterns of reactivity and are no longer pulled or charged by them, you can cultivate a heart that is open and receptive to whatever arises. Equanimity is a state of body and heart as well as of mind. As your nervous system heals, it is rewiring in a way that supports harmony and balance, returning to homeostasis and regulation. This is the basis for cultivating equanimity.

Equanimity rests on a combination of understanding and trust. The understanding entails accepting that life will happen: it is part of a larger plan. The trust entails the willingness to believe, feel, and sense that this is true. We are frustrated with the conditions of life only when we feel they are out of our control. This feeling is based on the assumption that we should have had some control. Part of the definition of unhealed trauma is that the traumatic experience felt out of your control.

Learning to accept that the trauma you experienced was beyond your control, and trusting in its importance as a part of your experience, is equanimity arising. To bring equanimity to your trauma is to love, regard, respect, and appreciate what has arisen to support your life. As your healing evolves, you can continue to meet whatever arises as a part of life. Whether an experience is pleasant, unpleasant, or neutral, you accept that it is not here for you to control: your role is to be present to its rhythms.

Developing Equanimity

The following practice and reflection/activity are intended to be completed consecutively. Allow twenty to thirty minutes to complete them.

Practice

Find a place somewhere in nature where you can experience many different environmental conditions (natural and human-made, hot and cold, dry or wet). Choose a posture that allows you to feel grounded, alert, relaxed, and open. You may choose to sit, lie down, stand, or walk.

Begin by bringing awareness to the breath. Feel the breath moving through the body as you inhale and exhale. If your attention shifts away from the breath to a thought, an emotion, or a sensation, be willing to simply feel the pleasantness, unpleasantness, or neutral quality of whatever arises. Be curious to feel what it's like to just let a moment be a moment, an arising experience. There is nothing for you to do — just allow yourself to be present with what is here.

Now expand your awareness to your surroundings. Connect to everything in the environment — the natural, the human-made, the weather conditions. Let what you hear, see, feel, smell, and taste be just as it is. Welcome these experiences as they arise and pass, feeling them as pleasant, unpleasant, or neutral. Let go of needing anything to be different from how it is.

Allow your heart to open, to soften. See if you can bring an openness, trust, and appreciation to what is here. You may want to repeat these phrases to yourself:

May I be balanced and at ease — here, now.
May I be open to life just as it is.
May I be compassionately present to and at ease with all conditions of life.

Meet whatever arises with kindness. There is no need to push away any thought, emotion, or sensation. Each moment is here to support your understanding.

You may choose to continue to offer these phrases of equanimity to yourself or direct them toward family or friends, to acquaintances or people you find challenging, to communities you know well, or to the Earth and all its beings. Be present to what arises as you cultivate equanimity for your own being and your interconnectedness to all beings.

To close this practice, offer appreciation and trust for what has arisen and for all conditions that support your being.

Reflection/Activity

You may wish to reflect on and journal about your experience of this practice. Do you sense balance, ease, or harmony in your body, mind, and heart? Do you sense contentment, trust, or confidence? How do you notice equanimity being expressed in your being now?

List three simple actions you can take today to support your cultivation of equanimity: for example, being okay with the arrival of something unexpected, appreciating feeling calm or at ease while engaged in a difficult task, or noticing a feeling of balance or organization in your body.

Taking Care

Nurturing the rhythms in your life and feeling connection with the rhythms of nature can sustain you and help heal your trauma. As you learn to trust the reality that all life is changing, that birth and death are present in each moment, and that you can find balance and equanimity amid it all, you can free yourself from trauma and suffering.

As you experience insights from these practices, you can integrate them into your everyday life. Here are some suggestions for practicing the inner seasons, moments of birth and death, and equanimity meditations during your day:

- In the morning, at midday, and in the evening, take one minute to observe your inner landscape. Sweep awareness through your body to sense its qualities in this moment: is it dry, arid, cold, warm, bright, dark, intense, quiet? Appreciate what you notice, and allow yourself to move into the next activity of your day.
- Attend to the beginnings and endings in each day: the beginning and end of a meal, break, task, activity, or conversation.
- Bring equanimity to your everyday life and interactions with others. In a moment of feeling imbalance, can you remember that this is as it is in this moment — unbalanced, uneasy, swaying with the movement of interaction? Can you let go of needing to change it or judging that it should be different and instead accept that this is what is here now? Be willing to express faith or trust in being with the experience as it is — pleasant, unpleasant, or

neutral. Choose your responses from this place of okayness and ease to be with how it is.

As you absorb these truths and rhythms into your life, you can begin to take healthy action. In awareness of our reciprocal relationships with what is within and around us in nature, you might consider taking action to protect the environment you live in, the community you are a part of, or the planet. Plant a garden, help clean up your neighborhood, or consider joining a group that supports an environmental cause.

When you see that the rhythms of birth and death are ever-present in your life, you might consider slowing down and taking the time to appreciate the simple things, like sipping tea, watching a bird soar in the sky, hearing and feeling the wind blowing gently through the trees and over your being, and appreciating a new leaf on a tree.

As you learn to cultivate balance and harmony, consider how you can experience the fullness of pleasant, unpleasant, and neutral activities of your day. Let equanimity support you in whatever arises. If it's too hot, let it be so; if it's too cold, let it be so. If your car breaks down, you are assigned unexpected work, or you experience a conflict with another person, let this be an opportunity to practice equanimity. Can you be like a mountain, solid and steady, letting the weather pass over you? Can you hold your poise and composure, letting go of needing to react to, resist, or change what is happening? Trusting the rhythms of your life, you can cultivate ease, contentment, and calm.

Chapter 12

EXPERIENCING INSIGHTS
of HEALING

Wisdom tells me I am nothing. Love tells me I am everything. And between the two my life flows.

— Nisargadatta Maharaj

As you continue to heal your traumas, you deepen your knowledge of yourself and your ability to skillfully engage in life. Insights about embodiment, presence and connection to energy, interconnectedness, curiosity, trust, mystery, and love bring a sense of wholeness and allow you to connect to the essence of your being. Now that you have released the reactive habits you developed to help you cope with trauma — such as resistance, avoidance, controlling, preparing, fixing, and ignoring — you have space within to welcome new ways to live.

Your courage, your strength, your persistence, and your willingness to explore the pain and the unknown in the terrain of your trauma have led you to a greater sense of embodiment. This is a feeling of being at ease and secure in your body, trusting yourself and your actions, and knowing how to move your body in and with the joys and challenges of life. As changes occur, you can feel in your body how to respond, and you can discern how to act in ways that support your well-being. You might be learning to slow down, choosing to set a boundary with someone you experience as depleting, or engaging in activities that allow your body, mind, and heart to feel alive.

As you come to trust your sense of embodiment, you can connect to energies moving within you and around you. This allows you to experience a sense of resonance and healthy action to guide you toward enhanced health.

A sense of embodiment gives rise to an awareness of our connection to all things. Thích Nhất Hạnh writes, "Everything relies on everything else in order to manifest." We are all part of one being. There is no sense of solitary beingness. Your body is alive in this moment as a result of multiple causes and conditions — actions by your ancestors and your immediate family; your own thoughts, feelings, and actions; the environments and cultures you've lived in; and the processes of the natural world.

When you bite into a tomato, your experience is the result of many actions and conditions. The tomato's existence has arisen from a seed harvested from its ancestor and planted; the soil, rich with nutrients contributed by earlier life; the warmth and light of the sun and the passing of the days, months, and seasons; the water from the rain, the rivers, and the oceans; the hands that tended to the plant and its rhythms of growth. As you eat the tomato, you are taking in nutrients of the Earth, eating a plant with which you have exchanged oxygen and carbon dioxide through the breath. All beings depend on one another to experience and be part of life. Sensing this interconnection brings awareness of our responsibility to care for ourselves and the world around us. With this awareness, we can begin to engage with the world more fully.

At a retreat I attended, all participants were invited to practice presence with a tree. The instructions were to invite embodied awareness and feel into the natural surroundings. I had been having some physical pain in my neck and had been working with somatic practices to support my healing. I chose to practice with a young pine tree nearby. I slowly walked in a circle around the tree, changing directions a few times to experience it from different perspectives. Then, seeing a pine cone full of pollen,

I came to a stop. I had never noticed that pine cones produce pollen. I stood still, breathing, being present to the soft, subtle edges of the newly forming cones extending from the thin green needles. As I slowly reached out my fingers to touch them, a cloud of pollen burst into the air and was gently carried away by the wind. I stood in awe at the beauty and aliveness of this tree. And my embodied, energetically resonant touch gave rise to the insight that my connection with this tree was now part of its history of growth and death. My heart soared with the pollen on the wind, wondering where it might land and whether it would grow into a tree that would produce its own pollen and seed, and eventually die and return nutrients to the soil. As this insight arose, I stood, silent and still, awed at the deep, interconnected mystery of life. On returning to awareness of my own body, I discovered that the neck pain had shifted. Along with the pain, I experienced a deep appreciation of how a single touch holds infinite possibilities for healing and connection. Walking back to the group from this solo practice, my body softened, opening and releasing what had been held in my neck, feeling a shift of my mind and heart. I felt restored and at ease.

Each of the practices you have learned and are integrating into your life brings you more aliveness and healing. Developing these practices will lead you to deeper insights and experiences. Let yourself be energetically present to your embodiment and connections with other life. You might consider returning to some of the earlier practices you found helpful and asking these questions as you end the practice:

- What am I present to in my body? What sensations and energies do I notice?
- How am I feeling aliveness in my body? What sensations, colors, images, energies, or vibrations do I notice?
- Where do I feel aliveness in my body? What sensations, movements, or energies are present in those places now?
- How are my senses — hearing, sight, smell, taste, and touch — offering me sensations of aliveness and interconnection?

• How is nature revealing her forms of embodied, energetic connection around me? How does each being express its aliveness, energy exchange, and connection?

Curiosity and Oneness

These practices are helping you to learn that it is okay to let go of what the mind thinks it knows. We have been taught since childhood to rely on our minds to discern, to figure things out, and to guide our actions — a top-down approach to knowing. Mindfulness and somatic meditations teach us to trust a different way of knowing, one that draws on the wisdom of the body and is centered on the present moment rather than on what we expect or what has been — a more bottom-up approach to meeting experiences. Often in mindfulness this is referred to as Knowing with a capital *K*. Through Knowing we learn to let go of constructs and thought processes such as identification, labeling, or creating duality and instead be open to curiosity, openness, and awareness of the present moment.

These practices can give rise to childlike wonder. You may notice that you are encountering experiences as if for the first time, even things you have experienced a hundred times before. This quality allows you to more fully experience possibility and discern different choices. If you are bound by what you think you "know," then there is nothing left to learn. Through Knowing, you can discover endless ways to experience and live your life.

Nature expresses her wonder and beauty to us anew in every moment. When we encounter an expansive vista, a delicate flower, a gentle spider, or majestic wildlife, we connect to the moment. When we sense that this is the only time that this particular experience can ever be, we fully Know this moment of nature. While we may try to preserve these experiences in our memory or with pictures, the grace, mystery, and beauty come from the wonder of meeting nature in that moment.

The mind loves to separate, to create duality. Its job (so it thinks — ha ha) is to judge, categorize, label, and describe. This way of operating is useful in many areas of life. It helps us work, make decisions, follow society's rules, and discern our choices. But all these processes create a sense of separateness. If we rely too much on these capacities of the mind, we miss the beautiful connectivity of everything.

A simple example is the classification of an experience as right or wrong, good or bad. The qualities of good and bad exist only in relation to one another. If we learn to welcome, be curious about, and be open to these coexisting states, we can begin to see the spaciousness and oneness of all things. Nature encourages us to let go of our tendency to create duality and opposites. The beauty of a dead grass amid a vibrant meadow and the snow-capped peaks of a sparse or barren mountain can welcome us to Knowing that both are part of the cycles of life, the mystery of oneness.

No two thoughts can ever be the same: thoughts are unique to the moment they are experienced. While a thought is the product of a myriad of causes and conditions, it can only be Known as it is in that moment. When we bring curiosity to our mind's patterns and habits, we are released and refreshed, able to perceive and experience life differently.

Not-knowing, welcoming uncertainty, allows us to loosen our tight grip on the way we view ourselves and life. This brings us to the insights of releasing the sense of self. With histories of trauma, we may hold firmly to a particular view or perception of our life and overidentify with our mind's construction of who we are. As we explored in chapter 10, releasing our relationship to trauma is a practice. When we realize we can let go of the "I" that has been defined in a particular way, and step into awareness of this moment, this being, our connection with all things, the self can dissolve.

While this idea might seem a bit unsettling, consider that it holds the possibility of freedom. Unconstrained by the definitions, constructs, images, and beliefs that define the self, we can enter into a fluid, constantly unfolding mystery of being! We can learn to distance ourselves in a healthy way from the thoughts, emotions, and history that we think of as constituting who we are, and rather become the experiences unfolding in our participation with life. Nature doesn't trouble herself with identification: she doesn't hold tightly to the need to be a rock, a tree, or a leaf. Instead, she reveals herself as shifting and changing, conditions that are part of the way things are.

Learning to let go of the sense of self is an advanced practice that may require years of mindfulness and somatic meditation. For the following practice, be curious, be open, and let go of your knowing as best you can.

This Being

The following reflection and practice are intended to be completed consecutively. Allow thirty to forty minutes to complete them.

Reflection

Reflect on the following questions:

- What within "me" is knowing this moment — through sight, sound, smell, and touch?
- Who is thinking this thought?
- Who or what is knowing this sensation now?
- Who am I?
- Where is the sense of "I" within me?
- What is it like to feel life as an array of expressions?

These questions point to the awareness that everything is a combination of arising and passing conditions — there is no localized sense of self to be found.

Write down what arises from this reflection. You may choose to bring these questions into your formal mindfulness practices; you may also choose to thread them into your everyday life to begin to experience what it's like to let go of the self.

Practice

Allow twenty to thirty minutes for this practice. Find a tree that you feel a sense of connection with, one that is part of your environment — a place you know and feel connected to. This might be a big oak tree, a tall pine, or a vibrant aspen. Take your time with each step of the instructions below to fully establish the experience that is being evoked. You may choose to practice only a few of these instructions.

Bring the body into connection with the tree. You may choose to lean against, lie under, hold, or climb the tree. Allow the body to feel a sense of groundedness, ease, relaxation, and openness in your chosen posture.

Now shift your attention to the breath. With each breath in, sense aliveness, awakening, uplifting. With each breath out, sense releasing, letting go, dissolving into the moment. Steady your attention on the breath and body in this way, allowing embodied awareness to arise.

Now direct your attention to everything around you that is supporting your presence. Feel and sense what is above — the spreading canopy of the tree's branches and leaves, the sky embracing and holding the tree. Feel and sense what is around you — the body of the tree, other plant life, animal life, insect life — vibrating and moving through the landscape and around your body. Now feel and sense what is below — the tree's roots reaching deep into the earth, holding strong and steady, connected to all life around and beyond. Sit in stillness, feeling this connection to tree-ness.

Gently move your awareness back and forth between this body, sitting with this tree, and the sense of this tree, sitting with this body. Explore the boundaries between them — the places that delineate where the body ends and the tree begins, or the body begins and the tree ends. Allow this body, heart, and mind to dissolve and become one with the tree. There is no longer this body, or this tree. Be open to sensing tree-ness, this-ness, oneness.

Continue to practice in this way, choosing the instructions that support your ability to sense and cultivate oneness.

A poem to close with, by Li Bai, a Chinese poet of the Tang Dynasty:

The birds have vanished down the sky.
Now the last cloud drains away.

We sit together, the mountain and me,
until only the mountain remains.

Allow a few moments at the end of this practice to reflect and write on what was felt or Known.

Intuition, Mystery, and Love

During my years of meditation, I have come to love spiders. Often when I have been deep in meditation practice, I have been graced with the presence of a spider. They have shown themselves high in the trees, connecting branches, leaves, and beings through their silvery, reflective webs; they have shown themselves taking shelter in the crevices of my windows, laying eggs that will give rise to new life; carried by the wind, they have graced my knee, sat for a while, spun webs between my legs, and then gently floated away with the next current of wind to spin webs of connections with other living beings. They have crawled and glided over the top of my computer and keyboard as I have been writing this book. Deep presence often gives rise to intuitive, mysterious connections.

I am always amazed by my intuitive ability to feel the presence of spiders, and I am in awe of their mysterious ability to weave their webs. Although spider webs might not appear at first glance to be a source or expression of connection, close connection provides absolutely the right conditions for weaving a beautiful web.

One lovely summer afternoon in the Colorado mountains while on retreat, deep in my meditation practice, I decided to let my intuition guide me through the forest. I meandered through a meadow, letting my inner sense of Knowing guide my steps. This led me to the river that ran through the meadow. I sat quietly with the river for a while, present to the rapids and flowing water, the sound of the current moving, the smells of the earth, and the trees around me. Feeling pulled to sit in the water, I found rocks to sit on where I could submerge my lower legs and feet. I let my legs and feet experience the river — the cold, invigorating, exciting water, the rocks, the sand, the algae. As I felt my body, heart, and mind awaken in attunement with this landscape, I felt a presence inviting me to turn around and sensed the message "Go against the stream." Carefully and gently I turned my body to face upstream.

As I turned, my eyes were graced with a beautiful spider — hovering in midair above the rushing river. My heart skipped a beat. How was this possible? As I investigated, I saw she had woven an intricate web above this river, anchored to the trees, rocks, and grasses, making her home above the center of the river. I sensed the strong strands of the web flexing in the winds rising up from the river, the sun illuminating its silvery sheen, the water spraying tiny droplets onto the strands, and the earth below the spider supporting her life. I felt mystery, awe, and love for the innate wisdom of this being, trusting and relying on the interconnected conditions of her life. I cried tears of love and deep gratitude for the blessings bestowed on me in that moment.

Intuition

The practices you have been learning are not only healing you but offering you a new way of experiencing life, enabling your mind, heart, and body to enter into new states of being. The ability to cultivate trust can be profoundly helpful in guiding your actions, freeing you from doubt, reactive patterns, and disconnection.

Intuition is an interesting word. It means "the ability to understand something immediately, without the need for conscious reasoning." As you attune to intuition, it allows you to trust the instincts that arise from thoughts, emotions, and sensations in order to inform your actions. You feel more confidence in yourself and the decisions and direction you choose for your life.

Intuition requires listening deeply to your inner Knowing. Letting go of expectant, problem-solving habits of thought will help you connect more deeply to your intuition.

Here are some questions to help you develop trust in your intuition:

- What in this moment lets me Know I feel at ease?
- What in my experience of this moment can I trust?
- How does my body Know what to do next?
- What emotions of ease are present in my heart in this moment?
- How is my mind open or spacious in this moment?
- Does this action align with a sense of calm, ease, and openness in my body, heart, and mind?

You can explore these questions throughout your day, or at the end of your meditation practices.

Mystery

When we are more attuned to our intuition, we are more receptive to the great mysteries of life. Infinitely many conditions arise in life that are not to be explained or understood but rather embraced. How can we grasp all the processes by which a cell comes into being and exists? Is it truly possible to know every aspect of interconnectedness? How has all of this come into existence? Without definitive answers to these questions, we can learn to abide in a deep respect for the majesty and mystery of life. Feeling the sense of mystery in the heart, mind, and body allows you to be open to the awe, the infinite expanse, the spirituality or divinity of life.

Most of us have a sense of what it "means" to be spiritual, to connect to the divine or to God. Whatever label or description you adopt, the truth at the center of it all is a beautiful mystery — something not to be figured out but to be received, graced by, and blessed. Whether this sense of truth arises from a moment of wonder about how a spider came to be in a certain place or from a contemplation of the vastness and origins of our universe, it's all a mystery. Welcoming this mystery with awareness allows more space and possibility to arise within us.

Reflection on mystery can deepen your practice. It can also open your awareness to the beauty, awe, and wonder of all life. You can ask these questions individually or in sequence, once or repeatedly, during your practices or in moments of everyday life.

- What in the mystery of nature is touching me in this moment?
- How is this moment possible?
- How did this expression of nature, of life, of connection come to be?
- What is unknown at this moment?
- What is unseen in the ordinary?
- What do I not know in this moment?

Learning to dissolve what we know, who we think we are, and what we think exists allows the mysteries of life to reveal themselves. In mystery we can experience awareness of stillness, silence, oneness, emptiness, connection, grace, and love — beautiful, wholesome, inspiring states to Know. Let yourself love the questions, the ability to not-know, to awaken to a mystery greater than anything that the conscious mind could ever know.

MYSTERIOUS NATURE

'Tis a mysterious thing to see the earth
Put on the fresh unfolded robe of spring —
To hear the liquid notes go up in mirth,
And melt in chorus from each living thing.

Noiseless the bud expandeth into flower;
Noiseless the forest robes its naked form;
Noiseless as thought in its mysterious power,
Or sunlight breaking through the clouds of storm.

Thoughtful we walk beneath the shadowy tree,
Dense with its canopy of leaves and flowers;
We hear aerial notes, or hum of bee,
And linger careless of the fleeting hours.

The rudest mind or dullest eye can see
This transformation of consummate skill;
For ice-bound streams and desolated tree,
The vernal robe, and gently flowing rill.

The flower at morn unfolds each silken leaf,
And lives its bright and beauteous day;
Then, chilled with age, it droops at dews of eve,
And thus the flowers successive pass away.

Each fragrant bud that opens its incense cup
Upon the air at early morn to pour,
Is filled with myriad life, in brilliant forms,
Whose day with flowers of setting sun is o'er.

Brief particles! minute, mysterious life,
In the material compact perfect made;

Atoms that breathe, and love, and reproduce,
And with the flowers at dews of sunset fade.

Each scene that moves the heart with deep delight,
Whose splendor unexpressed allures the eye,
Is but an atom, like the stars of night,
That shine, when millions hid beyond them lie.

Far, far beneath the waste of waters deep,
Are waving grottoes of perpetual green,
Where buds unfold and vines in beauty creep,
A world of life to human eye unseen.

In all the grand economy of God,
Where'er we gaze, whate'er our footsteps meet,
Through ocean's depths, the air, the verdant sod,
Atom on atom, life on lives complete.

Formed in obedience to stupendous might —
Before whose presence, veiled, in awe we bow;
Who yonder orbs swung loose in breathless height,
And bade them silent roll, since time, as now.

Lost in a reverie too deep for thought,
From these mysterious searchings set me free;
For who shall find out Him the change that wrought,
Or who explore the Power Supreme we see?
— O. M. Livingston

Love

When the body, mind, and heart are awakening into embodiment, inter-
dependence, oneness, and deep mystery as you heal from trauma, you

discover your true nature — love. This is not the kind of love that is attached to someone or something, seeking approval, validation, or security. It is a love that is based in the Knowing of the profound unity of everything, that expresses kindness, joy, compassion, and ease with all aspects of life. It is a love that is boundless.

Ram Dass, the psychologist, researcher, and spiritual teacher, taught that all we are is "loving awareness." When we are divinely present to life, anything that touches our awareness will be loved. Loving awareness releases our attachment to "I" and welcomes a different form of consciousness, one that knows our soul's true nature as loving awareness. This love is unconditional, freely offered, spontaneous, and boundless. Learning to direct love toward everything we perceive is a profound gift of these practices and the transformation of our trauma.

For example, this love enables you to be aware of a bee that buzzes next to your body without being caught up in the need to judge, protect, avoid, analyze, or understand, but simply welcoming its presence and beauty with wonder. With this type of love you can release yourself from fear. Over time, as you heal and your practice grows, you can begin to approach experiences in your life with this type of love — to love nature, your family, your community; to love your trauma; to love the people, places, and experiences that gave rise to your trauma; to love all beings; to love this Earth.

As you have traveled the path of healing, you have likely experienced moments of love — of a flower in its beauty, scent, or sacredness, or of a spacious, beautiful cloudscape. These moments opened your heart to love, to knowing your beauty, the sweet scent of your breath, and true sacredness.

We all have a beautiful light within us that, when it shines, is Known as love. Every form of life expresses its unique form of love. Knowing this love is liberating, affirming, and a source of connection to the divine. As you come to know yourself as love, the door opens to loving everyone and everything.

To nourish this type of love, we need to cultivate kindness, compassion, joy, and ease with ourselves and all life on this planet, in this universe, and beyond. There is no separation between our being and that of everything around us. Suffering or love is not an individual matter: one being's suffering is another's suffering, and your love is another's love. From this understanding we can begin to feel and sense the desire to act and live in ways that cultivate this truth.

Loving-kindness practice helps us to connect to our inner being and all other beings. Feeling the truth of your loving nature can support all beings and this Earth.

Practice: Loving-Kindness, All Beings

Allow twenty to thirty minutes for this practice. Find a location in nature that feels supportive, peaceful, and calming to your mind, heart, and body — a place you know well and love. Settle into a posture — sitting, lying down, walking, or standing. Feel your body grounded, alert, relaxed, and open.

Notice your breath, breathing in and out. Invite awareness of the expressions present in your heart in this moment. Notice the sensations of beating, pulsing, pumping; the expanding, the contracting, the quivering, or the opening. Be present to what is alive in the space of the heart.

Repeat the following phrases, or develop phrases of your own that resonate with you. As you practice, offer radiant energy from your heart to all living things.

May all beings be free from suffering.
May all beings be kindly cared for.
May all beings know happiness and the causes of happiness.
May all beings live in harmony and connection.

Allow your heart to radiate love in all directions — to the life in the skies, to the life in the waters, to the life that walks and inhabits the Earth, to the life deep beneath the surface of the Earth.

You may also choose to offer these wishes to yourself, to loved ones, to sentient beings, to nonsentient beings, to the land, waters, or climate, to the Earth, to the universe, and to the beings and mysteries beyond the universe.

Now shift to sensing your true nature as love, offering your love to be of service to all beings.

May my actions be of love to relieve suffering of all beings.
May my actions be of love to kindly care for all beings.
May my actions be of love to support and bring happiness to all beings.
May my actions be of love to live in harmony and connection with all beings.

In the last few minutes of this practice, notice how love is Known, felt, and sensed within you and in everything around you. Close by offering gratitude for what has arisen in this practice.

At the end of the practice, reflect on and write about your insights or experiences.

Taking Care

The path of healing is a choice. Along this path, you have encountered and will continue to encounter beautiful experiences to be welcomed and integrated into your life. Whenever you feel, sense, and connect to a sense of embodiment, interconnection, curiosity, oneness, intuition, mystery, or love, welcome and stay with these experiences. They are the fruits of your healing, and they will illuminate the next steps of the path and awaken you to fully living and loving.

Part 4

HEALING NATURE

We are now in the mountains and they are in us,
kindling enthusiasm, making every nerve quiver,
filling every pore and cell of us.

— JOHN MUIR

Now that you are embodying healing, you have a

new capacity to offer healing to the world around you. As we heal, we discover new ways to live. Our enhanced sensitivity, presence, and openness naturally lead to a desire to take action. As nature has been a part of this healing journey — providing support, respite, reflection, release, beauty, and wisdom — you may feel an inclination to give back, to help nature and all life heal too.

This beautiful and wise Earth needs our help. She is under constant assault from our ways of living and taking from her. We have grown into a culture that only takes from the planet rather than developing a relationship of balance and reciprocity with other life. These assaults are leaving this Earth scarred, wounded, and traumatized. She needs us to establish ways of living and interacting that will help her to heal.

The Earth has suffered from our ignorance, our greed, and our delusion that we can continue to take from her without attending to the damage we cause. In every moment, we harm the Earth with pollution of the air, destruction of land and water, deforestation, industrialization, generation of waste, and carbon dioxide and other greenhouse gas emissions. These actions affect every living creature and organism on Earth, including humans.

The practices you have explored up to this point have focused on transforming your own trauma with the support of the natural world. The trauma that was once stored in your body is transformed into energy that can redefine your relationship with all life. Healing allows reciprocity and gratitude to emerge, opening your heart into a new way of engagement with life.

You can be part of healing the Earth's trauma. You can awaken into feeling her pain. With compassion and care, you can discover how you are inspired and drawn to help heal the traumas the Earth is facing. This action may take the form of helping your family, friends, or work or spiritual communities in their healing of wounds and trauma. Or you may feel drawn to heal the Earth's trauma by taking part in global action to mitigate climate change. You may feel called to live with more care and compassion for nature, exploring sustainable ways of living. The mystery of your healing, and the support of nature in establishing new aliveness, health, and wholeness within you, can guide you in finding ways to help and heal other life.

Listening closely to the needs and messages of this Earth can awaken you to action, enabling you to be part of what sustains and allows all life to thrive. You are one with the Earth, part of the healing, sustainability, regeneration, and transformation of us all.

In the coming chapters, I invite you to dedicate the power and unique light of your healed heart, mind, and body to the possibilities of helping to heal nature — to find ways to offer the gifts that have unveiled themselves to you, through your healing, to the healing of the Earth.

Chapter 13

HEALING *to* HEAL
CONNECTIONS

We need to wake up and fall in love with the Earth. Our personal and collective happiness and survival depend on it.

— Thích Nhất Hạnh

Have you fallen in love with some aspect of nature, of the Earth, as you have been healing? Maybe it's the soft breezes that gently cradle your body, the blue sky that helps you see into the vastness of possibility, or the sweet touch of a plant gracing you with its presence. Likely there have been countless instances of your heart opening to the care and tenderness nature has been offering you on this journey.

Has nature helped you to love yourself differently, to appreciate your trauma, to Know the deep wisdom in the natural instinct of all life to heal and to be alive, interconnected, and mutually supportive? Your healing is a gift you have cultivated for yourself with the support of nature. Knowing how to care for and love yourself and show kindness to your trauma, you can now support the healing of others.

Loving-kindness practices invite us to radiate and extend love to all beings. As an extension of these practices, you can learn to offer your trauma healing in intentional ways to support the healing of your family, friends, and communities and all beings on the planet. By sharing your healing, you can transform and deepen these relationships. As awareness grows, trauma is healed, and you awaken to deep connections to yourself and to nature herself. When you are fully present and you have released the reactive habits and the trauma narrative that were limiting your participation in life, you have the capacity to extend this healing to your family, friends, communities, and other beings on the planet.

Before starting this journey, you may have had difficulty viewing yourself as healthy or engaging in healthy living. You may have also had difficulties connecting with others or maintaining healthy interactions. You may have been too numb or overwhelmed to see beyond your immediate survival. This is how we attempt to manage trauma when we don't know another way.

As you heal, you become more loving, open, caring, compassionate, and able to support and heal others and nature herself. As nature has offered her love to aid your healing, can you offer your healing love back to all of nature? Since we are all of nature, can you learn to extend this love in all directions, to all beings?

Breathe, and begin where you are. The possibilities discussed here for healing others may touch you, inspire you, uplift you. Some may create new currents of angst or challenge within you. Let these moments be the starting points for the next phase of your healing journey, one that involves healing others as well as yourself.

Family and Lineage

The experience of trauma can disrupt the relationships with family, friends, and communities, especially if you feel they failed to support you when you were in need. We have already explored ways to redefine these relationships and your view of yourself in the context of these relationships. Using this understanding, you can explore new ways to connect with the people closest to you.

Your family may be a source of your trauma. And it may be the place to explore the full possibilities of your healing. As a part of this family, you now have the opportunity to shift and change it.

Even if this family is no longer with you, or you have chosen not to engage directly with family members, what would it look like to interact with them now? The following exercise invites you to imagine your whole, healthy, resourced self in the presence of this family. Consider starting with one of the practices you have already learned to establish a sense of inner groundedness, strength, or presence — whatever you feel might be helpful. Take care, be kind. There is no rush.

Reflection: Healthy Being

Consider an aspect of nature you have connected to recently that reveals to you your whole, healthy being: maybe a tall, strong, vibrant tree, an expansive blue sky, or a stream of water flowing gracefully over boulders. Sense its qualities in your body.

Now imagine how you might express these qualities of your being in the presence of your family. What would you say to them? How would you act? What resources would you have for navigating challenging interactions that might arise?

Imagine this whole, healthy being as an expression of vibrant nature moving through the terrain of your family. Journal about what arises.

Everyone in your lineage has walked their own path, one that likely included challenges that shaped the history of your trauma. Maybe your family struggled with poverty, mental health difficulties, oppression, traumas similar to yours, or different traumas. Some of the struggles they endured may be known, and others may be forever unknown. You cannot change the past, but you can influence your family's future trajectory through your healing. Learning to not carry forward any reactive, survival-based patterns of engagement that may have been passed down in your family is a way of offering healing. Before engaging in the following reflection exercise, take a few minutes to practice one of the meditations you have learned that supports you in feeling rooted, connected, alive, or invigorated.

Reflection: Whole Ecosystem

Bring to mind the image of your family. This might be your immediate family — parents, siblings, children, partner — or your extended family, including aunts, uncles, grandparents, and great-grandparents. You may also want to include as many ancestors as you can call to mind who represent the cultures you are connected to — your ethnic origins, religion, communities, societies.

Holding this lineage in awareness, imagine a natural ecosystem you feel connected to: a deep canyon, a quiet lake, or a mountain vista, and all its living and nonliving components.

Now imagine how parts of this ecosystem reflect different aspects of your lineage. Who in your family is represented by the energy sources, the living organisms, the nonliving systems, the decay? How are you represented in this ecosystem?

Now imagine how your whole, healthy being is influencing the health of this ecosystem. Are you inviting new light, life, and nutrients, or dissolving into this system to allow it to heal and grow?

Let yourself feel what it's like to connect to your lineage in this way. Can you see how the healed ecosystem is nurturing new growth? Journal about what arises.

From a place of healing, you can see ways to shift your role in your family and support its health. To share the full benefits of your healing requires engaging with family members. At times these interactions may be challenging or not as deep or meaningful as you desire. The following are suggestions for integrating mindful communication practices into interactions with family:

- At the moment of communication or engagement, pause before speaking.
- Practice grounding and pendulating practices as you engage in difficult interactions, before and after you speak.
- Listen to others with kind engagement; notice any reactivity or judgment arising, and invite yourself to let go of it.
- Open your mind and heart to what is being said.
- Share what is true for you in that moment.

Drawing on the practices you have learned thus far can also help in connecting with family members. The following are some ways to share these practices:

- Take a walk or spend time in nature with a family member.
- Consider sharing some of the practices you've learned, or choose a practice to engage in as you connect with a family member.
- Consider sharing a meaningful topic, activity, or sign of appreciation that has arisen from your healing (e.g., by talking to your family about nature, mindfulness, or somatic healing; engaging in touch with family that feels clear and connected; expressing gratitude for parts of your life with them).

As your healing progresses, you will find wholesome and healthy ways to create new relationships with your family. If trauma begets more trauma, healing can also beget more healing. Trust that healing will unfold in the family you are a part of.

Communities of Connection

We are all connected to multiple communities — not only our family but also communities with whom we work; with whom we share interests, beliefs, histories, or circumstances; or with whom we participate in bringing about change. A strong community can deepen healing, both in ourselves and in the systems we are part of. Identifying the communities to which you feel most connected may be a way to support others in healing.

Eli's Story (Continued)

We met Eli in chapter 10. The story there ended when Eli was approached by the FBI to take action against the person who had abused him. With the confidence gained from his healing, Eli chose to participate in this process in order to find justice and reconciliation.

Through the investigation, Eli developed a new relationship with the school where his abuse had taken place, one that brought healing for both Eli and the school.

Eli shared his experience openly during the investigation. He met with members of the school board and school communities to help them bring about changes that would protect their students: instituting policies and practices to ensure students could speak up about sexual abuse without fear of rejection or retribution, creating sexual abuse awareness education and support programs, and establishing a mental health wellness center on campus.

Eli continues to share his experience with individuals and communities that have been affected by similar traumas. The transformation of his trauma into advocacy and support for others has not only enabled him to help others but also supported his own healing journey.

Your own healing may lend you special capacities to help those afflicted with similar challenges. If you have experienced oppression and racism, you may choose to offer your voice and experience to help your workplace or city heal the wounds of prejudice. If you have experienced a natural disaster, you may choose to offer your firsthand knowledge to help a community recover. As you engage in the healing of others, remember to care for yourself by practicing a meditation that helps you feel interconnection or oneness.

Reflection: Community Connection

Is there a particular community that lights up your heart and calls to your being? What connections do you feel with this community? What pain, challenges, values, and successes do you share?

In your mind's eye, picture all the beings of this community standing in a circle in a beautiful, supportive environment in nature. Imagine the community as one consciousness, one being, within nature. Think of one or two words that represent your connection.

Let these words point you in the direction of how to stand and voice the support needed for this community. Journal about what arises from this reflection.

While you may feel inherently connected to communities whose members share your history or interests, you may also be inspired to offer your support and presence to a different community. The Black Lives Matter movement is a recent and beautiful awakening of US culture to help heal generations of trauma endured by the Black community. We can use our practices of healing to understand how we can most effectively offer support to others who have been oppressed and marginalized. I am a privileged white woman with a history of trauma and healing from trauma; I also hold within me the trauma my ancestors may have inflicted on others. I have vowed the following to help support this community in healing:

- I vow to heal my ancestral trauma — the trauma inflicted by my race on the black community, indigenous people, and people of color.
- I vow to be more aware of what I represent to others who have experienced trauma inflicted by generations of people like me.
- I vow to support the healing of trauma within the communities of black, indigenous, and people of color, honoring what feels helpful and respectful to their needs.

When we allow trauma to remain stuck and unhealed in our nervous systems, it seeps into our community and social systems. This causes deep unconscious patterns and beliefs to operate within our cultural collective. Healing our individual trauma, feeling our deep connections to one another, can inspire, support, transform, and heal others. You, and the healing you embody, can be a part of this change.

Places You Inhabit

Where do you live now? What do you know about the land you inhabit? What life has existed here before you? How have the landforms, living things, and people shaped this place? How is this land now being supported or harmed by the ways humans inhabit it?

These might be questions you haven't been able to give a lot of mental space to in the past. When we are coping with trauma challenges, our focus is typically on survival, limiting our capacity and desire to explore the connections to our land and how we live in it. Also, most Westernized cultures have been taught and shown how to live *off* the land rather than *with* the land, leading to denial, disregard, and disconnection from nature.

As you heal from your trauma, you can begin to feel your intimate connections to the land you inhabit and are a part of. By using the skills you have learned for mindful and somatic connection to nature, you can enter into a new relationship with the place where you live. Before exploring the following reflection exercise, practice one of the meditations you have learned that helps you feel connected and present to the qualities of nature around you.

Reflection: History of Inhabited Land

Consider doing some research about what and who has inhabited the place where you are now living — over the past ten years, thirty years, one hundred years, and one thousand years. Imagine the plant life, the insects, the wildlife, the previous human inhabitants, the geographic features. How has all of this changed over time? What has remained? What has disappeared? How long have you been present in this landscape? How long have the various forms of nature been present in this landscape? Journal about what arises.

Reflecting on the conditions that have prevailed over a long period allows us to contemplate the evolution of the terrain and climate and the beings that have adapted themselves to life here. It can also show us the pain and hurt inflicted by human habits of consumption and extraction. Consider ways to expand your healing into the connection and protection of your land that has given you healing.

Practice: Neighborhood Nature Walk

Spend twenty to thirty minutes walking in the area where you live. What is the terrain like? What expressions of nature and the land support you? How do you inhabit this land? Who and what lives with you here? Stop and connect to what arises in your body, mind, and heart. Walk slowly, mindful of your breath, body, and senses.

Start by walking in the outdoor space around your home — your patio, out the front door, behind your apartment building, your backyard. Look for the insect life — where do the spiders, ants, and beetles reside? What do their homes look like? Consider the wildlife — birds, rodents, reptiles — where do they reside, and how do they make their home here? Where and how do the plants establish themselves? How do the soil, hills, and rocks make their presence felt? Curiously, slowly, intimately connect to all that is here.

Now extend your walk a few blocks around your neighborhood — or farther, if you choose. Observe all the life here. Reflect on one plant or patch of grass growing near your home. Where did the plant come from, how did it grow, and how is it establishing itself here? Now expand your reflection to all the plants, the wildlife, and the land itself.

As you move through the landscape, ask, How is it thriving? Who cares for the land and all beings within it? How are different kinds of life exchanging the forms of air (oxygen, nitrogen, carbon dioxide) they need in order to thrive? Where and how do the living things in this neighborhood obtain water? How are the warmth and light of the sun helping these beings to grow? Reflect on the web of support that connects all the people and living things here.

At the end of your walk, sit for a few minutes in a place you feel drawn to. Become aware of your breath and your body in this moment. Placing a hand on the ground, reflect and connect to all of the beings and life that have come before you here — the people, cultures, and species that have evolved in and with this land. Open your heart to feel the history of the land.

On returning home, take a few moments to feel and connect to what awareness of the land and its inhabitants has awakened in your mind, heart, and body. Close by offering gratitude for your practice and whatever has arisen in it, and for the land.

You may choose to journal about your insights or experiences.

As an act of healing, you may want to seek ways to support your land more intentionally in your daily life. You might consider cutting back on activities that pollute the land or air, or explore sustainable water use. You might choose to learn about practices that heal the land, mitigate climate change, and restore biodiversity, like regenerative agriculture, to encourage the planting of native species and plants that attract beneficial insects near your home, and to participate in efforts to protect sensitive local habitats.

Efforts to heal, sustain, and nurture the land can begin where we live. We can choose to learn more about the land we inhabit, become more intimately connected to it, and harness the energy of our healed trauma to help heal the land. Changes like this will ripple into larger communities, regions, and countries, and hopefully across the entire globe.

Beings on the Planet

There are seventy-five billion tons of living things (biomass) on the Earth. So far, 1.5 million species of plants, animals, fungi, lichen, and bacteria have been documented, with more being discovered every day.[1] This is almost an incomprehensible amount of life, and all of it is important and interconnected. Human sensitivity, compassion, and action are important to the survival of this life and of the Earth.

Human beings in the industrialized age have become disconnected from nature, and this disconnection is taking a toll on other life on this planet. Many species have been lost forever because of human activity, and the number of species under threat of extinction continues to grow. As of 2020, the International Union for Conservation of Nature (IUCN) Red List included thirty-two thousand threatened species.[2] According to one website, the biggest environmental problems in 2020 were poor governance, food waste, biodiversity loss, plastic pollution, deforestation, air pollution, agriculture, global warming from fossil fuels, melting ice caps, and food and water insecurity.[3] These phenomena threaten all the beings who inhabit this Earth.

What can we do to help? The task of healing the Earth and its beings can seem overwhelming. Once again, it begins with your own healing and what is arising in your heart and mind. If you were touched and healed by a tree, maybe you can consider supporting tree life in your community. If you were graced by a beautiful insect or wild animal, maybe you can look into how to protect its habitat and way of life. If you feel drawn to a particular form of aquatic life, bird life, insect life, or animal life in your community, you may want to care for its habitat by adopting more intentional ways of living.

You may also feel called to support the healing of these beings in a more activist way. This begins with knowledge, learning more about what is happening to the planet and its inhabitants. There are many groups devoted to specific aspects of environmental protection that can offer information and ways to become involved. You may also want to learn about what you can do on a daily basis to support threatened species in your location.

You can also direct your healing practices to supporting the beings of this planet. You have the capacity to turn toward, not away from, the pain they are enduring. Using mindful somatic healing, you can remain present to the anger, grief, or sadness you experience when you hear of an act of harm to other beings. You can ground yourself as a way of preparing to learn how you can help these beings heal and thrive. Practicing compassion for all the beings harmed by our disconnected relationship to nature can support their healing and survival.

Healing Continues

As you explore ways to support the healing of others in your family, community, and environment, it's important to keep attending to your own healing as well. Each reflection exercise in this chapter encourages you to begin with the meditation practices you have learned before you extend support to others. The ability to bear witness to and feel compassion for other beings' pain and trauma is a natural product of your healing. But with compassionate presence to their suffering will likely come pain, sadness, grief, loss, worry, and fear, all of which require you to continue with your own healing practices. Drawing on the capacities you have developed for embodiment, curiosity, interconnection, intuition, love, and a sense of mystery will help you maintain healthy engagement with others and help them to awaken and heal.

Chapter 14

LIVING *with* INTEGRITY

Each one of us matters, has a role to play, and makes a difference. Each one of us must take responsibility for our own lives, and above all, show respect and love for living things around us, especially each other.

— Jane Goodall

As you heal from trauma, you will feel a natural impulse to live in a new relationship with yourself, with other people, and with nature. This may take the form of attempting to live more ethically, pursuing healthy activities, or choosing to act with integrity in all you do. Healing enables you to follow your moral compass — to live wholesomely and with intention — and this in turn supports the integrity and health of the planet.

Our actions on this Earth matter. We are part of a living system that seeks to maintain homeostasis, just as our individual bodies, hearts, and minds do. Our lack of sensitivity, awareness, and care of the Earth has disrupted its ability to maintain and regulate itself.

We are nature; nature is part of us. By living in awareness of this relationship, we can make a real and immediate contribution to healing the Earth, and in turn we will experience a connection with the Earth that deepens our own healing. The goal of your healing journey has been to restore health, wholeness, and full capacity to your life. Can you now commit to offering the same to this living Earth?

Living Ethically

Every culture has morals, values, and rules to enable its members to support one another and interact skillfully. These include the laws of the city, state, and country where we live; religious or spiritual precepts; and inherited and cultural values. All of these help us to live in harmony.

Many subcultures have narrower and more specific ethical codes. During a traditional Buddhist silent meditation retreat, for example, participants are asked to accept the five precepts established for Buddhist laypeople. These include a commitment to abstain from killing or harming any living beings, from stealing or taking anything that hasn't been given freely, from harmful speech or lying, from sexual misconduct (in thoughts as well as overt behavior), and from intoxication in any form (such as alcohol, drugs, or media consumption). These agreements create a sense of safety, mutual regard, and care for all life in the community. They are an inspiring model for daily life.

It can be helpful to consider what ethical principles and actions inform and support your healing from trauma. Without the need to engage in fight, flight, or freeze behavior to survive, we have the capacity to live differently. Living a life guided by moral and ethical values can help to sustain and maintain our well-being.

Reflection: Ethical Daily Living

How do the five Buddhist precepts support your way of living, or how might they do so? List a few daily actions you might take to live in harmony with each precept.

• What actions can you take to avoid harming yourself or other beings? (Examples: eating healthy foods, engaging in healthy exercise or movement, not killing insects, following a vegetarian diet.)

- How can you share wealth and avoid taking from others? (Examples: offering unneeded food, clothes, or money, not buying more than you need, knowing where your food and clothing come from and the conditions under which they were produced.)

- How can you support being truthful and honest in your life and avoid speech that is harmful or hurtful to yourself or others? (Examples: speaking kind words to yourself and others, not saying things that cause harm, speaking from your heart, speaking what is true for you even if it is difficult.)

- How can you protect, respect, and care for your sexuality? (Examples: regarding your body as sacred, worthy of honor and respect; not engaging in sexualized language or unskillful actions.)

- How can you protect your mind from intoxicants and harmful influences? (Examples: being mindful about consuming substances or media content that may dull, disinhibit, or taint the mind.)

Living according to these precepts can bring more ease, health, and harmony to your life and to those around you.

Practice: Investigating the Five Precepts with Nature

Spend twenty to thirty minutes in a place where you can feel the sacredness of life — a special location you know well, or a place where you feel particularly connected to the terrain, vegetation, or animal life. Walking, standing, sitting, or lying down, engage the senses to feel your connections with nature.

Settle into awareness of your internal landscape. Feel the contact of your body with the earth. Sense the groundedness and the stability of the earth; allow your body to feel alert, relaxed, and open. Sense the breath, breathing in and breathing out in concert with the sacred life around you. Bring awareness to your senses — hearing, smell, sight, touch. Feel the sensations of being alive in the body.

Bring awareness to the practice of holding all life in respect and regard. Where are you placing your feet? What have you stepped on or sat on? How do you respond when you encounter insects: do you swipe at them or become agitated or fearful? See if you can let go of any reactivity and meet them with kindness. Can you invite a sense of care as you touch, feel, and connect to the living things around you? Cultivate an inner sense of reverence, regard, and care for the life in this place.

Now shift to investigating a sense of reciprocity and taking nothing from this land that isn't offered freely. Notice the oxygen, the sounds, the majestic presence of trees and other plant life, the colors, the light, the playful movement of the elements — all gifts of the sacredness of life, offered freely to you. If you connect to a bush, a flower, or a tree, do you ask its permission to touch it or take its offering of leaves or petals? Can you offer respect to life that has evolved intricately to find its place in the land, taking nothing from it, leaving it just as it is? Let this feeling of reciprocity and support for the land be present within, helping you sense your place in the web of life.

Now move to allowing kind thoughts and speaking heartfully to the sacred life that is here with you. Are you judging or comparing the forms of life around you? Are you expressing a preference for one over another, or making harsh judgments? Consider offering kind words to all the life you are connected to now. You might bow or offer appreciation to the insects, the elements, the plant life, the sky, space; or you might repeat a mantra of "Thank you," "I see you," or "I care about you" as you connect to the beings and forms of energy around you, acknowledging that life is an exchange of compassion and kindness.

Shift to sensing how you can inhabit this sacred land with sensitivity and respect. Letting go of the idea of sexual misconduct, consider how your body is intimately participating in the life and terrain around you, moving with grace, ease, consideration, and respect. Sense how all life is thriving, reproducing, and moving in concert with the conditions in order to enable life to continue. Feel care and reverence for the life of this land.

Moving to the investigation of avoiding intoxication or pollution, consider for a moment what enables your body, mind, and heart to experience and participate in the life of this land, and what causes you to disconnect from it. Do you try to dull certain difficult thoughts, emotions, or bodily experiences with intoxicants or habits of distraction (for example, checking your phone or taking pictures rather than being with what is here in the land)? Do you get lost in thought, overwhelmed by daily tasks, or distracted by emotion? Consider how you can offer the gift of full awareness to all the expressions of life here. Feel how your gift of clarity and vitality connects you to this sacred land.

At the end of this practice, let your mind, heart, and body feel the benefits of ethical awareness and action and the way you are learning to live with respect, regard, and care for all life. You may want to consider focusing on some aspect of this practice and put it into action during the rest of your day.

Take a few moments to write about any insights experienced in this practice.

Living with the Earth

The resources of the Earth are finite. For years we have been warned by climate scientists that our survival depends on changing the way we live. There are many ways to live more harmoniously and less harmfully on this Earth, in a way that offers to nature your gratitude for her support in your healing.

Reflection: Living in Harmony with the Earth

Take a few moments to reflect on and respond to the following prompts:

- A path to healthy living with the Earth is...
- Some activities I could undertake to live more harmoniously with this Earth are...
- The relationship I choose to have with the Earth in my everyday life is...

You may want to return to these questions later and expand on your answers.

There are endless ways to give back to the Earth, support its health, and act on climate change through small daily actions. You may already have your own list. Here I offer a few simple ideas you might consider if you aren't already following them. You may also want to explore other ways to reduce your impact on the Earth that are in line with your healing path.

- Pick up trash when you see it.
- Carry a refillable water bottle instead of purchasing bottled water, and be conscious of your water consumption in daily life.
- Recycle containers and paper; limit your use of plastic containers by buying in bulk in reusable jars.
- Drive or fly less, take public transportation, purchase an energy-efficient or electric car, ride a bike, or walk for transport.
- Consider becoming vegan or vegetarian, and buy foods that are organic, non-GMO, and not chemically treated or processed.

Your actions matter: when others see your environmentally beneficial actions, even small ones, they will feel more compelled to engage in sustainable practices too.

It's likely that you have already adopted some habits that support and reduce your impact on the Earth. Wherever we are on this path, we can all continue to look for ways to help, deepening our own healing through our commitment to healing nature. You may want to volunteer with local conservation communities, grow some of your own food, learn about regenerative agriculture, donate money to organizations that support sustainability, or live off the grid.

We often hear that the actions of an individual can't do anything to prevent or reverse the destruction of this planet. This isn't true. Our way of living on this planet is akin to living in survival mode after trauma. We freeze, check out, or deny the need to change because we don't know another way to cope. Yet we know from healing individual trauma that we can wake up to a new way of living with integrity, intention, health, and wholeness. The same is true of healing nature.

Jacob's Story

Jacob sought support for his intention to live with more integrity and attention to his well-being and that of his family. He felt that his career in construction was leading to harm of the Earth and disconnection within himself, and he wanted to shift to something new.

Through mindful somatic nature healing practices, he gained insights into the oppressive presence of his inner critic, which had arisen from challenges associated with drug addiction and traumatic parental dynamics that undermined his self-worth.

During one somatic experiencing session, Jacob noted a tightness that he felt as an old weathered rope, covered in algae and seaweed, wrapped around his spine and chest. As we sat by the harbor and explored this experience, he realized that this was the bound energy of toxic and unhealthy relationships. He connected it to his fear of being seen as a failure and to a narrative of success that he had learned growing up. As he somatically attuned to this experience, he realized that his definition of success and failure could change.

He came to define success as providing for his family through love, emotional and spiritual support, and financial stability. He could live more simply with his family and adopt green practices in his construction work that would align more closely with his values.

Jacob left his career in conventional construction. He redirected his construction and business skills and his understanding of the building industry into offering construction services that support the health of the planet, his employees, and his clients. He wants to make an impact not only within the green construction sector but across the entire industry.

Finding a New Way

Change requires us to move toward discomfort and the unfamiliar. This is what your healing journey has entailed. You have learned how to turn inward, skillfully attending to your inner landscape. You have learned how to transform the reactive habits of your body, mind, and heart and to respond to challenging experiences with care and kindness. This healing enables you to step into a new way of living.

In the same way, you can step into new ways of living in alignment with your values of caring for yourself and the planet. You can start by becoming aware of the reactive habits that aren't supportive of wholesome ways of living. Rather than judging yourself for these habits, investigate why they are here and what purpose they have served. You can then ask what it might be like to move toward a new way of living: what discomfort, difficulty, and unfamiliar experiences you may have to encounter, and how you can use your mindfulness and somatic awareness nature practices to negotiate these challenges. Then you can develop a more conscious and connected way of living.

Reflection: Local Connection to Food

Choose a form of produce that you consume regularly. Reflect on how you typically purchase this produce. As best you can, try not to judge these habits (they have evolved for a reason — out of necessity, because you did not know another way, or because you are disconnected from food sources). Reflect on where your food comes from, when it was grown, the labor and agricultural practices that were used to grow it, and how many steps the produce goes through on its journey to your local store. Hold what arises with compassion, even if it is difficult. Now ask how you can relate to the produce in a new way. Can you take time to see, smell, feel, and taste this produce? Can you act in accordance with what is meaningful and important to you as you become aware of how it reached you? You might consider finding a local produce stand, becoming friends with a local farmer, or learning what produce is available at your grocery store that is in season and locally grown. Journal about what arises from this reflection.

To enable more ethical participation in daily life, here are some suggestions for changing automatic patterns in activities such as shopping, eating, and traveling:

- Slow down; notice where the automatic habits are arising. Let go of judging the habits; they developed for a reason.
- Experience the pleasantness or unpleasantness of the activity. Bring compassion to the difficulties of reactivity.
- Notice a new way of being and relating. Invite the senses and body to be present in the activity.
- Sense a way to participate in the activity while aligning to what's meaningful and important to you in your relationship with the planet.
- Experience living with integrity. Feel the effects of your actions in support of all life.

The acronym *SENSE*, formed by the first letters of these guidelines, can help us to be more sensitive and present to the ways we choose to live. Each new ethical action you bring into your life is a choice to deepen the healing of your trauma and to increase your capacity to know the intimacy, beauty, and goodness of all life.

Healing Continues

You are change in action. At every moment, you can strive to live in connection with all beings. Recognizing and believing in your capacity to transform your way of living will contribute to global healing and awaken a commitment to live with integrity and reciprocity on this Earth.

The journey of healing is ongoing. As you continue to practice the meditations you've learned and to live with a greater sense of integrity, you may discover new places to heal within, traumas you didn't know needed healing. You may also experience ways of living that you never dreamed would be a part of your journey. This is part of living an ethical, embodied life.

Your entire life contains possibilities for healing and insight. Take time, be patient, and allow your practices and your ethical choices to transform you and the way you live now and for the rest of your life. Let yourself live fully, in harmony with all life.

Chapter 15

HEALING *the* EARTH

This is a dark time, filled with suffering and uncertainty. Like living cells in a larger body, it is natural that we feel the trauma of our world. So don't be afraid of the anguish you feel, or the anger or fear, because these responses arise from the depth of your caring and the truth of your interconnectedness with all beings.

— Joanna Macy

As you have deepened your relationship with the Earth and relied on that relationship to help you heal your own trauma, you may have become more attuned to the natural world and thus more acutely aware of the traumas the Earth herself is suffering: environmental degradation, climate change, and all of the related harms and losses. Realizing your oneness with the Earth, you may even be feeling these traumas as your own. You can draw on your experiences of healing your own past traumas to see how to begin to heal the trauma that humans have inflicted on the Earth and the grief, fear, and anger you may feel in response to it.

In this chapter we will connect to our oneness and through this truth help heal the Earth.

Let Your Heart Break Open

On the last day of a silent meditation retreat, the teacher I was sitting with led us in a sunrise meditation. We sat in a field and meditated as the sun rose over the Sierra Nevada.

The field contained a herd of cows — maybe twenty mature cows and six or seven calves. Our teacher invited us to be present with them as part of the vista.

Perplexed, I think, by a group of seated humans, the calves wandered toward us in curiosity. These movements caused the mother cows to call anxiously after them. There was a symphony of cow conversation as we sat. The sunrise came and went, and the practice became a cow meditation, a practice of presence to these beings interacting with us.

As I sat, my eyes met the eyes of a mother cow. Time seemed to stop. I sensed intimately our connection: we were not separate but present to one another, honoring and respecting life. I sensed and became present to this mother cow's angst and fear of our possible exploitation of her young and their probable fate; feeling a deep understanding of their needs, I wept and wept. My heart broke open to the need to care for all life. I vowed at that moment never to eat an animal again.

As you have cultivated your healing with nature and closely observed the state of the Earth, it's likely that you too have felt pain for the traumas she has experienced. Knowing that the challenges the Earth is facing stem from thousands of years of human greed, extraction of natural resources, and oppression of other beings, we may be left feeling helpless, believing our actions have little significance. This perspective can lead us to turn away and do nothing, keeping us complicit with the ever-worsening consequences and tuning out the reality that our lives and the life of this planet are at stake.

For most of us, an attitude of complacency or indifference toward the Earth's pain is a reactive pattern that allows us to cope with potentially overwhelming anxiety and sorrow. As we explored at the beginning of this book, traumatic reactive patterns are survival based: they are how we cope if we don't know any other way. Let yourself become curious about the reactive patterns you have used to cope with the challenges the Earth is facing or your feelings about them. Maybe you feel disconnected, or maybe you've adopted a pattern of denial or disregard.

On the journey to heal your trauma, you have learned that the first step is to recognize your reactive patterns. You have learned how to move toward the pain of the trauma rather than turn away, resist, deny, or avoid. So let your heart break open to feel the distress of the Earth. Becoming aware of and present to this pain is the first step in finding ways to relate to it and to act to heal the Earth's traumas.

Reflection: Feeling the Pain of the Earth

Reflect on any pain you notice related to the trauma the Earth is experiencing. Maybe you grieve over how species are being lost and habitats destroyed, or over pollution or weather extremes. Be curious about any tendency you may have to try to avoid feeling or acknowledging this pain. Are you pushing it away, checking out, resisting, rationalizing, feeling resignation?

Now reflect on how you might let your heart break open to the pain of the Earth. How can you use the practices of your trauma healing to be present to the pain, the fear, the uncertainty, the anger, the denial, the grief? Can you explore what this feels like in your body? What sensations are present? Meet whatever arises in the body, mind, or heart with kindness. Take a few moments to write about what you have experienced in this reflection.

Staying with the Pain of the Earth

My cow meditation allowed me to be present to and feel the cows' sense of fear and angst and the intensity of this within me and with them. What arose from that moment was an embodied feeling of connection beyond any intellectual conclusion my mind could have come up with. Using the practices we have developed to heal our own trauma, we can face and heal our sense of ecological trauma and the trauma of the Earth.

The environmental activist Joanna Macy, a scholar of Buddhism, general systems theory, and deep ecology, has developed an approach to healing the Earth that she calls "the work that reconnects." She describes the process as a spiral.[1] It begins with gratitude. When we feel appreciation for the Earth, we can connect to her differently. Gratitude gives rise to honoring the Earth's pain. Through this compassion, we develop an understanding of what needs to be helped and healed. We can see with "new/ancient eyes" how we are inextricably connected to all that is. With this sense of connection, we can harness our power to help our Earth heal. In the final twist of the spiral, we go forth and use our situations, gifts, strengths, and limitations to guide us into ways of helping to heal the Earth.

Let's begin this spiral with a reflection on gratitude for the journey of healing.

Reflection: Gratitude for the Earth

Reflect on what nature, this Earth, has offered in support of your journey of healing from trauma. Maybe you are grateful for a deeper sense of the presence of the wind and how it supports your body; maybe for the security you feel from being held by the Earth; or for the way birdsong awakens life within you. How do you give thanks and feel gratitude for the Earth and what has supported you? You might express this gratitude through a gesture, a bow, or an offering of thanks. Take a few moments to write about what you observed during this reflection.

Through gratitude for your healing, you can begin to explore your feelings of ecological trauma — the pain of the loss of ecosystems and species, or climate distress. We might grieve over the devastation of wild-fire aggravated by climate change. Experiencing the effects of pollution may cause us physical, mental, and emotional pain. Or we may feel hope-less when we consider the disconnection within our society and the way it damages our personal, social, and environmental health.

Ecological trauma can be experienced as a double trauma. We feel the traumatic pain not only of the ecological crisis on our species but also of knowing that we humans are the cause. This realization is part of turning toward the trauma. Exploring the connections between our suffering and that of the Earth can give rise to a stronger intention to help in the healing.

We know that unhealed trauma begets more trauma. We also know from our own healing that we can stop and heal the reactive habits of trauma. The deep interconnection of our trauma and the planet's creates new possibilities for healing. Our awareness, intentions, and actions can break the cycle.

Reflection: Healing the Earth

What aspects of the traumatic pain the Earth is experiencing touch your heart most deeply? Why? Do you feel pain for yourself, your family, or your community? Do you feel compassion for the suffer-ing of nature? Do you feel intimately connected to and healed by nature? Take a few moments to write about your reflections.

As you respond to these questions, connect to what arises within your body. Do you feel a sense of contraction, ache, pain, tightening, tension, heaviness? Notice and stay present to these sensations. If you find yourself becoming reactive, wanting to grasp onto, figure out, avoid, withdraw, resist, deny, or question things, can you see these responses as opportunities to simply stay with what is arising, being kindly present to it all and curious about where it leads?

You may experience a new type of movement in the body, a healing emotional response, or an inspiring new thought. You may feel an impulse to express deep gratitude, offer amends, or perform a small, compassionate act of healing. Continue to use the healing practices you have learned to aid in the investigation and healing of the Earth's trauma. Take a few moments to write about your experiences during this reflection.

Caring for the Earth

The tenderness you may feel as you explore the pain of ecological trauma is the heart's willingness to feel and offer compassion for what has been done to the Earth and what continues to cause her pain. Meeting and staying with the pain invites something new to emerge — the possibility of change in our relationship to ourselves, to others, and to the Earth.

Practice: Forgiveness for the Earth's Ecological Trauma

This practice explores forgiveness for our collective responsibility for ecological trauma, for the ways our lack of knowledge and awareness may have contributed to harming the Earth. In this practice, we invite awareness to awaken and connect to the pain of ecological trauma.

You may choose to start with just one part of this meditation and progressively expand it. The phrases offered are to be recited inwardly. Allow what arises to be held with care and in loving awareness. Remember, forgiveness is not to be forced: it is the capacity of the heart to freely offer compassion.

Spend ten to twenty minutes in a place where you can feel the pain and trauma the Earth is experiencing — a polluted or degraded landscape, a dump, near trash in nature or in your house. Choose a comfortable posture, walking, standing, sitting, or lying down.

Begin by feeling the breath in your body as you inhale and

exhale. Steady awareness on the movements, the rhythms, and the sense of ease or relaxation in the breath.

Now shift awareness to sensations of groundedness, ease, calm, and relaxation in the body. Become curious about the sensations arising and passing in the body.

Bring awareness to any barriers of reactivity or sense of disconnection in your heart in relation to the traumatic pains of the Earth (e.g., exploitation or overuse of resources) — any pain, numbness, tightening, aching, sadness, fear, grief, or anxiety.

Breathing softly and with ease, extend forgiveness to yourself and humanity for this sense of disconnection from and contribution to ecological trauma. Notice any images, emotions, or embodied feelings that arise.

First, offer forgiveness to yourself by repeating the following sentences:

There are many ways I have chosen to deny, resist, and turn away from seeing the harm of the Earth, my community, and myself.
For the ways I have turned away from the trauma of the Earth, I extend full and heartfelt forgiveness to myself.

Continuing to contemplate the ways you may have turned away from the pain and trauma of the Earth, offer yourself kindness and forgiveness for your lack of understanding or mistakes you have made.

Next, ask forgiveness from the Earth by repeating the following sentences:

There are many possible ways I have misunderstood and been disconnected from this Earth.
For the many ways I have knowingly or unknowingly caused harm or pain, I ask forgiveness.

Looking around you at the damaged landscape, acknowledge the ways in which you have contributed to the Earth's traumas. Let yourself feel the fear, confusion, regret, sorrow, shame, or guilt. As these feelings move into awareness, continue to ask forgiveness.

Now turn to sensing and feeling the environmental harm caused by others. To the extent that you are ready, feel the despair, sorrow, anger, confusion, and fear and the wounding of body, mind, and heart that you have suffered through the harm inflicted on the Earth, and offer forgiveness by repeating the following:

> *I offer my forgiveness to you for the harm you cause me and this Earth. I remember the many ways others cause harm out of denial, pain, confusion, disconnection, and despair, and I offer forgiveness.*

Continue as best you can, in small and manageable ways, to offer expressions of forgiveness as you encounter pain and trauma resulting from harm inflicted by others on the Earth. No matter what arose in this practice, invite a kind and caring response to what is here. To close the practice, offer gratitude to yourself for the goodness of your practice and your willingness to care for your heart and the Earth in this way.

You might choose to write in your journal about any insights or experiences you encountered in this practice.

Through the healing of your personal trauma with mindfulness and somatic practices in nature, you have developed a close connection with the Earth. This connection enables you to use the unique qualities of your being to help her heal. Let yourself continue to explore what emerges from this way of connecting to the Earth to support our collective healing.

Going Forth with Fierce Gratitude

If the world is to be healed through human efforts, I am convinced it will be by ordinary people, people whose love for this life is even greater than their fear. People who can open to the web of life that called us into being.

— Joanna Macy

When we sense the heart's capacity to be touched, cared for, and healed by this Earth, what naturally arises is a profound sense of reverence and gratitude for her healing energy. A sense of fierce gratitude allows us to reciprocate this gift by responding to the Earth's pain with actions that will make a difference. Amid the pain, trauma, and suffering of the planet we can find a sense of hope and true potential for change.

There are many steps we can take as individuals to live in a more skillful and reciprocal relationship to the Earth. To have a greater impact requires that people come together in community, sharing our fierce gratitude, reverence, and love for this Earth. Fierce gratitude is a heartfelt and powerful way to respond with actions that show appreciation and return kindness to the Earth for the support and healing energy she provides. When we act with fierce gratitude the ripple effect of change can stream into the healing of the Earth.

Many groups around the globe have formed to support the healing of the Earth and mitigate the effects of climate change. You may want to learn more about some of these groups, participate in their activities, or support their work with donations. Some of the more notable organizations are the Sierra Club, the World Wildlife Fund, Earth First, Greenpeace, the National Wildlife Federation, the Forest Stewardship Council, the Rainforest Action Network, the Nature Conservancy, Friends of the Earth, the Intergovernmental Panel on Climate Change, the International Union for Conservation of Nature, the Wildlife Conservation Society, and the National Geographic Society.[2]

A few groups that I want to highlight are 350.org, Extinction Rebellion, One Earth Sangha, and the Work That Reconnects Network. (For links to these groups' websites, see the resources section at the back of the book.) Each of these groups embraces intentional ways to move toward and heal the challenges and ecological traumas of our planet.

350.org is an international movement of people working to end the age of fossil fuels and build a world of community-led renewable energy generation for all. As their website states, they seek "a safe climate and a better future that is just, prosperous and equitable, built by the power of ordinary people." They demand "a fast and just transition to 100% renewable energy for all, no fossil fuel projects anywhere, and not a penny more for dirty energy."

Extinction Rebellion is a global, decentralized, politically nonpartisan movement that has engaged in nonviolent direct action and civil disobedience to persuade governments to act justly on the climate and ecological emergency. They demand that governments tell the truth about the climate and ecological emergency, act now to halt biodiversity loss, reduce greenhouse gas emissions to net zero by 2025, and go beyond politics to allow citizens to assemble on behalf of climate and ecological justice.

One Earth Sangha brings the wisdom and practices of the Buddhist teachings to a collective engagement with the ecological crisis. On the premise that the Buddhist tradition offers significant resources that can support action on the world's interrelated ecological and social crises, it supports the practice of mindfulness in the context of Sangha (spiritual community) to apply these teachings to heal the collective suffering of the planet. It asserts that activism is most effective and sustainable when rooted in mindfulness and compassion and that social engagement is a part of the spiritual path. It offers training, events, and a global sangha for growing and deepening the practice of mindfulness in relationship to ecological crises.

The Work That Reconnects Network, based on the work of Joanna Macy, helps people transform their views of challenge, disconnection, and pain into healing. It seeks to enable people to discover and experience their innate connections with all of life, to see the self-healing powers of the web of life, and to transform despair and overwhelm into inspired and collaborative action. Macy has developed many teachings and experiential exercises to support awareness of the needs of the Earth and efforts to address them. In her teaching and many books, she has proposed frameworks and paradigms to help us understand how we can actively support one another and heal the Earth. The Work That Reconnects Network offers training and resources to help us collaborate in caring for this Earth.

Whichever community or other mode of action speaks to you, follow your heart. The light of fierce gratitude will lead you to new and inspiring ways of healing within and allow you to be a part of the bigger changes needed to heal this planet.

At the end of the sunrise meditation described earlier in this chapter, I experienced another moment of heartbreak. We had just broken the silence of the retreat, and I was sharing some of my experiences over the week with my group. When we were finished, I looked out toward the Sierra Nevada. In the midmorning light, I saw an ashen haze enveloping the peaks and the valleys below. Particles of pesticides, fertilizers, and fossil fuels filled the air, stifling the trees, the bird and animal life, all life. Knowing the impact of agricultural pollution from my childhood, my heart ached for the harm we humans are inflicting on all life, including ourselves, and I cried. I took another vow in that moment to commit to helping others awaken, through their own healing, to help heal this Earth. From that vow came this book.

Healing Continues

Feeling the traumas of our Earth and our collective is a radical act of compassion. It takes a fierce love to walk toward this intense pain. As we do so, our healing journey continues and deepens. Harnessing the wisdom of your healing to support the healing of our Earth is a beautiful and bountiful gift.

The word *Earth* is an anagram for *heart*. To me there is a beautiful and synchronous mystery in this. The Earth's love, care, kindness, compassion, and interconnected life allow us to know we are all one heart, one Earth. Go forth with a full heart on your journey to help heal this planet.

Chapter 16

TRUSTING *the* MYSTERY

If you wish to know the divine, feel the wind on your face and the warm sun on your hand.

— Buddha

This life is a mystery, a constant unfolding of the unknown. As you heal, you sense your true being, ready for whatever life will bring. You feel a willingness to trust your heart in following what it loves. It may lead you to different types of healing, to spirituality, and to recognizing your calling in life.

Often the stuck energy of unhealed trauma limits the ways we can experience life. As you have transformed your experiences of trauma, you have probably experienced a sense of blooming. Maybe you now experience simple joys more fully, noticing that the touch of a cool breeze brings contentment and ease. Maybe you have felt greater confidence and security in your friendships, family life, or work as you have become less reactive and more aware. Or maybe you have come into a deeper and more spiritual relationship with nature. The energy released from your trauma now allows you to access your whole, fully alive self in which to live, experiencing new encounters and explorations in your life.

And this life is part of the beautiful web that encompasses all of nature, every creature, system, landscape, element, and energy force. Your being is inextricably linked to all of this, part of the dance and mystery.

There is no end to the healing or this journey. It is always unfolding and deepening. This chapter suggests ways that you can continue to explore and delight in the mystery of life.

Nature's Energy Connections

Energy fuels life. It is essential for all life in order to form, grow, thrive, and evolve. A flower seed is formed by energy consumed by the parent plant; the seed draws energy from the sun and the soil as it sprouts, blooms, and produces seed in its turn. When it dies, it returns energy to the Earth. This seed's plant ancestors, the elements, and the conditions of time and the seasons all influence the qualities of its energy.

Awareness of nature's different energies can help you connect more deeply with what is around you. We may feel the stillness of a tall tree, the quiet of a snowy forest, or the uplift of an expansive sky; in those moments we can sense the resonance of the energy that is present within us and all around in nature.

While forms of energy and energy exchange can be understood in scientific terms (and these are helpful to learn about), this chapter explores the qualities of energy in nature that bring teaching and healing.

Plants, Trees, and Flowers

One manifestation of nature's energy is the medicinal properties of plants, long known to herbalists and practitioners of traditional medicine. The chamomile flower is well known for its ability to relieve stress and aid sleep when it is made into a tea. It also has many other healing properties, like lowering blood sugar, reducing the risk of osteoporosis, reducing inflammation, supporting cancer treatment, alleviating cold symptoms, and relieving mild skin conditions.[1] It's amazing how one little flower can offer so much healing. The same is true for many plants, lichens, and mushrooms. The natural world is full of healing energy. Learning to feel, sense, and absorb the goodness of the energy of plant life offers healing and deeper connections to nature.

Reflection: Connecting to Plant Energies

Think of a plant that has touched you in your journey of healing. Find a place where this plant grows, or hold it in your mind's eye. Think about how its leaves or petals are formed, the forms of the stems or branches, the place where it touches the Earth, the roots reaching down into the soil.

What form of energy do you feel is present in this plant? Is it a gentle, quiet, slow energy; a vibrant, robust energy; or a delicate, graceful, light energy? Imagine the energy flowing through this plant, allowing it to form, grow, thrive, and evolve.

Reflect on how this plant energy supports your healing. What is it teaching you? How is it offering healing medicine to you? Write about the insights you experienced during this reflection.

Wildlife

Wild animals, birds, insects, and marine life are full of unique and beautiful forms of energy: the patterns of bird flight, motion, and song; the walking, swimming, and flying motions of insects; the patterns of flow and propulsion of marine life; and the abilities of animals to move through, burrow into, scavenge from, and blend into the landscapes where they reside. Encounters with the energy of these beings offer us medicine and teachings. A hawk gliding and soaring through the air might fill us with awe at its strength, precision, and grace. Its energy enlivens our own body, mind, and heart.

For many thousands of years, humans have identified certain animals as totems or symbols of the highest ideals. Jesus was called the "lamb of God." The serpent and eagle are sacred symbols in ancient Greek and Mesoamerican societies. More recent cultures have also adopted animals as symbols. The lion is the symbol of England; in France the honeybee symbolizes immortality and resurrection; the bald eagle represents might and freedom in the United States.[2] The qualities and energetic expressions of these forms of life symbolize the aspirations of individuals and social groups. Indigenous spiritual traditions have long used the wisdom of animals to help guide people into their full and true potential in life. Drawing on your connections to wildlife and their energy can support your healing and deepen your connection to all the beings on Earth.

Reflection: Connecting to Wildlife Energies

Think of an animal, bird, insect, or aquatic creature that has touched you in your journey of healing. Imagine its colors, textures, shape, and ways of engaging with its world: the sounds it makes, the ways it moves, how it sees or senses its habitat, where it lives, how it forms and grows.

Imagine the energy present in every cell of this being. Is it grand, awe-inspiring, fierce? Stealthy, subtle, quiet? Light and whimsical? Invite yourself to imagine the life force that permeates this being, the energy that allows it to live, thrive, and evolve.

Now reflect on how this form of life supports your healing. What medicine and teachings does its energy offer? Journal about the insights you experienced during this reflection.

Elemental Energies

Nature's energy forms exist among the energies of elemental forces. All life is bound to the energies within the elements of earth, fire, water, air, and space. We have looked at ways to cultivate deep awareness of these elemental forces within us and around us. Continuing to explore and connect to these forces can continue to deepen your healing and allow intimate connections with all of nature.

Each element has a particular energy within it. Earth holds the energy of rootedness, groundedness, and solidity. Fire contains the energy of heat, vitality, and pulsations. Water holds the energy of fluidity, flow, and cohesion; air, the energy of lightness, movement, and circulation; and space, the energy of emptiness, formlessness, and vastness. Learning to trust and use these energies to invigorate and nurture yourself is a beautiful way to extend your healing practices.

Reflection: Connecting to Elemental Energies

Recall one of the elemental forces that has supported your healing in this journey: earth, fire, water, air, or space. Sensing the particular energetic qualities of this force, imagine the colors, shapes, forms, and textures that represent the energy of this force to you.

Now imagine the conditions that have arisen to allow the full expression of this elemental force (for example, the distance the sun's rays have traveled to offer warmth, and the gravitational force that compressed matter in space to create the planet Earth). What other combination of elemental forces or expressions of nature allow this particular force to exist?

Imagine this element as it offers energy to help life form, grow, thrive, and evolve. Reflect on how this elemental energy supports your healing. What medicine and teaching does it offer? Journal the insights you experienced from this reflection.

Learning to feel the flow of energy movements in your life and your intimate and reciprocal relationships with plants, trees, flowers, animals, birds, insects, marine life, ecosystems, and elemental forces can help you heal, flourish, and find direction. Be curious, be open, invite a different kind of listening and sensing — attending to the interplay of energy in all the life around you. This will let you Know a connection to life that will deepen your healing, your sense of reciprocity, and your ability to partake in the experience of all of life.

Connections to Spiritual Experiences

What does spirituality mean to you? You may associate it with the practice of an established religion, or you may sense it as connected to your soul or some form of divine being or force. You may not hold any belief about life or energy beyond what we can observe here on Earth. Or you may have a sense of spirituality that is undefined but open and curious. My discussion here is based on the belief that there is something greater than ourselves, something that supports a greater sense of peace, purpose, interconnection, and meaning in life.

Our capacity for spiritual connection can sometimes be constrained by stuck trauma. If you experienced oppressive forms of religious observance or traumas in which you felt the failure of a spiritual being or force to care for you, it can be difficult to consider returning to these connections. As you have transformed your traumas, spirituality may be another dimension to explore in your healing journey.

A spiritual experience is a sense of peace, purpose, and connection that can range from a sense of aliveness and interconnection to something deeply sacred or transcendent. While many people link these experiences to organized religion, some find them in individual prayer, meditation, or a connection to a deity or a higher power. Some people also experience these connections through art and nature. Allow yourself to redefine and explore your idea of spirituality.

On your healing journey, do you recall an experience during a meditation, a moment with nature, or a movement of healing that gave you a deeper sense of peace, aliveness, purpose, or connection to yourself? Moments like this are the doorways to connections with spirit, the divine, God, the universe, or oneness.

What might it look like to create a spiritual path that cultivates more of these moments? Maybe you want to explore what is at your spiritual core, investigating questions like Who am I? What is my purpose? What do I value most? Maybe you want to look more deeply into how to live a fulfilling, happy, and healthy life. Maybe you want to explore forms of creative expression that give you peace and purpose. Maybe you would like to find a spiritual home, such as a religious group that aligns with your beliefs and values, or would like to study and learn from Indigenous cultures' spiritual and healing practices. Or maybe you seek spiritual connection with the wisdom of the Earth. The path is yours to create and follow. You can choose whatever supports you in continuing to transcend the challenges and traumas of your mind, body, and heart and moving into a fuller sense of being.

Reflection/Activity: Connecting Healing to Spiritual Living

The intent of this reflection and activity is to connect to the qualities that have been cultivated through your healing journey and create art that reflects the spiritual path you have formed. You may want to take a walk in nature as you reflect and engage with this activity. Take all the time you need or desire to complete it. You will need a piece of paper large enough for painting or brainstorming, along with crayons, colored pens, or paints.

What spiritual experiences have arisen on your healing journey to reveal a greater sense of your true self? How is this now expressed in your being? Are you more present, alive, centered, grounded, connected, joyful, content, playful, creative, strong, courageous, outgoing? Allow yourself to feel these expressive qualities. Write words that express these qualities anywhere you like on your paper. If you can, use a different color for each word.

Now consider how these qualities relate to the purpose and meaning of your life. Can you embody these qualities while you are with family or friends, while working, when engaged in everyday activities? For example, if you are practicing being more present in your conversations with others, might this give rise to speaking with clarity, truthfulness, and purpose? If you seek to embody creativity and playfulness in your work, might this give rise to engagement in new, more meaningful work? Reflect on how integrating these qualities into your daily life might bring more purpose and meaning into your life. Now draw images of how these qualities might be expressed as actions. Place them around the words you have written.

Reflect on the beautiful, spiritual experiences you have had and how they emerged. Remember the conditions, the settings, the places, the forms of nature, the beings, the connections that helped give rise to these expressions of your being. For example, you may have felt the qualities of strength and groundedness embodied within you through a moment of deep interconnection with a tree. Allow yourself to reflect on the limitless connections and conditions that arose to allow these new qualities to emerge within you on this healing path (including all the forces of your own life, the support of the practices, and the energies of nature). Now create images, representations of movement (such as lines or squiggles), or written words that show and express the deep interconnections that gave rise to the beautiful, expressive qualities that you now radiate into the world. Allow yourself to see a path of spiritual connections forming.

To close the activity, you may want to reflect on, write about, or create images that will continue to inspire you and deepen your connection to yourself and that which is beyond you.

Trust the Mystery of Life

This life is full of beautiful and mysterious possibilities. We've explored how the wisdom gained from healing our trauma can bring us into a greater sense of wholeness, health, and well-being. We've seen how this body is miraculously designed to orient us to healing, to a sense of being alive, to fully expressing our true nature. We've discovered that nature can reveal healing, deep wisdom, divine love, and spiritual connection.

As the forces of mindfulness, somatic experiencing, and nature have helped you heal your trauma and live more intentionally and in closer connection with the Earth, you may be contemplating what is next.

What is next is this moment. And this moment. And this moment. Breathe. Feel this body, heart, and mind now. Meet this moment with clear and kind awareness, present to what is within and all around you. This moment is always where we return to, where we begin, and where we continue. Awareness and deep Knowing will guide the way.

Often social expectations or rigid planning has determined what we do next. Now, with a deeper understanding within your healed being, you can begin to listen to, trust, and follow what is calling you.

Trust your heart. What have you come to love through your healing? This is the guidance to follow. Maybe you have been inspired to plant a garden where you can continue to practice the meditations and healing practices you have learned. Maybe you want to take on a project to help the healing of a particular group you are closely connected to. Maybe you want to read, learn, or study with a teacher to explore a particular topic, theory, or spiritual practice that has inspired you on this journey. Maybe you would like to expand your contemplative practice by learning and practicing various forms of meditation or prayer. Maybe you want to be more active in efforts to care for and support the Earth.

Through these healing practices, you can come to trust more and more in what life is presenting to you. Trust in the guidance of the divine mystery of presence and interconnection. Be open to new and surprising opportunities that may present themselves to you.

Practice: Mystery with Life

Continue this practice for as long as you choose. Find a place in nature that holds a sense of sacredness, mystery, or spirituality for you. Choose a comfortable posture — walking, standing, sitting, or lying down. In addition to the meditation prompts here, you may choose to incorporate other practices you have learned along the way that may help you fall into the mystery of life.

Begin by attending to what is here with you — plants, trees, birds, insects, wildlife. Become aware of the breath, inhaling and exhaling with this place. Now become aware of the senses — what you hear, see, smell, and feel. Notice the sensations arising and passing. Now invite your body to lead the way. Begin to move. You might walk, dance, flow, or stand with or next to an expression of nature. Feel the body pulsing, vibrating, and resonating with the energy around you.

Now let yourself meander, guided by the qualities and energies of your mysterious being: your playful energy, your grounded and solid energy, your sensitivity to the life around you. You might skip, hug the trees, or laugh with the leaves.

Allow the spirit of wonder and curiosity to infuse your body, mind, and heart. Let go of the knowing mind and step into the mystery and the unknown. Get down close to the earth to investigate the soil, the terrain, the small creatures; feel the ground and touch what you encounter as if for the first time. Let the top of your head be tickled by a leaf, energized by the power of a tree trunk, kissed by a petal of a flower. Feel the energies flowing around you and within you.

As you feel these energies, immerse yourself in the moment. This is life — full of connection, openness, oneness, spirit, divine love, God, and mystery to be felt and known.

Trust what arises. If you feel an impulse to engage in another practice or to experience presence to nature, yourself, or the mystery of it all, let that guide you.

To end the practice, offer reverence and gratitude for what has been cultivated. Lovingly offer to yourself and to all that is around you appreciation for the goodness that is here, felt, seen and un-seen, known and unknown.

Healing Continues

Every ending is a beginning. Upon reaching the end of this book, you may choose to begin again, returning to explore the practices and ideas you've learned in greater depth. Maybe you will focus on experiencing the goodness of your healing in daily life, feeling the fruits of healthy relationships and community connections. Maybe you now feel called to help others to heal from traumas similar to yours or to help heal our Earth.

Let the mystery and transformative power of living consciously continue to lead you. As you continue on your path, may you feel connected to your true and whole self, alive, healed, and connected with all beings. May the power and wisdom of your healed trauma be carried forward to support the healing of all beings and this planet. Healed, we heal the Earth.

ACKNOWLEDGMENTS

There are many people, beings, and experiences I would like to thank for supporting me in writing this book. First, I thank New World Library and Jason Gardner for agreeing to publish this work and support my heart's calling to help people to heal with nature. To my editors: Jess Beebe, thank you for your passion and guidance as this book formed; Erika Bűky, thank you for your support in achieving greater clarity as I completed it.

I am grateful to the many teachers who have shared their wisdom and experiences to support my practice. To the teachings and traditions from which these meditations come, I offer a deep bow of gratitude and respect. I offer a special thank you to Mark Coleman for his wisdom in sharing these teachings in nature, and for guiding and supporting me in teaching others.

In my garden in the canyon, I want to say thank you to the succulents, ferns, aloe, and spider mums that grow as the heritage of my mother's and grandmother's gardens. To the canyon herself, I express appreciation for the grasses, hawks, squirrels, rabbits, redbirds, sparrows, doves, pine trees, eucalyptus trees, brush, snails, spiders, scorpions, rocks, soil, roots, waters, and land. I thank the Kumeyaay, Yuman-speaking people of Hokan stock, for caring for this land for ten thousand years.

I am so grateful to my family for their support and encouragement to pursue what I love — thank you, Jason, Lorissa, Zach, Aidan, Mom, Dad, and Grandmas. I am also thankful for my faithful writing companion, Karuna. To my dharma sisters, for your never-ending presence and support as this has all unfolded, thank you.

I also offer thanks to all of the traumas I have experienced. There are many seen and unseen conditions, many things I know and others that I will never know, that brought those moments into my life.

Thank you to the land that has supported me throughout my life — the rows of peach trees, ditches to play in and catch tadpoles, the fields of dirt where I built forts and made mud patties, the forests of New Mexico and the deserts of southern California that have offered me rest and refuge. And thank you to the beings I have encountered in my healing — mama cow, all spiders, the birthing pine of the Jicarilla Apache and Ute Indians in the mountains of New Mexico, and the heavy air of the Central Valley, breaking my heart open to love this Earth and help her heal.

To the healing of all trauma and to nature and her infinite ways to support our aliveness and health. May all that is transformed through the teachings of this book aid the healing of the Earth.

NOTES

Introduction

1. C. Benjet, E. Bromet, E. G. Karam, et al., "The Epidemiology of Traumatic Event Exposure Worldwide: Results from the World Mental Health Survey Consortium," *Psychological Medicine* 46, no. 2 (2016): 327–43, https://doi.org/10.1017/S0033291715001981; R. C. Kessler, S. Aguilar-Gaxiola, J. Alonso, et al., "Trauma and PTSD in the WHO World Mental Health Surveys," *European Journal of Psychotraumatology* 8, sup. 5 (2017): 1353383, doi: 10.1080/20008198.2017.1353383.

2. Kirk Warren Brown, J. David Creswell, and Richard M. Ryan, *Handbook of Mindfulness: Theory, Research, and Practice* (New York: Guilford Press, 1997); Jeremy Smith, Kira Newman, Jill Suttie, and Hooria Jazaieri, "The State of Mindfulness Science," Greater Good Berkeley, December 5, 2017, https://greatergood.berkeley.edu/article/item/the_state_of_mindfulness_science; Alvin Powell, "When Science Meets Mindfulness," *Harvard Gazette*, April 9, 2018, https://news.harvard.edu/gazette/story/2018/04/harvard-researchers-study-how-mindfulness-may-change-the-brain-in-depressed-patients/.

3. Peter Levine, *In an Unspoken Voice: How the Body Releases Trauma and Restores Goodness* (Berkeley, CA: North Atlantic Books, 2010).

4. T. E. Andersen, Y. Lahav, H. Ellegaard, et. al., "A Randomized Controlled Trial of Brief Somatic Experiencing for Chronic Low Back Pain and Comorbid Post-traumatic Stress Disorder Symptoms," *European Journal of Psychotraumatology* 8, no. 1 (2017), www.tandfonline.com/doi/full/10.1080/20008198.2017.1331108; N. E. Windblad, M. Changaris, and P. K. Stein, "Effects of Somatic Experiencing Resiliency-Based Trauma Treatment on Quality of Life and Psychological Health as Potential Markers of Resilience in Treating Professionals," *Frontiers in*

Neuroscience 12 (2018): 70, https://doi.org/10.3389/fnins.2018.00070; D. Brom, Y. Stokar, C. Lawi, et al., "Somatic Experiencing for Posttraumatic Stress Disorder: A Randomized Controlled Outcome Study," *Journal of Traumatic Stress* 30, no. 3 (2017): 304–12, https://doi.org/10.1002/jts.22189.

5. Tristan Roberts, "We Spend 90% of Our Time Indoors. Says Who?" *Building Green*, 2020, www.buildinggreen.com/blog/we-spend-90-our-time-indoors-says-who.

6. Quentin Fottrell, "People Spend Most of Their Waking Hours Staring at Screens," *Market Watch*, August 4, 2018, www.marketwatch.com/story/people-are-spending -most-of-their-waking-hours-staring-at-screens-2018-08-01.

7. Florence Williams, *The Nature Fix: Why Nature Makes Us Happier, Healthier and More Creative* (New York: W. W. Norton, 2017).

Chapter 2: Sensory Awareness

1. Peggy Trowbridge Filiponne, "A Brief History of the Strawberry," The Spruce Eats, April 20, 2019, www.thespruceeats.com/history-of-strawberry-1807668.

Chapter 3: Body Awareness

1. Adapted from Bob Stahl, "32 Parts," http://32parts.com, accessed August 28, 2020.

Part 2: Somatic Knowing in Nature

1. Rhitu Chatterjee, "Where Did Agriculture Begin? Boy, It's Complicated," NPR, July 15, 2016, www.npr.org/sections/thesalt/2016/07/15/485722228/where-did-agriculture -begin-oh-boy-its-complicated.

Chapter 6: Finding the Healing Currents

1. "Lotus Flowers: Meaning and Care," Flower Glossary, www.flowerglossary.com /lotus-flowers-meaning/, accessed June 20, 2020.

2. Peter Levine, *In an Unspoken Voice: How the Body Releases Trauma and Restores Goodness* (Berkeley, CA: North Atlantic Books, 2010).

3. Tiffany Field, "Massage Therapy Review," *Complementary Therapies in Clinical Practice* 20, no. 4 (2014), 224–29, https://doi.org/10.1016/j.ctcp.2016.04.005.

Part 3: Living into Your Aliveness with Nature

1. "Academy Scientists Describe 71 Species in 2019," www.calacademy.org/press /releases/academy-scientists-describe-71-species-in-2019, accessed July 3, 2020.

Chapter 10: Reexperiencing Relationships and Yourself

1. "Components of Ecosystem," Toppr, www.toppr.com/guides/biology/ecosystem/components-of-ecosystem/, accessed July 15, 2020.

Chapter 11: The Rhythms of Nature

1. "Learning with the Natural World," *First Nations Pedagogy*, https://firstnations pedagogy.com/earth.html, accessed August 1, 2020.

Chapter 13: Healing to Heal Connections

1. "How Many Living Things Are There?" University of California Santa Barbara Science Line, http://scienceline.ucsb.edu/getkey.php?key=1388, accessed August 14, 2020.
2. "The IUCN Red List of Threatened Species," International Union for Conservation of Nature and Natural Resources, www.iucnredlist.org, accessed August 14, 2020.
3. "The Biggest Environmental Problems of 2020," Earth.org, September 14, 2020, https://earth.org/the-biggest-environmental-problems-of-our-lifetime.

Chapter 15: Healing the Earth

1. Joanna Macy and Chris Johnstone, *Active Hope: How to Face the Mess We're in without Going Crazy* (Novato, CA: New World Library, 2012).
2. "25 Environmental Agencies and Organizations," Ecoist, https://webecoist.momtastic.com/2008/09/24/25-environmental-agencies-and-organizations/, accessed August 21, 2020.

Chapter 16: Trusting the Mystery

1. "What Is Chamomile Tea?" Medical News Today, January 6, 2020, www.medical newstoday.com/articles/320031#what-is-chamomile-tea.
2. "What Is a Power Animal?" The Four Winds, October 3, 2016, https://thefourwinds.com/blog/shamanism/what-is-a-power-animal/.

RESOURCES

While healing from trauma, you may want to seek additional forms of support. The following list offers suggestions for finding groups, retreats, organizations, and individual practitioners who can help you with specific aspects of your healing.

There are many therapists trained in the exploration of trauma. This book is rooted in a mindfulness and body-based approach. You may wish to seek support from a therapist trained in this approach. It may also be helpful to seek the assistance of trained mindfulness teachers to support your development of these practices.

Trauma

Organizations and Websites

The Somatic Experiencing Trauma Institute is a nonprofit organization dedicated to supporting and resolving trauma and developing resilience through culturally responsive professional training, education, research, and outreach in diverse global communities. It maintains a database of trained somatic experiencing therapists at https://traumahealing.org.

The National Institutes of Health has created a list of online resources for various types of traumas, available at www.ncbi.nlm.nih.gov/books /NBK207198/.

The National Alliance on Mental Illness provides advocacy, education, support, and public awareness to help individuals and families affected by mental illness to build better lives. Information about diagnoses and resources is available at www.nami.org/support-education.

Books

Among the many books available that support healing from trauma, the books I list here offer additional resources for exploring somatic-based therapies and mindfulness-informed understanding for the healing of trauma.

> *The Body Keeps the Score*, by Bessel van der Kolk
> *Trauma-Sensitive Mindfulness: Practices for Safe and Transformative Healing*, by David Treleaven
> *Waking the Tiger: Healing Trauma*, by Peter Levine

Mindfulness

Organizations and Websites

The International Mindfulness Training Institute oversees national and international mindfulness training. It maintains a list of trained mindfulness professionals around the world at www.imta.org.

Insight Timer is a website offering free access to thousands of mindfulness and other types of meditations, as well as courses, at https://insighttimer.com.

Mindful is an organization that provides resources for learning and exploring mindfulness. The organization's magazine (available both in digital form and in print) provides information about mindfulness offerings. Information is available at www.mindful.org.

Retreats can be a wonderful way to practice mindfulness and benefit from supportive teaching. Here I list the two retreat centers in the United States that are most closely associated with teachings on mindfulness in nature:

Vallecitos Mountain Retreat Center, Vallecitos, New Mexico, www.vallecitos.org

Rocky Mountain Ecodharma Retreat Center, Ward, Colorado, https://rockymountainecodharmaretreatcenter.org

Books

The books I suggest here explore mindfulness in nature, practical approaches to understanding mindfulness, and a deeper exploration of the four foundations of mindfulness, which I introduce but do not discuss in depth.

Awake in the Wild: Mindfulness in Nature as a Path of Self-Discovery, by Mark Coleman

From Suffering to Peace: The True Promise of Mindfulness, by Mark Coleman

Fully Present: The Science, Art, and Practice of Mindfulness, by Susan Smalley and Diana Winston

Mindfulness: A Practical Guide to Awakening, by Joseph Goldstein

Nature

Organizations and Websites

350.org, https://350.org

Extinction Rebellion, https://rebellion.global

One Earth Sangha, https://oneearthsangha.org

Work That Reconnects Network, https://workthatreconnects.org

Books

Active Hope: How to Face the Mess We're in without Going Crazy, by Joanna Macy and Chris Johnstone

Becoming Animal: An Earthly Cosmology, by David Abram

Braiding Sweetgrass: Indigenous Wisdom, Scientific Knowledge, and the Teachings of Plants, by Robin Wall Kimmerer

INDEX

269

ABOUT *the* AUTHOR

Rochelle Calvert is dedicated to sharing the power and healing potential of mindfulness, somatic awareness, and nature. She has studied and taught for the past eighteen years and knows personally the transformational potential of these techniques and approaches to healing. Rochelle leads courses and retreats in mindfulness, somatic experiencing, and Awake in the Wild (nature-based mindfulness). She also facilitates professional training in mindfulness for clinicians and leads seminars across the United States.

She is a certified mindfulness teacher with the Mindfulness Training Institute and the International Mindfulness Teachers Association. She has also trained with and assisted Mark Coleman as an Awake in the Wild teacher. She practices mindfulness-based meditation rooted in the Buddhist Theravada tradition, meditating in nature daily.

Rochelle is the founder and clinical director of New Mindful Life, which offers mindfulness, nature-based, and somatic experiencing therapies. She teaches individual meditations with nature that assist in healing from trauma. She supports her clients and takes them into nature with the aid of Bertha Grace, a Sprinter van that serves as a mobile therapy office.

Rochelle lives in San Diego, California, and enjoys spending her free time in nature, hiking, practicing yoga, exploring the land's Indigenous heritage, and resting with trees.

https://newmindfullife.com/